Restartup

A Founder's Guide to
Crisis Navigation

Restartup

A Founder's Guide to
Crisis Navigation

ARUNKUMAR KRISHNAKUMAR
MAXSON J.Y. TEE

WILEY

This edition first published 2021

© 2021 John Wiley & Sons, Ltd

Registered office

John Wiley & Sons Ltd, The Atrium, Southern Gate, Chichester, West Sussex, PO19 8SQ, United Kingdom

For details of our global editorial offices, for customer services and for information about how to apply for permission to reuse the copyright material in this book please see our website at www. wiley.com.

Wiley publishes in a variety of print and electronic formats and by print-on-demand. Some material included with standard print versions of this book may not be included in e-books or in print-on-demand. If this book refers to media such as a CD or DVD that is not included in the version you purchased, you may download this material at http://booksupport.wiley.com. For more information about Wiley products, visit www.wiley.com.

Designations used by companies to distinguish their products are often claimed as trademarks. All brand names and product names used in this book are trade names, service marks, trademarks or registered trademarks of their respective owners. The publisher is not associated with any product or vendor mentioned in this book.

Limit of Liability/Disclaimer of Warranty: While the publisher and author have used their best efforts in preparing this book, they make no representations or warranties with respect to the accuracy or completeness of the contents of this book and specifically disclaim any implied warranties of merchantability or fitness for a particular purpose. It is sold on the understanding that the publisher is not engaged in rendering professional services and neither the publisher nor the author shall be liable for damages arising herefrom. If professional advice or other expert assistance is required, the services of a competent professional should be sought.

Library of Congress Cataloging-in-Publication Data:

Names: Krishnakumar, Arunkumar, author. | Tee, Maxson J.Y., author.
Title: Restartup : a founder's guide to crisis navigation / Arunkumar
   Krishnakumar, Maxson J.Y. Tee.
Description: First edition. | Chichester, West Sussex, United Kingdom :
   Wiley, 2021. | Includes index.
Identifiers: LCCN 2021000105 (print) | LCCN 2021000106 (ebook) | ISBN
   9781119754404 (hardback) | ISBN 9781119754596 (adobe pdf) | ISBN
   9781119754626 (epub)
Subjects: LCSH: New business enterprises. | Financial crises. |
   Business enterprises—Finance.
Classification: LCC HD62.5 .K75 2021 (print) | LCC HD62.5 (ebook) |
   DDC 658.4/056—dc23
LC record available at https://lccn.loc.gov/2021000105
LC ebook record available at https://lccn.loc.gov/2021000106

Cover Design and image: Veda Kasireddy

Set in STIX Two Text 10/12

C9781119754404_100321

This book is dedicated to the spirit of entrepreneurship.

To those who don't take NO for an answer. To those who believe they can change the world and to those who actually have. To those who work through nights to protect their firm even when they have a young family to attend to in the morning. To those who live their passions sacrificing time, money and relationships.

To those who dare to hope!

Contents

Preface

It was January 2020 when we were just hearing about COVID-19 in China. It already feels like a decade ago. That's been the nature of the year 2020. We had unprecedented forest fires, geopolitical tensions between Iran and the US, the Beirut blast, the Brexit episode, the American elections and Harry and Meghan moving to the US. A year of chaos, not just crises.

In early 2020, I was on a panel at an event focussed on women entrepreneurs. At the end of the discussion, I had over a dozen founders asking me questions around how I thought the startup landscape would change if COVID-19 hurt the economy. I am not sure if the air around us in the room had the virus, but I could sense that it was filled with anxiety. I felt I had to do something about it, more than just giving them piecemeal answers.

I came home and started working on a blog series with several topics on how a startup could deal with a crisis. I looked across my portfolio firms and how they were dealing with it. They all had different plans, some of them felt they would fly, some of them felt they may have to slow down, a few others wanted to see how the market changed for them through February and March 2020 to then make a decision. There was a minority who felt they would be irrelevant if lockdowns happened.

It was quite clear that a crisis didn't have a homogenous effect on the innovation ecosystem. Yet, there was one homogeneity across these startup founders I spoke to. They were all anxious, if not depressed, because they didn't have enough information about the nature of the crisis. Remember, we are still in early 2020.

As we entered March 2020, it was dawning on us how bad the world was going to get hurt by this crisis. My portfolio firms had by then drafted several plans – A to B to C – and some of them had implemented their plans, too. A couple of them got lucky as the lockdown brought growth. Yet, one common theme across the firms was that founders who were agile and quick in making clear and tough decisions seemed to be do better.

By then my idea of writing a blog series had grown just because of the number of topics I could cover. In the past few years, I have had the pleasure of working with Max at our VC firm, Green Shores Capital. We had a little office at Mayfair in London and had numerous discussions, brainstorming sessions and heated debates using the glass walls of the office as our whiteboard.

Both Max and I felt that we should come up with mental models and thought road maps to help entrepreneurs be better prepared for a crisis. We spent a few days working on Miro mind maps and putting together various strategy topics that we would like to discuss in the book. We still hadn't considered one critical topic that this book now has – mental health.

However, as we started talking to entrepreneurs through March and April of 2020, we understood that even those we rated as the best entrepreneurs were too close to the problem, too stressed and had trouble communicating effectively to their teams. We also saw many of them struggle with time management and a couple of them struggle with anger issues. These interviews were eye-opening for us because we hadn't ourselves realised the criticality of mental health amongst entrepreneurs.

We spent quite a lot of time researching about the topic, speaking to professional coaches and mental health experts. Legends in the venture capital industry such as Jerry Colonna, author of *Reboot,* and Brad Feld, the managing director at the Founding Group, openly discussed their depressive episodes with us when we reached out to them. In a world where we are taught to brag 'I am Superman' and 'I am immune to the deadliest virus', we found vulnerability refreshing and genuine.

We also spoke to more than 50 CEOs, VC professionals and central bankers for their thoughts on how founders should respond to a crisis. In essence, this book is a summary of personal and professional experiences of all these experts that are structured into frameworks and mental models that startup founders can benefit from.

We have 3 key themes across the book. The first is about the macro environment that startups operate in. Entrepreneurs must understand the functioning of capital markets, the flow of cash and how this flow could help or hurt their progress. This would also help them understand the impact that an economic shift can cause to the market they are serving.

The second theme of the book is mental health. Of its 3 themes, this is the one where most work needs to be done globally. From Silicon Valley to Bangalore, from Scandinavia to South Africa, founders fear talking about their mental health. It is considered taboo; worse, it is considered a sign of weakness even by the most accomplished CEOs and VC investors.

All members of the innovation community across the world must spare a thought for the entrepreneurs. In crude commercial terms, entrepreneurs are the ducks that lay golden eggs. We cannot be more focussed on the golden eggs and less focussed on the ducks. That's madness. It is the responsibility of the investors, board members, mentors and all others who feel they are part of the innovation community to respect, understand and support the entrepreneurs they work with.

The third key theme of the book is strategy. Max and I quite enjoyed working though this part of the book. Our approach to the strategy part of the book was to look at a topic of discussion and come up with the simplest way of articulating it as a framework. I had several 4 am moments, when I would come up with an idea, write it on a piece of paper, improvise it digitally, hoping I would get a 'wow' from Max.

Max would then do his due diligence on these models: ensure they add up and help refine them and in some cases further simplify them. It has been one hell of a journey. The strategy part of the book starts with the tactical aspects of going lean and mean in response to a crisis. We then look into how an entrepreneur can assess the market landscape, customer behaviour and slowly steer the firm in the right direction. When none of this is possible and a drastic pivot is needed, we have discussed how that can be achieved, too.

This book has been an intellectual rollercoaster for us. We came up with a few basic hypotheses (with our frameworks), validated them with the market (through our interviews), enriched them (with mental health angle) and are presenting it to you hoping we will hit product–market fit. Here is a little poem from an amazing mind to kick-start your journey with this book.

As you took the mirror
Outside your home,
You knew not how to hold it –
That which your passions made.
It crumbled to several pieces –
Each piece sharp and hurtful.
Passersby suggested how to fix it,
But each time you did and looked in,
Another form of yourself you saw.
And each felt wrong and distorted.
You finally shut them all out
For you knew this was your job
To fix, To mend, To heal.
And that you did,
With long thoughts in silence,
Reflecting where each piece belonged,
If it did, and in what shape.
Finally done it was and
You looked at yourself
Wondering what you had created.
What you felt you knew not
Except that one voice loud and proud,
That this was your work.

A poem by Meera Ganesan

Happy reading.

Startup is like an invisible mesh of trust.

Akshay Sharma, CTO at Doc.AI

If you have a warm introduction, you are 13 times more likely to get funded.

Alice Wagner, managing director at the British Business Bank.

A crisis triggers a flight to quality behaviour amongst investors. The top quartile of startups typically gets the lion's share of the capital.

Arvind Purushotham, global head of venture investing at Citi Ventures

A startup is trying to find what works in a series of experiments, many of which fail.

Brad Feld, managing director at Foundry Group

A lot of things change in a crisis. As an investor, you are not really backing a business or a market in a crisis. You are backing the founders to find the right opportunities in the market.

Camilla Dolan, partner at Eka Ventures

As the crisis hit, we focussed a lot on ecosystem work and bringing people together. I felt like if we VC investors were lost, I couldn't imagine how founders felt.

Carmen Alfonso Rico, partner at Blossom Capital

Don't just do a pivot for the sake of attracting funding and or trying to show product-market fit for whatever you have. So I think the biggest question is, why should you pivot?

Chitresh Sharma, former CEO of Swipii

If you're in a fintech startup, where the team is young and visionary, you might be missing something, which is someone who's been on the block. Find a grey-haired person who has dealt with regulatory bodies.

Chris Skinner, author and nonexecutive director at 11FS

If you are in Europe, tap into government funding. It can be a good source of capital during a crisis.

Christophe Pechoux, partner at Consilience Ventures

A startup working with a CVC investor would need to be very good at building relationships not just with the person writing the cheque but also the business lines who could have synergies with their proposition.

Claire Calmejane, chief innovation officer at Societe Generale

Based on my own experiences, a lot of mental health issues boiled down to people not recognising and asking for help when they need it.

David Fogel, cofounder at ADV and Alma Angels

Your values are the lenses through which you see the world. And so for me, you've just got to stay true to what your values are.

David Brear, CEO at 11FS

Focus on the customer's pain; focus on wins for the customer.

Emma Maslen, vice president and general manager,
EMEA & APAC at Ping Identity

They say great companies are built in times of crisis because if you survive that shit, you come out on the other side pretty lean and pretty mean.

Fred Destin, founder at Stride VC

A VC investor's job is to help manage crises. If everything goes well, nobody needs me.

Ganesh Rengaswamy, cofounder at Quona Capital

When you have legends on your cap table, and you have a good idea at the right time, it's pretty hard to mess that up.

Howard Lindzon, founder at Social Leverage

Founders really need a coach and a mentor to be the impartial third-party support systems.

Hussayn Kassai, CEO and cofounder at Onfido

True grit is kind. Resilience is the path; equanimity is the goal.

Jerry Colonna, author of Reboot: Leadership and the Art of Growing Up (HarperCollins) and co-founder of the executive coaching firm, Reboot.io

As a woman entrepreneur, I knew how hard it's going to be. I knew that I wouldn't be able to do the marathon if I didn't invest in my mental health.

Joyeeta Das, cofounder and CEO at Gyana

A lot of money comes with a ton of expectations. When you raise a lot of money, you [must] become more careful and disciplined in terms of how you deploy that capital.

Kelvin Au, head of Ventures at Founders Factory

Experiences during a crisis can help us find a sense of perspective and rethink what we want to do in life.

Kunal Mittal, chief product officer at FrontM

I've learned that negative momentum is almost as powerful as positive momentum. We always need some kind of momentum. Up or down is better than flat.

Lizzie Chapman, cofounder and CEO at ZestMoney

I've told a number of CEOs to just reach out to me as a friend. Forget that I'm an investor, just call me as a friend, share with me the uncertainties that you're facing as a person and as a leader of an organisation.

Manuel Silva Martinez, general partner at Mouro Capital

As the crisis unfolds, the messenger is often as important as the message.

Mari Sako, professor of management studies at the University of Oxford

A lot of success is based on whether or not the founder is able to tough it out to a certain point with things. This makes it imperative for founders to keep a lookout for their mental health.

Mary McKenna, expert advisor to the European Commission

Even something as simple as putting an out-of-the-office and saying, I'm not available or blocking your calendar can be the modelling behaviour that the founders can do. The notion of being available 24/7 is not sustainable.

Monica Brand Engel, cofounder at Quona Capital

I just believe that if you know what your values are, if you can know what makes you tick and if you can make good decisions and be happy with those decisions, then there is a really powerful ripple effect from that.

Natasha Chatur, associate coach at People Untapped

Unlike previous crises when the impact was largely on the Western world, with the COVID crisis, the entire globe is shrinking at the same time.

Managing Director of South Asia and MENA at Ripple

Most young companies identify and exploit an error in a regulated area in such a way that the incumbents think they're protected by it.

Nicola Persico, professor at Kellogg School of Management

Entrepreneurs often solve the world's problems, and there're always the brave ones, the pioneering ones who will go in and fight the cause. I think a crisis can be a massive opportunity for entrepreneurs to lay their claim.

Nicole Anderson, managing partner at RedSand Ventures

Painting pictures and stories for people in the hearts of crisis is really important to the way they can connect to you.

Nigel Morris, nonexecutive director at Guardian Media Group PLC

As funding dries up for fintechs, they may have to rely on partnerships with incumbent financial services firms, which could potentially lead to consolidation.

Pinar Ozcan, professor of entrepreneurship and innovation at the University of Oxford

For VC investors in emerging markets, the accelerated digitisation in 2020 might come as a boon. LPs would likely double down their investment in us as their allocation for technology innovation increases.

Rabeel Warraich, founder and CEO at Sarmayacar

In most corporates, and particularly banking and financial environments, they still kill the guy who fails. That needs to change.

Richard Turrin, author at Innovation Lab Excellence

Disruption is not adding a new product to the product line if it's being sold to the same set of customers in the same way and just creates a different form of revenue generation.

Ron Shevlin, director of research at Cornerstone Advisors

Founders are time travellers who have seen the scene or lived in the future, and they come back to the present to build that future.

Rory Stirling, partner at Connect Ventures

Crisis is an excellent time to re-evaluate a startup's problem statement, altering positions based on the current situation.

Sabine VanderLinden, cofounder and CEO at Alchemy Crew

Ensuring that there is clear and consistent communication is extremely critical. What is impeccably important is that you deliver the messaging honestly to the team; don't sugarcoat it.

Sachin Jaiswal, cofounder and CEO at Niki

It's a huge generalisation, yet, I think women have always struggled to raise money. We learn to do more with less even in the good times. That comes in handy during a crisis.

Sarah Turner, cofounder and CEO at Angel Academe

I think a key differentiator is that very early on when we set up our cost model, we kept it as variable as possible. That kept our cost structures efficient.

Simbarashe Rusike, VP of finance at Assurance IQ

I normally look at crises in three buckets. There's this structural crisis, like the global financial crisis, which is a balance sheet issue. Then, there is a cyclical crisis, which is inflation, unemployment, things like that. And there is something called an event-driven crisis.

Sopnendu Mohanty, chief fintech officer at
Monetary Authority Singapore

Whenever we go out to pitch, you always want to talk about who you have in the cap table as a hook for them to come on. It says a lot.

Victor Chang, corporate legal counsel at Curve

That is one of the really clarifying things about a crisis. It calls so many previously forgotten assumptions into question.

Victoria Fram, cofounder and
managing director at VilCap Investments

You need to be resilient and optimistic to get through the rejection that comes with being a founder. But to be a leader, you need to be a good listener, be insightful and potentially vulnerable.

Yifhat Ernstein, Executive Coach

Acknowledgements

Arunkumar Krishnakumar

With another book began another journey, yet those whose life faced disruption supported it unconditionally. Thanks to my wife and my daughters for allowing me the time to do this.

The book wouldn't have happened without Max, who kept us honest on the quality of the content, stories and the completeness of the models we created for the book.

Maxson Tee

Never have I ever thought that I would be writing a book. It has been a hard but rewarding journey. None of this would have been possible without my coauthor, colleague, mentor and friend, Arunkumar. I am forever indebted to him for his patience, kindness, friendship and guidance.

To my family – thank you, Josephine Chai, my mum, for always being the person whom I could turn to during my darkest periods. Alfie Pok, my mum's partner, for being a father figure to me when I needed it the most. My little brothers, Jason and Dickson: thank you for your care and support in my life.

We thank ...

We thank all the entrepreneurs, VC investors, innovation thought leaders, academics and central bankers who contributed to this book. It was a difficult period for the whole world when we started writing this book, and they were very generous with their time. Some of them even offered to spend more time with us than initially planned and provided introductions to help us with more interviews.

We thank all these super women ...

- Our friend and colleague Theodora Lau, who has kindly written the foreword but also provided critical feedback on the coverage of topics that helped us.
- Dr Rajeswari (Arun's mom), who helped us with the Shakespeare quotes for every chapter. It was an interesting experience explaining the gist of a chapter in a business book to a professor of English literature. She would then come up with several pages of quotes per chapter, and we would choose one of them.
- Veda Kasireddy for doing the cover art for us. We weren't the easiest to please, and she did a patient and a tremendous job of nailing the theme of the book with her artwork.
- Meera Ganesan, for allowing us to use her poem in the preface of the book.

- A special shoutout to Doris and Raji at Firebrand Labs (FBL). Without these two amazing women, the visual deliverables wouldn't have reached us in time and in style. Team FBL have added a spark to the design elements of the book.

- To the awesome Wiley editorial team – Susan, Purvi, Gemma and Gladys. Thank you for keeping us honest with our content, language and timelines.

This book is a result of several amazing minds contributing selflessly to give back to the entrepreneurial community. Thanks to that spirit of giving!

About the Authors

Arun

Arun is a venture capital investor at Delphos International, and previous to that at Green Shores Capital. He sits on the board of several of his investee firms. He is a managing trustee at Aram Foundation, an NGO in India focusing on water conservation. Previous to becoming a VC investor, Arun spent most of his career in Barclays and PwC within data and technology.

In 2020, Arun published a book *Quantum Computing and Blockchain for Business*. He is the founder and podcast host at *One Vision* (one of the top 5 fintech podcasts in the world). He was a blogger on *DailyFintech*, which is the second most read fintech blog in the world, where he has contributed more than 150 posts over 3 years.

As a by-product of his investing and writing career, Arun is also one of the top 100 Onalytica fintech influencers and one of the top 100 Refinitiv's global social media leaders in sustainable investing.

Arun holds a master's in finance degree from the London School of Economics and a postgraduate diploma in global business from the Said Business School, University of Oxford.

Max

Maxson is a product manager, strategy professional and an investor. A scout for Green Shores Capital and Founders Factory, he has spent the last few years reading and learning about the technology entrepreneurial ecosystem. Prior to his current role, he was a product manager, building award-winning technology software at Finastra and a founding team member at AgriLedger, working with The World Bank to support smallholding farmers.

Maxson holds a master's in engineering with finance from University College, London. He lives and works out of London. You can visit him online on Twitter (@maxsontjy).

CHAPTER 1

Even Shit Floats in High Tide

All that glisters is not gold,

Often have you heard that told:

Many a man his life hath sold

But my outside to behold.

Gilded [tombs] do worms enfold.

— William Shakespeare, The Merchant of Venice

Introduction

Five years back, I was pitching to an investor for my venture capital (VC) fund. I showcased the startups I had invested in and explained how well they had all performed since the investment. He was quiet for a few seconds and responded,

"Even shit floats in high tide."

He had observed that all our investments were made during bull markets. He continued to push me onto my backfoot, saying our investments should withstand a crisis to really stand apart. I was shaken by his comment because he was right. I remember telling myself, 'This is it, I've lost it'.

All the investments I showcased to him had happened in 2014–2015 when the market was pretty healthy. He had seen through my sales exercise. Somehow, miraculously, I won him over and he became my cornerstone investor. One thing led to another and we later partnered to set up Green Shores Capital. Together, we have so far invested in more than 15 startups, and many more individually. However, the philosophy has often been about assessing how well a startup would perform at times of stress.

In 2019–2020, we have closely followed trends about the rise of investments into late-stage startups, fall in VC investments in Asia, the rise of corporate VC and the rise, and subsequent struggles, of the Softbank Vision Fund. These were macro trends that we have been keeping tabs on. We also witnessed a slowdown in funding for early-stage startups during 2019. However, as the COVID-19 crisis has unfolded, we've seen activity fall off a cliff.

We reached out to all our investee companies, discussed their plans and suggested ways they could navigate the crisis. We made several observations during those conversations. There were differences in the way each of them approached the crisis. We saw nervousness, resolve, confusion, hope and, in a few cases, excitement.

Everyone entered the same crisis, yet the way companies have reacted to the crisis varied remarkably. This is largely because of how they had set themselves up for crisis. That led us to think through the 'Why?' behind the way our investees have responded. During our due diligence process at the time of investing in these companies, we analysed their preparedness for a crisis. But very few will disagree if I said, 'You cannot be completely prepared for a crisis'.

In this book, Max and I will go through the journey of a startup getting into a crisis, living through that crisis and emerging out of it. In the process, we will bring together insights from across the world – from VCs, startup CEOs, central bankers and ecosystem stakeholders. We have chosen a few case studies that we will pick best practices from and highlight them throughout the book.

In this chapter, we will discuss why it is important to understand that the bull (market) has been running for too long. This comes from regularly keeping tabs on the key markets across the world, understanding how the macros affect the startup ecosystem, assessing the potential scenarios that could unravel and staying sufficiently nimble to respond effectively.

If you are an entrepreneur, you might want to ask, 'Why should I be interested in all that? I have enough on my plate with just building my product and selling it'. Remember, successful entrepreneurs are generally compensated so well, not just because they have built and sold a product. They equip themselves with information to navigate their firms through both market highs and lows. Now, let us turn to why the macroeconomy matters and how an understanding of that helps an entrepreneur to make informed decisions.

The Macros Matter

Be it in fitness or finance, the macros matter. Let us first start with the scenario we were in before the COVID crisis hit. A raging bull market that just couldn't be stopped. The Brexit vote was finally behind us and market sentiment had improved. Europe saw a huge influx of institutional capital and there were VC funds with a lot of *dry powder**.

Dry powder refers to the amount of cash reserves available with VC and private equity funds.

We knew things were unsustainably rosy and on the surface we celebrated every single win: new client contracts, investments at crazy valuations, expensive hires, glossy PR and the list goes on. The *Burn rate** for businesses was so ridiculously high that we asked ourselves, 'What do they spend so much money on every month?'; however, we ignored them because times were good. I wouldn't go as far as claiming there was a systemic bubble forming before the COVID crisis hit, but there were sporadic signs of an overheated market.

Burn rate refers to the cash outflow that businesses incur every month.

Startups claimed crazy valuations during investment rounds. I remember sitting at a pitching lunch session at Mayfair in London. There were about 15 family office and VC investors sitting around the table, and there was one firm pitching to us through the expensive lunch that was served. The firm pitched for a £12 million funding, had an artificial intelligence (AI) component that was revenue-generating and were building a Blockchain component to enrich their product offering.

They had a burn rate of £1 million per month, had raised £9 million only a few months ago and had made about £300K in revenues over the previous 12 months. They weren't fundraising to grow their clientele on an already revenue-generating AI component; instead, they chose to invest into a potential add-on using Blockchain. The £12 million, they claimed, would help the whole product to be rolled out in 9 months' time, after which they were planning to fundraise again. They were valuing their firm at £72 million.

Pitches like these make me cringe. However, they did win some investors from that pitch. Those were times when investors had a lot of capital. When we see consistent deployments of capital into low-quality propositions such as the one I described, it is often a sign that people do not know what to do with their money and are desperate to deploy. That leads to bad investment decisions, and when a wave of bad investments collapses at scale globally, it can result in a recession, as it did in 2008.

We saw a bit of that when Softbank Fund I struggled after the WeWork episode and hasn't been able to raise its second fund since. If you are a startup, you could be asking, surely Softbank is a multi-billion-dollar player, and why would it have a capital crunch? Hold on to that question; it will be clear when we discuss the *capital pyramid.*

During several events, discussions and social media interactions, I have been asked why VC investors don't deploy in certain types of assets or at certain times of business cycles. That is because not all the capital deployed by a VC is from the partners of the firm. There are other investors behind the scenes, called *limited partners* (LPs), and they can dictate terms. So, the risk appetites of VC investors differ in line with the risk appetites of their LPs.

Therefore, it is critical that entrepreneurs understand the macro variables that could potentially hurt or help their business: events that are not close to their day-to-day reality, such as an interest rate hike or fall, a sovereign default or a large institutional investor failing to raise its second fund. All these have an impact on the innovation community and the flow of capital into startups. A good understanding of these macro events and their potential repercussions help startups and their management team stay prepared for any structural events.

This might not seem as important when the markets are booming, but, much like bad times, good times don't last either. Therefore, it is always prudent to stay on top of macro trends that affect capital flows. Without further ado, we shall dive into the money pyramid that the capital flow is built on.

Capitalism: The Pyramid Scheme

The world of capitalism can be visualised as a money pyramid. It can be imagined as a pyramid that has capital flowing from top to bottom, with a few, mighty firms at the top. As capital flows from one tier of the pyramid to the next, value is added and the organisations in the tier are compensated for the value addition. Let's go through the institutions that make the pyramid work (see Figure 1.1).

Tier 0

Central banks sit at the top, ensuring there is liquidity (money flow) in the system. They are also interested in ensuring that the markets are behaving and consumer appetite is optimal. They keep track of their region's business landscape, trade balance, inflation, consumer spending, foreign direct investments and market sentiment. They have a few tools, such as interest rates and quantitative easing, to manage some of these factors that they continuously track. The amount of liquidity within the pyramid is often influenced by the policies that central banks enforce.

Tier 1

Wall Street banks and large blue-chip firms schematically sit below the central banks on the pyramid. In the context of understanding liquidity in the capital markets, they can be viewed as Tier 1 organisations. They are the means through which capital is distributed across the system. The health of these financial institutions and large corporations often reflects the health of the economy.

On top of facilitating liquidity throughout the pyramid, in recent times these organisations have directly interacted with technology startups through innovation labs, corporate venture funding and joint ventures.

Tier 2

Tier 2 of the pyramid is where institutional investors such as endowments and pension funds operate. This tier receives capital from organisations and their employees who contribute to pensions and endowments. Endowment and pension funds distribute capital to other parts of the system from this level. Based on their risk appetites, they allocate capital across different asset classes from equity, fixed income, real estate and PE.

Tier 3

Tier 3 is what entrepreneurs need to understand closely. This tier of the capital pyramid comprises of the specialist money managers who run niche investment vehicles to address specific categories of investment. They have

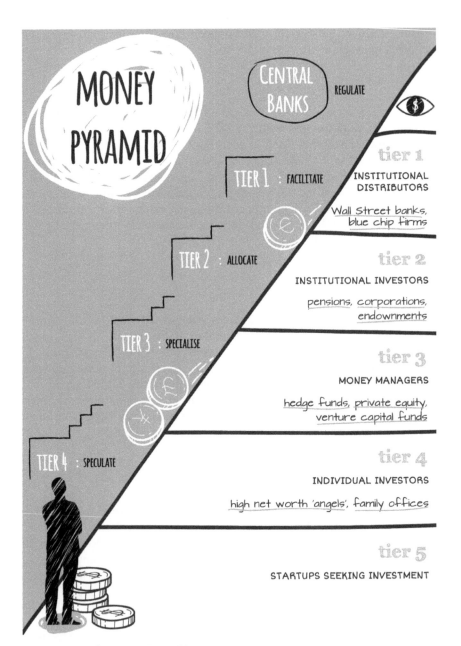

FIGURE 1.1 The Money Pyramid

specialist skills to address an underserved market or find the much-needed alpha for Tier 2 organisations.

Tier 3 can be categorised as VC and PE organisations that are private market players and hedge funds that invest into public markets. In more recent times we have large corporations setting up their venture investing arm. These are called *corporate venture capital* (CVC) firms. CVCs are Tier 3 organisations that have been a growing segment of institutional investors since the 2008 crisis.

Private market investments involve deploying capital into firms that have not yet been listed in the stock market. Public market investments are those that are deployed into assets listed on an exchange.

CVC has been a recent addition to the list of institutional actors in the capital pyramid. CVCs are typically venture arms of big corporations who have allocated funds to invest in startups. When CVCs fund startups, they typically look for two key dimensions. One is the return on investment through appreciation of share value, which is similar to a VC. The second criterion is strategic synergies between a firm and the startup they have invested in. This criterion is a key difference between VCs and CVCs. CVC investors can often take a firm they have invested in to their clients, do joint ventures and, over a period, can acquire them, too. In that sense, CVCs do feel as if they are smarter and more strategic money for startups because they not only help in funding the firm but also could become a client or the distribution.

As a result, as soon as the investment is made, many CVC investors can look to use the product or the services of the startup in their own organisation's business units. It is both capital and client for the startup winning the cheque. However, CVC investors also typically invest slightly later than VC investors do. More on the VC–CVC comparison in Chapter 6.

Tier 4

There is another group of investors in Tier 4: family offices, ultra-high-net-worth individuals (UHNWIs) and high-net-worth individuals (HNWIs). These are typically families, their wealth managers and individuals who have made or inherited millions of dollars and are looking for investment opportunities.

The primary difference between these stakeholders and the institutional investors is that Tier 4 investors have the ability to make investment decisions with less formality. Tier 4 stakeholders can also be convinced quickly because they typically do not have onerous investment processes in place. They are also seen as the least-sophisticated set of investors in the pyramid.

Tier 5

At the bottom of the pyramid are the startups and the small- and medium-sized enterprises (SMEs), which are looking up the pyramid for capital to flow down. Despite being categorised as the bottom of the pyramid, SMEs make a big contribution to the health of the economy. As per the UK Small Business Statistics (**www.fsb.org.uk/uk-small-business-statistics.html**), there were 5.82 million small businesses in the UK that account for half of the turnover in the private sector. They also employed 60% of the UK workforce (16.6 million).

Please note that not all of these SMEs are the technology startups that this book focuses on. The statistics include all small businesses, from a grocery store to a coffee shop.

Often, depending on the maturity of the startup, and the business and market conditions, money can flow directly into them from Tiers 2 or 3 of the pyramid. For ease of understanding the flow of cash in the form of transactions through the economy, you can visualise consumers in this tier of the pyramid, too. However, consumers buy products and services from businesses, and the health of the large corporations in the top tier is often reliant on the buying capacity and appetite of these stakeholders.

Let us now discuss what drives capital flow from or into each of these actors, thus keeping liquidity in the system.

Role of the Central Banks and Regulators

We briefly touched on how central bank policy can affect capital flow across the economy. Central banks and regulators have a pivotal role in driving capital through the pyramids. This, in turn, has an effect on investor appetites and funding for startups. The purpose of central banks is to ensure they maintain a healthy economy through the balancing of essential economic variables. For instance, economic policies can trigger inflation during good times, which in turn can push the central banks to react with interest rate hikes.

The human brain has already become digital. Policy making should be a supporting mechanism, instead of a hindrance, to ensure large-scale digital adoption.

Sopnendu Mohanty
Chief fintech officer at The Monetary Authority of Singapore

However, during previous market downturns and recessions, central banks have employed quantitative easing and interest rate cuts to introduce liquidity into the system. But, too much cheap money can cause a currency market crisis and increase sovereign debt. If a major economy starts accumulating debt, it can potentially lead to their investment grade being cut by rating agencies such as S&P and Moody's.

During a recession, central banks need to pump oxygen into the economy while also making sure they do not risk a rating downgrade. If a country's ratings are cut, it could hurt their ability to borrow money and might also result in foreign direct investments (FDIs) drying up. Central banks have the unenviable job of striking the right balance among all these different variables. From a startup perspective, it is worth understanding how policy could affect FDI inflows, thereby limiting capital available for them to grow.

These three ingredients essentially propel innovation and drive economic growth.
- Venture capital investors willing to support ideas (means and motivation).
- Policies designed to support new innovation.
- Society and consumer confidence in the market economy.

Sopnendu Mohanty
Chief Fintech officer at The Monetary Authority of Singapore

Let us now look at how central banks and regulators have taken a more proactive role in engaging with the innovation ecosystem. In recent times, some regulators have taken on a more hands-on role to support their innovation ecosystem. Innovation policy from these regulators across the world has had a major impact on the innovation community in the region.

In some countries, such as Singapore and India, the regulators and the government have proactively pioneered the infrastructure required for startups. For instance, the unified payments interface (UPI) developed by the government of India has been the foundational building block for digital payment infrastructure in the country. Fintech firms such as PayTM, PhonePe and global players such as GooglePay and WhatsApp pay have used this infrastructure to accelerate their services to the end customer, thereby triggering the adoption of digital payments in the country.

On a similar note, the Monetary Authority of Singapore (MAS) has paved the way for digital KYC (know your customer) and digital payments for technology firms to leverage. Firms that need to perform KYC on their customers do not have to rely on a repetitive, document-intensive and time-consuming process. They can just reuse the KYC solution that the MAS has facilitated.

Although Asia has taken a more hands-on approach to building its digital infrastructure, Europe had more legacy infrastructure to start with. Therefore, European regulators have been more collaborative with technology startups and provided more of a hand-holding process in guiding innovation in the right direction.

European regulators such as the Financial Conduct Authority (FCA) and the European Central Bank (ECB) have facilitated innovation through regulations such as the Payment Services Directive (PSD). That has triggered the application programming interface (API)-driven innovation paradigm called *open banking*. These regulators have catalysed change through policy making rather than building the necessary infrastructure to lead innovation. The FCA also has a sandbox that works with startups and helps them understand the regulatory implications of the solutions they are working on.

Therefore, regulators can help the innovation ecosystem not just through monetary policies but also through infrastructure support. This is especially critical in emerging markets economies where legacy infrastructure is largely absent. A lack of legacy infrastructure is an opportunity for both regulators and innovators. In developed countries, infrastructure policies can open up opportunities for new players and increase competition.

We will revisit the importance of regulations and infrastructure policy in Chapter 6 in more detail. Let us now look at how the economy behaves during good times.

Virtuous Cycles

During good times, the economy sees a flow of capital through transactions that act as the oil and keep the capitalism engine running smoothly. Consumers' appetite is at a high as they are actively buying products and services from large corporations. For the sake of simplifying this process, let us understand that the economy sees transactions happening from the top tier in the pyramid to the bottom tier of startups and small businesses.

Organisations at the top of the pyramid do well, thanks to consumer appetite. Banks see a rise in deposits and credit decisions are typically easier. If you are looking for a mortgage during these times, you are more likely going to be asked fewer questions and require fewer documents. Banks also act as distribution channels of capital to businesses. Therefore, with ample liquidity in the system, businesses are able to access the capital needed to build and expand.

As a result, these are times when large firms are making good revenues, healthy margins and, consequently, expanding operations. They are hiring aggressively and employee salaries, bonuses and pensions are on the rise. This results in the flow of capital into the next tier.

As a result, endowments and pension funds that are Tier 2 institutions have a good influx of capital from these flourishing organisations at the top. Tier 2 institutions are vehicles set up to deploy capital efficiently across a broad range of asset classes. Two such asset groups into which funds are allocated are listed and private equity (PE).

A vast portion of capital from Tier 2 institutions is allocated for public markets. This is deployed into funds that invest in public markets. A part of capital deployed in the public markets will be used to take positions in shares of the firms whose employees contribute back to the pension funds. This creates a virtuous cycle in good times (see Figure 1.2).

A similar cycle can be seen as pension funds invest in private equity and venture capital, which, in turn, invest in startups/businesses. Startups thrive on creating value through innovative services and products, resulting in higher consumer spending, thereby keeping the cash flowing through the system.

Since 2008, a low interest rate environment has definitely been driving more resources into ventures, just because of the perception that you can get better returns than the public markets.

Manuel Silva Martinez
General Partner at Mouro Capital

The allocation of capital into PEs and VCs increases during low-interest-rate environments as cash gets cheaper. As LPs see yields from traditional investment vehicles and public markets fall, they turn to the riskier asset classes such as PEs and VCs.

It is worth noting that these virtuous cycles become vicious during recessions. As liquidity dries up, all parties stop interacting with each other. As trust in the system goes down, the cost of capital typically increases. There is less motivation for LPs to look at risky asset classes such as PEs and VCs in such a climate. A stock market crash can also create a liquidity crunch that breaks these virtuous cycles. Often, there is a lack of trust between counterparties that do business with each other during a liquidity crunch. It is the role of the central banks to break these vicious cycles and get the virtuous cycles back in motion.

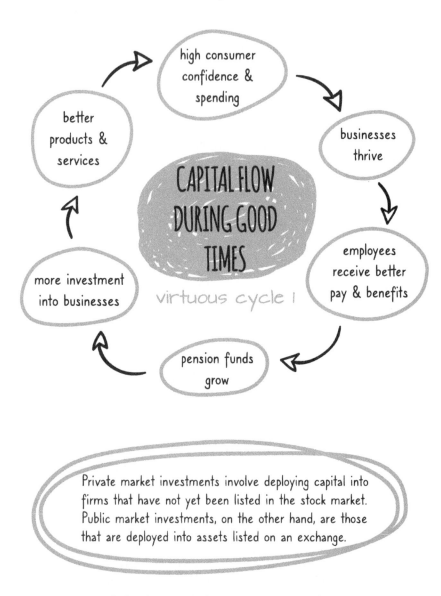

FIGURE 1.2 Capital Flow During Good Times – Virtuous Cycle 1

The capital pyramid has good liquidity during a market boom (see Figure 1.3). Stakeholders at different tiers of the pyramid can access capital with relative ease. Even banks relax their lending rules during this time. As the market rises, it is invariably accompanied by growth in the real estate market. As residential real estate booms, we often see a phenomenon called the *wealth effect*.

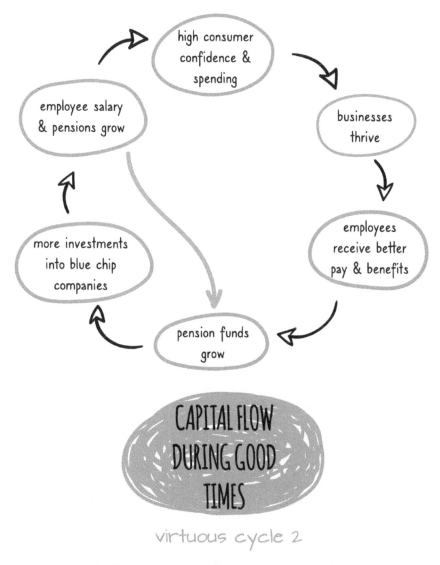

FIGURE 1.3   Capital Flow During Good Times – Virtuous Cycle 2

The Wealth Effect

The Wealth effect is a behavioural economics concept that articulates that consumers spend more as the value of their assets (properties) increases. There is a sense of abundance when property prices increase, which leads them to to their ebullience. This, in turn, brings more transactions, more liquidity and more confidence into the economy, acting as yet another virtuous cycle.

The wealth effect is noticed at different levels in different economies based on homeownership. In the UK, for instance, homeownership is the most prominent form of wealth and a rise in property prices has a higher correlation with a healthy economy. In other economies, such as Germany, where renting is widely preferred, homeownership has a lesser effect on consumer spending.

Therefore, if we must choose one *north star key performance indicator* (KPI)* for the economy, it should be consumer spending. If consumers keep spending healthily, the economy performs well. The moment consumer spending falls due to a credit crunch, unemployment or other structural issues, the economy goes into recession.

> *North star KPI* is the single most important key performance indicator to track progress on the growth of a business or the economy (in this case)

We have looked at ways the economy reinforces itself during a bull market. An understanding of these macroeconomic behaviours is essential for entrepreneurs to plan a course for their businesses. Let us now look at the motivations of the institutions in different tiers of the capital pyramid to understand it better. Let us start with the large corporations at the top.

An Interplay of Incentives

Thanks to the capitalistic society we live in, corporations are mostly interested in increasing short-term shareholder returns. In the process, they look at expanding their top line and bottom line, business lines, products and services, global presence and brand equity. As firms adopt a 'winner-takes-all' approach, hiring the right skills becomes crucial. Companies often pay competitive and, at times, predatory salaries to attract and retain talent. This results in better employee salaries and benefits.

Employees in an organisation play two crucial roles related to keeping the capital pyramid efficient. They contribute to pension schemes that will help with their retirement. They also play a critical role as consumers who are getting prosperous along with their organisations through a bull market. It is essential that employment numbers look healthy to keep the market sentiment positive.

> As the COVID-19 crisis peaked, the world was watching the US unemployment numbers closely. Just before the announcement of the unemployment numbers the US Federal Reserve announced an injection of capital into the economy. This was to mitigate the risk of the markets collapsing as unemployment numbers hit an all-time high in record speed. More on this in Chapter 2.

As corporations flourish, pension funds receive a healthy amount of capital. These funds look for ways to deploy the capital to ensure their assets under management appreciate. They have their risk appetites and holding periods to adhere to. They deploy capital into the liquid public markets and the illiquid private equity markets. Because private equity investments take longer to make returns, pension funds will have to wait for a few years before they see any meaningful returns.

PE and VC funds deploy their capital into private businesses and startups where the returns can be high, typically above a 25% internal rate of return (IRR). PE and VC investment thesis rely on their portfolio businesses getting them returns that are several times the invested capital. When these funds get it right, such as in the following instances, they make up for the losses from other investments in the portfolio.

> **The Facebook IPO:** The VC firm Accel Partners invested in Facebook in 2005 when they were valued at $12.7 million. In 2012, when Facebook went public at $104 billion valuation, Accel Partner's shares were worth $9 billion.
> **The Alibaba IPO:** In the year 2000, Softbank invested $20 million in Alibaba to own 30% of the firm. In 2014 when Alibaba did their IPO at a $231 billion valuation, Softbank's shares in the firm were worth $60 billion.

As PE and VC firms exit their investments and disburse their returns, they typically charge 'carry fees' from their investors or LPs. It is often easily said that PE and VC firms receive capital from their LPs, without highlighting the challenges involved. The usual suspects of the VC world have a track record of investments. As a result, they are often reached out by LPs (endowments, pension funds, fund of funds).

In good times, VC funds have dry powder, which sometimes puts them under deployment pressures from their LPs. LPs have committed capital to the VC funds hoping the VC investors would start deploying their capital. However, there are times when VC investors do not find good enough investment opportunities and are still under pressure to invest.

This sometimes forces VC investors to make a hasty investment decision to keep their LPs happy. VC investors who have capital during bull markets can do that with relative ease. During good times people want to invest actively all through the pyramid. Therefore, as VC investors raise capital, they are also keen to deploy them into startups.

Public and Private Markets

In the public markets, you can pay up for something. I can buy Zoom shares today. I don't care about the valuation. Valuations to me in the public markets don't matter to me much. It's all relative in the public markets. It's like if Zoom is worth this, can it be worth that?

In the private markets, you are betting on the time value of money. For instance, I rejected a Zynga investment opportunity a few years ago. When I saw the term sheet for the investment from Fred Wilson, I felt the deal was overvalued. But the $100k I could have invested in the deal then would be worth about $10 million. What I didn't see is that having the right investors on your cap table is priceless.

Howard Lindzon
General partner at Social Leverage

First-time funds typically have a harder time raising funds from LPs. It is often much easier to raise capital for a startup that has a specific business model, a known market, a stellar team and some product–market fit. However, when LPs invest in first-time VC funds, they are relying on a team that could make them huge returns from a blind pool of capital. As an investor, a blind pool of capital can feel more intangible than investing in a startup.

Innovation also takes place within incumbent banks. When corporates tend to allocate money from revenue-generating business lines into new experimental projects if they can afford to, that in itself is a reflection of their perspective on the economy.

During the bull market, corporations reserve extra capital for innovation. It's a hedge against the bear market.

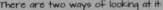

There are two ways of looking at it:
• Corporates are anticipating a downturn; therefore, they will need to invest heavily into products that can scale to make a dent on their P&L and balance sheet.
• Corporates now have extra cash to invest as a result of a bull market, thus, they spend more money on innovation.

Sopnendu Mohanty
Chief fintech officer at The Monetary Authority of Singapore

Many of these first-time VC investors focus on early-stage startups due to the limited amount of capital they can raise with their track record (or the lack of it). Often, they have to operate akin to a startup themselves, show progress through deployments and raise funds in parallel. These VC investors often have to wait a few years before they can start showing their portfolio performance and push for bigger funds.

Now that we have discussed the motivations of investors through the pyramid let us take a closer look at interactions between startups and VC funds during a market boom.

Investor Dilemma

A bull market is a time when excitement is everywhere and, even for the analytical investor, mediocre startups might look like excellent investment opportunities. As a result, this is a time when startups can call the shots and be choosy about the investors they take money from.

I was recently in a conversation with a VC friend who is focussed on growth-stage firms. He mentioned that in 2017, he was on a call with a portfolio firm and its potential investor for a subsequent fundraising round. Just by throwing in some hyped jargon into the conversation, the entrepreneur was able to get the investor excited. He got a commitment from the investor for several million dollars within an hour on the phone.

This is not how VC investors (should) operate. However, there are three different pressures I see VC investors going through during the good times that can perhaps help explain this behaviour:

- There is a good supply of capital from LPs and an urgency to deploy.
- There is a lot of demand for capital from startups, and it is hard to separate the noise.
- The market is quite active, increasing the fear of missing out (FOMO).

Even the best and the biggest VC investors can sometimes struggle to get into the best deals during these times. Entrepreneurs who know what they are doing line up several investors they can choose from. Therefore, they are careful about whom they want to take capital from. It is a market when people at the bottom of the pyramid do have some say.

95% of startups chase the VCs, but as a fund, we strive to partner with the top 5% of high quality startups instead

Ganesh Rengaswamy
Partner at Quona Capital

As a VC, if you screwed up 19 times but the 20th time you hit 100X, you are good. Not doing 100X is what you will get fired for. If Zoom walks in the door, and you say no, that's grounds to be fired. If you screwed up 10 times before you got Zoom, it may not matter as much.

In a family office, the payouts don't work that way. You're far more focussed on the downside, because the upside doesn't really get you very much. And you know, even if you pick the next great venture fund, they will deliver a 5X or a 7X for you. The payoffs are not gonna be so asymmetric like in a VC fund.

Hussein Kanji
Founder of Hoxton Ventures

You see your friends, colleagues, your company and everybody having a party time and then you're like a fool. You are the one who's sitting by the corner not investing when the party is going on. It's very hard for you to take the opposite view, to dig in and say, 'Hey, I'm preparing for a correction in the economy, I'm preparing for hibernation, I'm preparing for winter and that's totally contrary to what everybody else is doing'.

Navin Gupta
Managing Director of South Asia and MENA at Ripple

Some new attractions for VC investors have been Fintech between 2014 and 2018, Blockchain at the same period and the other hyped up technologies such as AI and Quantum Computing. These technologies are used by entrepreneurs in their pitch decks to lure investor attention. Some investors see through these hype words and focus on the 'So what?'. They like to see that the technology is used to solve a genuine problem. However, in most cases, investors succumb to the FOMO pressures and go with the crowd.

From the perspective of a startup, there is one group of investors whom they should not ignore. They are the rich families, UHNWIs and HNWIs who have typically made their money through other ventures or inherited wealth that they would like to invest. This group of investors operate differently from institutional investors such as pension funds and even VC funds.

HNWIs often make decisions quicker than institutions, thus saving precious time for an early-stage entrepreneur. A business looking at a quick fundraise should definitely consider this group of people. There is more structure if not science to the investment decisions of institutional investors.

When businesses are at an early stage, there is very little data to demonstrate the viability of their business models. HNWIs and family offices can generally tolerate that and can get the vision of the entrepreneur without needing too many data points. The due diligence processes with these investors are shorter and lighter than institutional investors. More tips and techniques in approaching investors are provided in Chapter 6. Please see Figure 1.4 for the gist of this chapter.

CHAPTER SKETCH

Employees in an organization play two crucial roles in keeping the capital pyramid efficient.

They contribute to pension schemes that will help with their retirement.

They act as consumers who are getting venture capital investors focussed on early-stage startups due to the amount of capital they can raise.

Three different pressures on VC during good times:

» Urgency to deploy from LPs

» Demand from mediocre startups

» Fear of missing out (FOMO)

When a wave of bad investment decisions collapse at scale globally

it results in a recession

Wealth Effect

a behavioural economics concept that identifies that consumers spend more as the value of their assets increase

WHEN CONSUMER SPENDING FALLS THE ECONOMY GOES INTO A

recession

FIGURE 1.4 Chapter One Sketch

Fund Manager vs. Angel Investor

As a professional fund manager, you have a thesis and governance to go through before making investments. You are not at liberty to make investment decisions at will, if that contradicts the fund's thesis. You don't want to get into trouble for doing unconventional things.

But when it's your own money you are investing, no one is going to fire you for backing something you believe in, even if it is not purely aligned to your thesis of investing. But when you break your own rules, you have to really understand why you're breaking them, whether it is domain experience, or experience with the founder, or just some unique edge that you think you have.

Howard Lindzon
General partner at Social Leverage

Seed funds can get screwed when they invest too fast and the market turns. You can end up with a number of hungry mouths to feed and companies going through refinancing right when the markets are tight.

You might also have invested too much of your portfolio when valuations weren't that friendly, or raised too much in hot markets. That's why temporal diversification matters.

Fred Destin
Founder of Stride VC.

Conclusion

In this chapter, I wanted to bring to light the macroeconomic factors that an entrepreneur needs to understand. When a central bank slashes interest rates, when oil prices fall, when a data policy takes effect across a region, there are ramifications across the innovation ecosystem. A good understanding of this will help entrepreneurs make contextual decisions.

We discussed the capital pyramid and how capital is distributed across the different tiers. We went through the motivations and the incentive structures of various stakeholders in the pyramid. We focused on VCs, CVCs, NWIs and family offices a bit more than the other actors because they are more relevant from a funding standpoint. Startups need to see this structure as a chain of actors who make money work for the whole system.

VC investors are not where the buck stops, and they have their own capital raising to do. Their investors, called limited partners, are typically endowments, pension funds and sometimes large family offices and corporations, too. Therefore, startups need to understand the source of funding for VC investors and how that source will behave during times of market ups and downs.

We see several virtuous cycles in a booming economy due to transactions that happen throughout the pyramid. The balance of these cycles must be maintained in a healthy optimal economy where there are no systemic issues emerging. That is the role of central banks in an economy. They strictly monitor several macroeconomic variables and fine-tune the economy through tools such as interest rates and quantitative easing.

During market highs, there are several pressures on investors to deploy capital. There are psychological pressures on them as they fear missing out on a deal even when it is a mediocre one. They might also have demands from their LPs who may make them deploy capital with a sense of urgency. This starts as sporadic investor behaviour and soon becomes systemic resulting in an overheated economy, needing to be corrected.

In Chapter 2 we will see how crises have happened in the past and understand key patterns and takeaways from the recessions since the 1980s.

CHAPTER 2

Hindsight's 2020

When devils will the blackest sins put on,
They do suggest at first with heavenly shows, . . .
— William Shakespeare, Othello

Introduction

I am a venture capitalist and I believe in capitalism. It is not without its faults; however, this is the best system that we have today. I was in school in 1991 when India, which had been a closed economy until then, chose to liberalise. The Indian economy was in crisis and was struggling to choose between communism in the USSR, its closest ally at that time, and capitalism. It was a watershed moment in July 1991 when the decision was made to open its door to capitalism.

Until that point, the country's economy was surviving on a month-to-month basis. The government was cash-strapped and it had to get innovative to keep the country afloat. The economy needed a reboot and something drastic had to be done. The collapse of the USSR helped accelerate the decision to liberalise the economy; however, it was more the country's crisis that drove the transformation of the markets and resulted in growth and a booming middle class. Crisis makes us focus on the things that matter and often accelerates change. For many who grew up in India during the 1980s and 1990s, capitalism has always been king because it has led to prosperity such as never before.

Since the 1991 liberalisation of the economy, the Indian markets have been considered as a precious jewel that both the West (the US) and the East (China) want a part of. The Indian middle class has grown in wealth and confidence on the global stage. Top Silicon Valley firms have brought in CEOs with Indian origin, most of whom were quite young in their careers when India began its journey towards capitalism.

Yes, capitalism has created inequality, but it has helped millions of people out of poverty too. In India alone, between 2006 and 2016, more than 270 million people got out of poverty and started making at least $10 a day. Therefore, the system clearly works, at least in certain contexts. I wouldn't disagree that capitalism is still a work in progress, but it is the best system we have. So, of what relevance is the India story to this chapter?

In this chapter, we will walk you through the crises that have hit capital markets in the internet era and the causes and effects of these market slowdowns. However, I wanted to highlight the fact that I am pro-capitalism, because I have seen how it can change the lives of a billion people within a decade. In my eyes, capitalism is just a system, and people need to use the system wisely. Despite several market crashes, with a little tweak, capitalism can help create sustainable economies.

For those who have been badly hit by the COVID crisis and do not want to hear the *c* word any more, please bear with us as we walk you through how and why some of these crises have occurred since the 1980s. You will see light at the end of the tunnel shortly. It is critical that entrepreneurs understand the macro environment that they are operating in.

An understanding of the macro factors of the economy is helpful during good times, but it is quintessential during a market slowdown because it helps you decide how well you can navigate your way through a crisis. As recessions shut doors on certain business models and industries, they invariably open them to a number of new business models and industries. We have seen survivors of recessions thrive and grow very quickly as they emerge out of it.

Entrepreneurs must understand the cause and effects of recessions and be able to read into the fundamental shifts they often bring. A solution framework that helps people navigate through a crisis begins with an understanding of how well they have understood crises in general.

I must stress that this book is about carrying your hopes through a crisis. Although this chapter describes the four biggest crises of the technology era, the intention is that we understand them and the patterns that are typically seen before a structural crisis.

Structural versus Event-Driven Crises

The internet era has witnessed four major market crises so far. We can categorise them broadly into two: structural and event-driven crises. Economists would add cyclical crisis to the list, but as discussed in Chapter 1, capital markets work in cycles and respond to policy makers. However, in my view the crises of the technology era have all been either structural or event-driven.

Structural

The Black Monday market crash in 1987, the dot-com bubble at the close of the millennium and the Great Recession of 2008 can all be categorised as a structural collapse of the economy. Each crisis had different triggers that started the market crash, but there were fundamental issues with markets, systemic risks and overheating of economies. As the system was getting too toxic, market players started losing confidence, leading to a quick drying-up of liquidity in the system.

As a result, the structural issues had to be fixed by monetary policies and banking regulations. Markets had to go through a period of correction before the return of the bull markets.

Event-Driven

For the first time in the post-War era, we have seen an event-driven global crisis through the COVID-19 virus. The world had no idea how to deal with a pandemic that had little trouble spreading across the world within weeks and brought most key economies across the globe to a standstill. The immediate response was to ensure the death toll didn't get out of hand. It was hard to strike the right balance between protecting lives and saving economies.

Several world economies stabilised markets through various monetary tools, went through the flattening of the COVID curve, and have slowly started to open up their economies. However, even before the virus triggered the crisis, there were talks of a recession looming on the horizon. There were overvaluations from time to time and the system was starting to creak.

We're going to see some mortality (for startups) in several markets that are going through their first venture cycle. I think people are going to become more sane, thoughtful and philosophical in general, which I think is good. I keep telling people that a lot of venture investing and the work we do with companies, boards and more is so much about human psychology and having a philosophy of life and not just about making money.

Seed funds are going to be under stress. They may not be able to raise the next funds, as a number of their portfolio companies will disappear and they will have a tough time answering to LPs.

Ganesh Rengaswamy
Partner at Quona Capital

In the case of the COVID crisis, consumer inactivity happened at an alarming rate. The rise of unemployment in the US was also unprecedented.

Although these issues were caused by the COVID virus, we cannot directly link them to a structural economic issue. But the COVID crisis has started to expose the structural weaknesses of several economies across the globe. We might see a lagged structural recession if the global economy can't bounce back soon.

The response to the COVID crisis has been more humane from policy makers than purely structural. Several countries have announced funding to protect small businesses, entrepreneurs and employees with a 'universal basic income' type of model. This move was unprecedented, yet understandable. Interest rate cuts and quantitative easing have also been employed.

The key difference between a structural and event-driven crisis is that in a structural crisis policy makers might not necessarily look at the humanitarian factor. If an event such as a pandemic causes a recession, the response must begin with humanitarian measures followed by economic measures. An event-driven crisis can be followed by a structural crisis with a lag. Let us now look at the crises since the 1980s.

The Crisis Timeline

In a recent conversation with a portfolio startup CEO, I asked what it felt like at the beginning of the COVID crisis. The entrepreneur's answer was, 'I am married, and I run a startup. You think a virus can be worse?' But unlike marriage or a startup, a crisis often blindsides us. If we are not familiar with the symptoms of a crisis, the surprise factor will hurt us more than the crisis itself.

Market crises have occurred since the tulip mania in the Netherlands in the 17th century. However, the most relevant crises to discuss here are those that have happened since internet and technology firms have become relevant (see Figure 2.1).

Let us first start with the 1987 market crash.

I usually look at crises across three categories:
- Structural crisis - Global financial crisis in 2008, which was a balance sheet issue, is an example.
- Cyclical crisis - Inflation, unemployment, which the central banks and regulators manage.
- Event-driven crisis - COVID-19 crisis.

Sopnendu Mohanty
Chief fintech officer at The Monetary Authority of Singapore

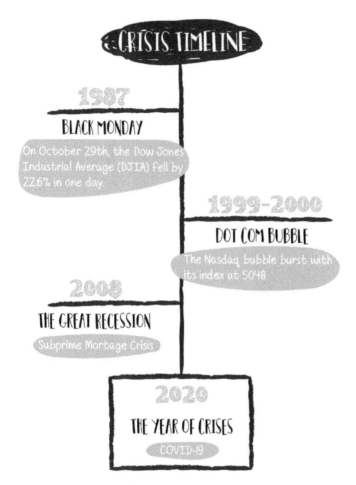

FIGURE 2.1 Crisis Timeline

Black Monday 1987

Apple was 11 years old and Microsoft 12 when the Black Monday crash took place on 29 October 1987. The Dow Jones Industrial Average (DJIA) fell 22.6% in one day. The next biggest fall had happened in 1929: a 12.8% fall of the DJIA in a single day.

In the build up to the crisis, stock markets across the world were booming through the mid-1980s. The Dow had risen from 820 in May 1980 to 2560 in September 1987. Price-to-earnings ratio had crossed 20 and most investors saw the market as overvalued. Inflation was rising and the Federal Reserve had to respond with interest rate rises. From just below 6% in 1985 interest rates rose to 10% at the market peak in 1987.

Figure 2.2 shows how interest rates rose to unsustainable levels during the mid-1980s and, as the markets crashed, it shows how rates had to be slashed back to single digits. The chart demonstrates another key trend worth noting. There is a relative rise in interest rates before every crash. This is due to increasing consumption resulting in inflationary pressures.

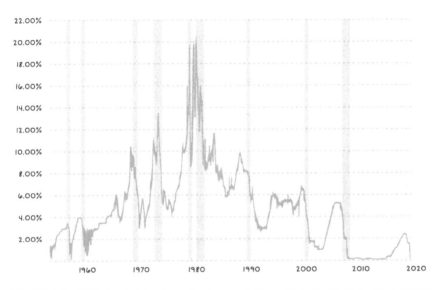

FIGURE 2.2　US Interest Rate. *Source: Investing.com, US Interest Rates. © 2020, Fusion Media Limited.*

There were two other fundamental factors involved in the 1987 crash. Several institutional investors used *portfolio insurance**, which gave them a false sense of security. As a result, these market participants had higher risk appetites than usual, knowing that their portfolios were insured.

> *Portfolio insurance* is the strategy of hedging a portfolio of stocks against market risk by short-selling stock index futures.
> *Source:* **www.investopedia.com/terms/p/portfolioinsurance.asp**.

The other factor that contributed to the market fall was programme trading. It was in the early days of computers being used in market trading. Computers were executing trading strategies without the right governance and controls. In a more mature environment, these programmes would have been put through testing to understand how they would behave in times of market stress. However, the regulators didn't have the foresight. As a result, the institutions using these systems, and their regulators, failed to see how these systems would react when a market slide was triggered.

Therefore, as macroeconomic factors caused a fall in the stock market, computer programs triggered a further downward slide as soon as prices fell past a certain threshold. These programs also turned off all the buying, making the situation worse. As the selling spiralled and buying shut down, the market ended up by losing more than 20% in a single trading day.

The computer program contributed to the losses; however, the fundamental issue was the macroeconomic triggers. During peak times, there is 'irrational exuberance' in the market, which is similar to a house of cards. Most market participants want to ride this wave into glory and do not want to miss out. FOMO further exacerbates market exuberance. Money flows into businesses and investment opportunities where there are no sound fundamentals.

When this house of cards is exposed to a mild storm, it starts to collapse. However, an astute investor knows when the market is overvalued. As the master investor Warren Buffett puts it,

'We simply attempt to be fearful when others are greedy and to be greedy only when others are fearful'.

In a survey conducted by Robert J. Schiller in 1987 for the National Bureau of Economic Research (www.nber.org/papers/w2446.pdf), a questionnaire was sent to institutional and retail investors to understand what triggered the collapse on Black Monday. More than 1,000 responses were received and one of the key findings was that both buyers and sellers thought before the crash that the market was overvalued. Let us now move on to the crisis when the dot-com bubble burst.

Dot-Com Bubble 1999–2000

The 1987 Black Monday crash was perhaps the first time technology had a hand in a market crash. However, in that instance, it was an operational issue. The dot-com boom and bust was directly related to technology businesses. As the market recovered from Black Monday, there was tremendous growth when the Federal Reserve cut interest rates. Thanks to the policy makers at the top of the money pyramid, there was cheap money available, and it only took two years for the markets to return to pre-crash highs after 1987. This is in stark contrast to the 1929 crash when the market took 20 years to return to pre-crash highs.

As discussed in Chapter 1, the capital pyramid was seen in full action through the 1990s. The interest rates set by the Federal Reserve fell to about 3% in the early 1990s from 10% just before the 1987 crash. As the Federal Reserve slashed interest rates, cheap money flushed through the pyramid. It made its way through VC firms into technology startups.

Let's talk in a bit more detail about how VC investors make their money. As discussed in Chapter 1, VC investors receive investment capital from their LPs: pension funds, family offices and endowments. The VC's role in a capitalist economy is to deploy these funds into private businesses, make handsome returns for their LPs and take a commission.

These businesses will be early-stage startups, often with very little or no revenues. There are VC investors who invest in slightly more mature startups, too. However, the economics are similar across VC investors who invest at different points in the business cycle of a startup.

VC investors invest in private firms early on and help them grow and create value. Once they are big enough, they exit the investment through a sale of their shares in the company to a bigger investor or into the public markets through an initial public offering (IPO). This can be quite lucrative, when they get it right. Therefore, in a portfolio of say, 10 investments, if two or three performed exceedingly well, the VC fund would have still made a good return for their LPs.

There is a risk in both good and bad times. In good times, as the value of the investments appreciates, VC investors are still looking at an unrealised paper increase which cannot be realised until there is a sale or an IPO. Until these exit opportunities, also termed *liquidity events,* happen it is generally not possible for investors to get their monies back. The risk of not being able to exit a start-up investment until such an event happens is called liquidity risk.

If the investment was in the stock market (that is, liquid) instead, and if the investment didn't do well, it would be possible for investors to exit their positions, get some of their money back and cut their losses. It is important to grasp this risk–return dynamic of the VC industry to help understand the dot-com bubble better.

As investments into technology start-ups hit unprecedented highs, many of them turned bullish and went for premature IPOs. Without viable business models, sufficient revenue and a huge percentage of VC investment being allocated to marketing budgets of these startups, it was really a house of cards. 'Jargon mania' was in full swing, as investors piled money into any business that had a .com angle to it.

Through 1999 and the first quarter of 2000, 386 technology companies had their IPOs. Most of these were in Nasdaq, the US index that has a large proportion of technology firms. This resulted in Nasdaq growing from 1000 in 1995 to 5000 in 2000.

After a few years of irrational exuberance in the private and public markets for technology businesses, the bubble finally burst. The Nasdaq index was at 5048 when technology firms started to sell their own shares, which triggered panic selling. In a few months, most technology stocks on the Nasdaq had become worthless, and even blue-chip companies were trading at historic lows.

It would be hypocritical for me to say that I wouldn't want to make such crazy money. However, one of the first things entrepreneurs need to do is to ensure they have a viable business model in place. The Silicon Valley model of grow, grow, until you can take the whole market and then figure out how to make money could work too, and there is no denying that there are technology firms who have done it.

However, it is very important for the management of a company to assess that their business model is viable, at least before they get listed through an IPO. Until the point of an IPO, it is largely accredited investors who have signed cheques for the firm. They generally understand the risk–return profile of the private equity asset class. But, once a firm is public, retail investors who do not understand the viability of business models will invest into it.

In my opinion, it is irresponsible for the management team, the board and the regulators to let a firm that can't demonstrate profitability list on an exchange. Let's now go back to how spectacularly the Nasdaq crashed in 2000.

Throughout the rest of 2000, and into 2001, markets tumbled. The situation was made worse by the terrorist attack on the twin towers on 11 September 2001. We all knew the world had changed and would no longer be the same.

Let us now move on to 2008, when the US housing market collapsed.

The Great Recession of 2008

I was working at Barclays Capital (Barcap) when the Great Recession struck the world. As a foot soldier in front-office technology, it was nervous times because budgets were being cut across the organisation. However, as Lehman Brothers collapsed, Barcap spotted an opportunity to acquire their equities business in the US. We all knew that things were never going to be the same at Barcap, which was until then a new kid on the block amongst giants in investment banking. At Barcap, I had the opportunity to witness how smart leadership can turn a crisis into a life-changing opportunity.

I was an investment banker between 2005 and 2010. I had the opportunity of working on mergers and acquisitions deals during the peaks of the market and again in 2008 as the recession kicked in.

It is not just in PE and VC that overvaluations happen during a bull market. Even in the public markets often transactions are overvalued I remember a travel company acquisition, where the firm wasn't the best and the margins weren't great either. Unit economics weren't in a steady state, however, the acquired company had a huge customer base. The acquirer was well aware of this and overpaid for the deal.

Kelvin Au
Head of venture at Founders Factory

Unlike the 1987 crisis or the dot-com bubble, the Great Recession of 2008 didn't have much to do with technology or technology companies. The crisis was triggered by the US real estate market; more specifically, the US *subprime** mortgage industry.

> *Subprime* borrowers are those who have a bad credit history and a high risk of defaulting their credit obligations.

Starting in 1999, after the dot-com crisis and the 9/11 attack, the US Federal National Mortgage Association (Fannie Mae) made mortgages more affordable to subprime borrowers. This resulted in an increase in homeownership, which caused increased levels of systemic risk (see Figure 2.3).

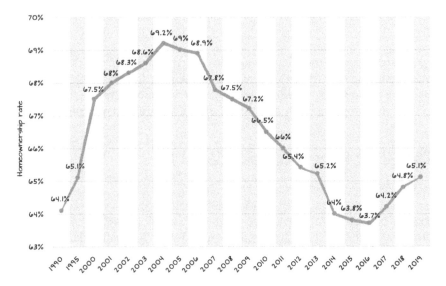

FIGURE 2.3 Homeownership Rate. *Source: Statistia, Homeownership rate in the United States from 1990 to 2019 © 2019, Statista, Inc.*

For instance, many of these subprime borrowers were being charged variable interest rates or were started on low interest rates that would soon increase. These low interest rates were fixed for a period of two to three years, after which the lending institutions increased the rates alarmingly. Often, as homeowners struggled to meet their mortgage payments, they would have to sell their property and make money from the sale. This worked when property prices were going up because homeowners had equity in their property.

If you own equity in a startup or have invested in real estate in the middle of 2006, everything seems fine. Everybody is having a party time, you fear looking like a fool if you are not investing.

Navin Gupta
Managing Director of South Asia and MENA at Ripple

This plan of increasing homeownership to subprime borrowers was supplemented by a product that banks had gotten very fond of, called *mortgage-backed securities (MBS)*. These securities allowed banks to borrow money from investors, pay them a periodic coupon, and lend the monies to these subprime borrowers. Banks would take a cut in the middle without taking on too much risk. As a result, they were able to offload most of the lending risk to the investors who bought these MBS.

The quality of the MBS was only as high as the quality of the mortgages that the banks had offered to their borrowers. This worked well as house prices kept increasing until 2006. However, when house prices stalled and people's debts kept growing, defaults were inevitable. Homeowners had to give up their properties because they couldn't pay their mortgages. As these defaults increased, banks couldn't honour their obligations to the investors of the MBS.

This triggered a systemic collapse through 2007 and 2008. Lending from banks came to a standstill and liquidity within the economy evaporated. This was made worse when financial institutions tried to lend to each other, but they often didn't have a view on the credit health of the institution (the counterparty) at the other end of the transaction. This loss of trust across capital markets made it more difficult for institutions to find some liquidity to address their short-term obligations.

The 2008 financial crisis exposed the fragility in our financial system. Some of this has been resolved today in terms of the provision of capital that firms need to hold, and the risk management within financial services.

David Brear
Founder and group CEO of 11:FS

On 15 September 2008 the crisis hit its climax with Lehman Brothers, the fourth-largest investment bank on Wall Street, filing for bankruptcy. They had over $600 billion in assets, yet were not able to escape the fall from grace. The markets lost over $10 trillion in the following months, and the US Treasury had to intervene by providing a $1 trillion package to buy toxic assets through a programme called the Troubled Asset Relief Program (TARP).

The market stayed volatile over the remaining months of 2008 and through the first quarter of 2009. The recovery started in 2009, and it took about four years to get to the pre-crisis highs. The 2008 crisis is perhaps not as directly related to technology startups as the dot-com crisis. However, startups must realise that they are part of an ecosystem that relies heavily on the larger economy functioning optimally.

As Lehman Brothers collapsed, our investment banking team shrank from 16 people to 5. I was one of the fortunate ones to keep my job. All the large cap deals basically dried up and I started leading coverage on SMEs. That's when my firm started covering small caps. That was when I personally got involved in the startup space in 2008. It gave me the opportunity to work with many entrepreneurs and venture capital investors. I wouldn't be here if not for the crisis.

Kelvin Au
Head of venture at Founders Factory

In 2007, we were feeling good in the venture world, and then 2008 happened and brought the economy to a standstill. Each crisis had a different cause. The 2001 crisis was more of a dot-com and a tech bubble. 2008 was a broader, sort of systemic issue that hurt Wall Street more than technology firms.

One of the first things that happened was flight-to-quality in the startup world. The best startups, perhaps, the top quartile of the startups continued to do well and to get the lion's share of the capital that was available.

Arvind Purushotham
Head of ventures at Citi

As the recovery from the 2008 crisis was well underway, the global economy saw a few minor tremors from Brexit and instability in Europe. As a result, central banks and regulators have largely kept interest rates at historic lows, making that the new normal. This has meant there has been easy cash in the capital pyramid that has flown into the innovation ecosystem. VC investors have come swinging hard and have had several home runs in the decade since the 2008 crisis. Some of the large VC-backed exits and mergers and acquisitions (M&As) of the decade are shown in Figure 2.4.

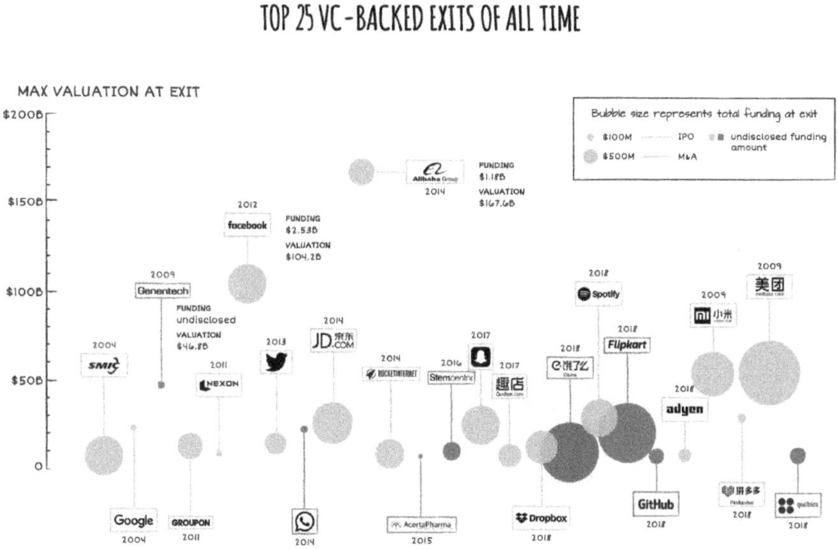

TOP 25 VC-BACKED EXITS OF ALL TIME

FIGURE 2.4   Top 25 VC-Backed Exits of All Time.

As this trend of easy money continued, the decade from 2008 to 2018 was a pretty good one for the VC and start-up community. At the start of 2020, for instance, there were several US VCs setting up shop in Europe. This was said to be because the US market had heated up and valuations were pretty high, and they considered European investments 'better value' for money. Although that gave us European VC investors hope on the health of our ecosystem, something that none of us foresaw blindsided us.

The Year of Crises – 2020

I was in school during the Black Monday crisis of 1987. I didn't remember the event until I had to study it as a capital markets professional. But the COVID crisis that we find ourselves in as I write will be etched in our memories forever. It has affected all our lives, be it children going to school or the oldest member of the family walking down to the grocery store for a pint of milk.

Recently, my four-year-old daughter Diya asked me if she could go out with me to the beach and have ice cream, once the coronavirus is 'killed'. I am sure she will remember the year 2020 for some time to come. Never in the post-war era have we had a crisis of this proportion affecting and perhaps transforming our lifestyle, work and markets. Yes, the 2008 economic crisis hit people's livelihoods, careers, economies and more. But 2020 has felt more personal, at least it has for me.

It was also the first time since World War I that the world saw a recession triggered by a virus. The year started with a bang, quite literally when the US assassinated an Iranian official. That was joined by the continuing Brexit upset driving poor market sentiment.

As we all wondered if it could get any more eventful for the year, COVID-19 hit us. When I look at the FTSE 100 index between December 2019 and May 2020, apart from the slight volatility that the index showed at the end of January (because of Brexit), it's largely flat, until COVID-19 of course. The crisis hit us at such a brisk pace that, by the time we realised we were entering we had already slipped deep into it.

> It hits you more severely when it hits you suddenly.
> Alexander Dumas, *The Count of Monte Cristo*

This crisis was different from previous ones, which since the post-war era have affected specific regions or markets in the world. Although there were secondary effects felt across the globe during the previous crises, this time most major markets across Asia, Europe and the Americas were directly slowed within a matter of a few days. The speed at which that happened was unforeseen too.

In order to soften the blow from the crisis, the Federal Reserve had to pump in several trillion dollars into the market to keep the economy from crashing further. As unemployment numbers in the US hit 36.5 million in May 2020, it remained to be seen how soon the lockdown would ease, allowing people to get back into their jobs. Although some economies across the world have started to open up, it is safe to say that life will not be back to pre-COVID normalcy until the efficacy of a vaccine is achieved at scale.

It is surprising to see how quickly the COVID crisis brought the world economy to a standstill. The other worry is the amount of money that the Federal Reserve pumped into the economy to create liquidity. Although this might have appeased a distressed market, it may turn out that the injection of such vast amounts was not good for the economy in the medium- and long-term and instead sowed the seeds for another recession.

In 2008 we saw primarily a banking crisis. It was a western world crisis, affecting markets in the US, UK, Europe to some extent and a bit of Japan. But everybody else only felt the secondary effect. Therefore, in some way, the 2008 crisis was contained, because it was not a global crisis. It was not a crisis in which every country would be drawn in.

The COVID crisis on the other hand has affected every meaningful market across the world directly. The whole globe is shrinking at the same time. This is a humanitarian crisis that is causing economic impact at scale.

Navin Gupta
Managing Director of South Asia and MENA at Ripple

During the 2008 crisis, banks were bailed out very fast compared to now, to keep the markets functioning. The impact on the public markets was mostly clear in 12 months. The venture ecosystem, however, always operates with a lag. The impact of the 2008 crisis was felt until 2011, as funds were struggling to raise money.

Today (through the COVID lockdown) when you look at the Nasdaq, it has regained its losses since March 2020 because the technology firms in it helped the rise. However, oil has struggled to see the same level of support. Therefore, you see technology stocks grow by 80% and oil going down by 60%.

David Fogel
Cofounder of Alma Angels, ADV, and Israel Tech Parliament

We are a healthcare AI company based in Palo Alto, California. One of the advantages we have in Silicon Valley is that we get access to information early on through the rich startup ecosystem. We had access to early data of what's going on with COVID.

Silicon Valley figured it out quite early on. Google and Facebook immediately went on 'work from home' policies, and we followed them as well. We had insights on what Stanford University was thinking because we work with them. So it was very obvious to us that this would be a pandemic quickly. Typically the run length of pandemics is 18 to 24 months. If you look at Ebola in 2013, for example, and the history of pandemics, it would help understand how long COVID will last.

Akshay Sharma
CTO at Docai

We have looked at the crises that occurred during the technology era. Let us now discuss what could be some early signs of a crisis and how start-ups can prepare proactively as they spot these signs.

If It Smells Like Funk

As an investor, I have had the privilege of looking at several hundred start-ups in a year. As Max would point out, we closely evaluated 403 start-ups in the 2019–2020 financial year. Over my modest VC career, I must have looked at more than 2000 companies. I am sure there are investors who have seen more opportunities come to them during this period.

Assessing businesses, interacting with them, and understanding the challenges and opportunities in relevance to their business landscape are day-to-day activities. Therefore, investors often have a hunch about market trends in relation to the innovation ecosystems, and good investors often have the right hunch.

Investors are able to stay on top of these market trends because they are able to plug themselves into the information grapevine of the macroeconomy and the local ecosystem. An understanding of the large moves at play and how those dynamics affect their innovation ecosystem is essential for an investor. An entrepreneur looking to navigate through a crisis must also develop some of these instincts.

Top economists across the world have struggled to predict the start or the end of a crisis. However, some structural issues can be spotted in an overheated economy. Let us now look at how entrepreneurs can identify those issues.

Greed Is Good, or Is It?

It is very hard to separate the phrase *irrational exuberance* from a crisis. Some economists argue that greed can be a good thing in driving innovation and creating value. However, it is also this human nature that leads to a market crash. Irrational exuberance has been the culprit behind every single market slowdown that has resulted in a liquidity crisis across the capital pyramid.

This exuberance doesn't happen without top-down support or a trigger. Central banks and regulators are often called out as responsible for setting policies that trigger human greed. Their role at the top of the pyramid is to ensure there is liquidity in the economy. Therefore, during times of crisis they use interest rate cuts and *quantitative easing** to bring back liquidity.

> *Quantitative easing* is the introduction of new money into the money supply by a central bank.

Both these tools bring cheap cash into the economy, resulting in orga-nisations such as banks taking more risks, investors being more lavish and consumers tapping into the opportunity. However, most of these actors in the economy are reacting to these monetary policies and often do not have a method of proactively optimising their investment strategies or spending patterns. As a result, a bull market is unleashed, leading to valuation bubbles, high inflation and general bloat.

Capital markets have developed a habit of hopping from one bubble burst to another. This behaviour affects the innovation ecosystem. Let us look at what those effects and trends are. Please note that there are very few astute minds in the world who have predicted a crisis successfully. Therefore, these trends are only going to tell you that there are structural issues emerging. They are not going to tell you precisely when an economic crisis is going to occur.

Consistent Overvaluation

As an entrepreneur, when you see a few investment rounds in your ecosystem that are at unrealistic valuations, you are at liberty to tell yourself that irrational exuberance is rampant. As a VC investor, I wholeheartedly ask you to tap into that exuberance. However, do not lose sight of the fact that you are at the top of the peak and, without care, you might soon find yourself sliding down the hill at a brisk pace.

What is the worst thing you can do in an overheated market? Invest too much too fast right as you might be heading into a difficult environment. When COVID hit we had no idea what we were in for and had no mental model for how this would impact the market, but we felt the balance of risk was on the downside. So we didn't stop investing, but we slowed the pace a little and moved earlier on the curve, to gently reduce our risk. We also worked hard and quickly to make sure everyone was properly financed.

Fred Destin
Founder of Stride VC

Consistent overvaluation of startups in funding rounds can become a new normal during the peaks of a bull market. Such overvaluations typically mean that there is a lot of easy cash and investors are desperate to deploy their capital. Start-ups have several funding options and can choose the ones that give them the best valuation. This is a sign of irrational exuberance at the top of a bull market. There are signs to note as the market starts to slide, albeit slowly initially.

Failed Funding Rounds

As the slide begins from the top of the bull market, initial signs start to show. Investors who get wind of macroeconomic creaks will (be forced to) take a break. This could mean that LPs of VC funds might fail to respond to a capital call from the fund. As LPs pull out, VC investors have little option but to put their deal-making on hold until capital is available.

This might come at a bad time for a start-up that is perhaps a couple of weeks away from closing a funding round that has been negotiated for a few months. If the venture capitalist who is pulling out is a lead investor for the funding round, that round might fail. These are sporadic instances that we typically would notice as a capital crunch begins. Do not expect to see such instances across the ecosystem, though. If you have begun seeing too many failed funding rounds, you are already well in the midst of a crisis.

Down Rounds

Down rounds are those where a start-up is funded at a share price lower than a closed previous funding round. This can happen for various reasons, and sometimes because of a combination of them:

- The start-up hasn't made the progress it had promised.
- The start-up has suddenly seen a cash flow challenge and is desperate to raise funds.
- The markets do not have the same dynamics anymore.
- Investors do not have the appetite to invest in previous valuations anymore.

The start-up not making the progress is sometimes a reflection of market conditions. If consumer spending and demand is cooling down, start-ups will have less traction than they anticipated. Cash flow issues for a start-up could arise from a vendor missing a payment or a highly lucrative contract not materialising or prematurely coming to a close. Start-ups with cash flow challenges get desperate and investors smell desperation from a mile away. All these issues often lead to down rounds for start-ups and are signs of trouble in the economy.

Funding Gaps

As liquidity dries up across the capital pyramid, funding gaps start showing up across the system. In 2019, for instance, as VC funding data across the world were released, it was clear that early-stage funding was slowing down. Late-stage firms still received good investments. Figure 2.5, from KPMG's Venture Pulse report, released in January 2020, highlights that the market peaked in 2015 for the number of investments and in 2018 for the value of investments. It also shows that early-stage deals that closed in 2019 were below 2018 highs. I don't intend to say that these drops in volumes or numbers of deals are a sign of a looming market crisis. However, it is important to note that often the number of deals can be a better indicator of the health of the venture eco-system than the quantum of investment.

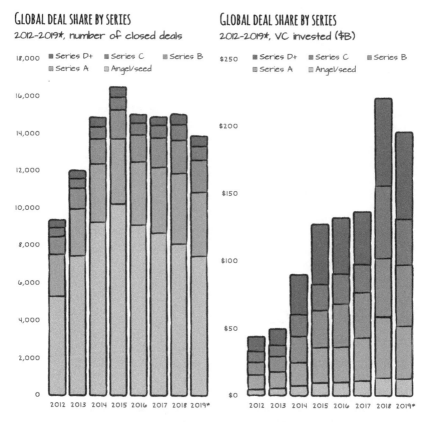

GLOBAL DEAL SHARE BY SERIES
2012–2019*, number of closed deals

GLOBAL DEAL SHARE BY SERIES
2012–2019*, VC invested ($B)

Source: Venture Pulse, Q419, Global Analysis of Venture Funding, KPMG Private Enterprise. *As of 12/3/19. Data provided by PitchBook, 1/15/20.

FIGURE 2.5   2019 Global Analysis of Venture Funding. *Source: KMPG, Venture Pulse Q4 2019, Global Analysis of Venture Funding, © 2019, KPMG International.*

If the numbers are increasing for growth-stage deals and are falling for early-stage startups, it indicates that investors' risk appetite for early-stage firms is falling (see Figure 2.6). It is a lower risk proposition to deploy capital in growth-stage firms because they have more data to demonstrate the health of the business. It is harder to substantiate that in early-stage start-ups. There-fore, early-stage start-ups take the hit first when investor risk appetite for the VC asset class falls.

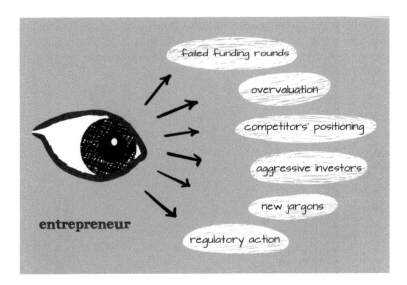

FIGURE 2.6 Crisis Watch List

We have discussed some key indicators of an overheated economy. Consider looking at some data collection and planning at this stage if you think a recession might be around the corner.

Data Collection

'The more you sweat in peacetime, the less you bleed in wartime'.

Running a business effectively as an entrepreneur can be a hard-enough task. Ensuring the product development milestones are achieved, the sales pipeline is rich, clients are happy and the team is staying together can easily exhaust even the best-prepared business person. Therefore, I would understand if data collection and scenario planning in preparation for a 'potential crisis' is the last thing you want to be spending your time doing, especially because you will likely still have to do tactical and strategic planning once a crisis hits. More on that in Chapter 4.

Creating a separate plan for crisis management in anticipation of a market crash might sound like b-school bullshit. However, the suggestions in this section need not necessarily be a separate stream of operational activities to perform in anticipation of a crisis. You can integrate this thinking into your day-to-day operations to save yourself time and effort once a crisis hits.

It is essential that you focus objectively on data collection and not jump into acting on them straight away. A crisis often creates market pivots and the data that you collect now might point to a different set of actions once the crisis has arrived. Please note that this data collection is happening pre-crisis. Let us first look at how you can tap your ecosystem for information before looking internally into the firm.

Ecosystem Pulse

I sometimes find myself talking to entrepreneurs who have no clue about what is going on in their own *ecosystem**. As a business owner, it is important to ensure you know who the actors are in your ecosystem, how you can reach out to them if needed, and try and keep them informed about what you are doing, directly or indirectly. It is also important that your ecosystem knows what you are doing and feeds you information from time to time, even before you ask for it.

> By *ecosystem,* I refer to the organism that is made of other start-ups that operate in the same space, angel investors and VC investors who are active and relevant, accelerator programmes and events. This can also be extended to regulators when a start-up is focused on a space that is highly regulated.

I am critical of entrepreneurs who spend too much time at events and less time focussing on their business. Entrepreneurs need to tap into events to build brand equity, albeit in moderation.

Entrepreneurs who are well plugged into their ecosystem often find information at their disposal. Failed funding rounds, overvaluations, mind-less investors, competitors' positioning, acquisitions, regulatory risks and 'new jargon that sells' are all critical news feeds for entrepreneurs. These are trends that help entrepreneurs prepare their firm for a crisis if they have spotted any systemic issues.

In November 2019, we felt that the balance of risks shifted to the downside. There were too many storm clouds on the horizon.
So we decided to do a few things to adjust our risk: we invested a little more slowly, a little earlier on the curve, and primarily in businesses that were less path dependent and less funding dependent. We also took advantage of a hot market to make sure all our companies were properly funded, even if it meant raising earlier than planned.

Fred Destin
Founder at Stride VC

You might also want to keep receiving intelligent feeds about the field you are operating in. Spending 15 minutes every day going through this feed to understand market trends will be helpful. It not only makes you sound cleverer in conversations with your team, peers and investors, but also helps you understand what your competitors are doing.

An understanding of competitor activities, positioning and strategies is an attribute I look for in my portfolio founding teams. This is also important for VC investors who pitch to their LPs for funds.

When I pitched for funding to Banesh Prabhu, a former C-Suite executive at Citigroup Consumer Bank, we had an hour-long discussion on where financial technology (fintech) was headed. I had to match his knowledge about the field with my understanding of the ecosystem and the most recent trends to impress him and win him over as an investor and subsequently as a business partner.

Team

If there is only one thing that you can proactively attend to as you sense a crisis coming - it's your team. A top-class team can even create a new market where there is none existing. People are the biggest assets in a start-up. Therefore, you need to ensure that your best people are engaged, informed and up for the roller coaster ride ahead (see Figure 2.7).

Some steps to take:

- **Toppers:** Engage with your team to identify your top people. If you have a 10-member team, you might not have to do this exercise because you know where each person stands. But once you grow past a 50-member team, it is hard to keep track of the top talent you want to hold on to through a crisis.

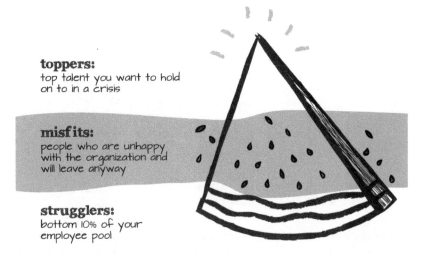

toppers:
top talent you want to hold on to in a crisis

misfits:
people who are unhappy with the organization and will leave anyway

strugglers:
bottom 10% of your employee pool

FIGURE 2.7 Team Makeup

- **Strugglers:** It is also critical to know the bottom 10% of your employee pool. This is to ensure that if you have to act quickly when the market crashes you know who would be the first to go.
- **Misfits:** Try to spot team members who are unhappy with the organisation, the vision, their role in the firm or just feel they are a misfit culturally. These are people who will likely leave your firm anyway. Therefore, making a note of these people will help make quick personnel decisions once you are in a crisis.

You might want to use a simple model such as this even in normal times to decide compensation on an ongoing basis, not just to prepare the firm for a crisis. Keeping this information up-to-date can help with quick and decisive action when needed.

Product

The pre-crisis planning is all about data collection and not about action. Therefore you will need to work with your product head to understand the road map of the product. Most have three broad categories of functionality that make sense to the board or the management team:

- Market-driven
- Experimental
- Product debt

Market-driven functionalities are those that are being driven by client or market demand. If you have a software as a service (SaaS) solution providing a better email experience and your iOS solution is selling like hotcakes, you would want to focus on rolling out an Android experience, too. That is a big market that you can't ignore after your success with iOS users. These product enhancements would result in revenues in the short term.

Experimental functionalities are those for which you have a core product and you plan to introduce either new functionality or a new product line. You are at a stage when your new product line will be rolled out in a lean fashion as you assess the market uptake for the new product. These functionalities are not necessarily going to bring in revenue in the near future.

Product debt is an aspect of the product that needs to be fixed. Oftentimes, as technology teams work with time and budget constraints, they have to make compromises on the design or performance of a product. However, they always know that they need to come back and fix the tactical work sometime in the future. Although these functionalities might not necessarily bring revenues all by themselves, they can enhance customer experience and satisfaction.

It is important to understand the proportion of the product road map and the associated costs that fall under these categories. This will help you understand the investments you are making into product development that directly contribute to a quick revenue opportunity, the ones that could make your product better and the ones that your product team thinks are potential opportunities in the future.

You can go a little further with this data collection and map your team members who are working on each of these types of functionality. In doing so, you will be able to understand who in your team is on the critical path to revenue-making opportunities. That information, when combined with performance details, will serve you well in making personnel decisions once a crisis hits (see Figure 2.8).

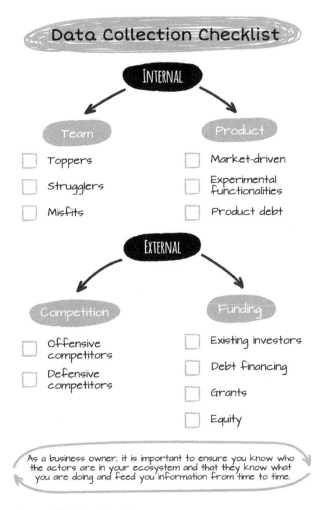

FIGURE 2.8 Data Collection Checklist

Although most product teams have a clear view on priorities of deliverables they are working on, they might not necessarily classify product functionalities like the above. It is important for the product team to provide information in the way management would consume, to help them make quick cost-saving decisions during a recession.

Competition

As a start-up, it is important to stay on top of your competitive landscape and ideally even their strategies. You should do this even during good market periods.

About five years ago, I was talking to the chief product officer of an Adtech firm. He mentioned to me how he shares some of his plans with his competitors and gets their feedback on them. He called them 'frenemies' with whom he doesn't have a problem sharing his road map. In return, he gets to know what they are working on and planning in their road map. He stressed that sometimes, despite having similar product road maps, it is the execution that makes the difference.

This might not necessarily work for all start-ups. It does give a refreshing view on how competitors could help each other with a better understanding of the landscape. It is important to understand your competition and how they are positioned from a product strategy and financing perspective. Your competition is going to react either in an offensive or defensive way once the crisis hits.

If **offensive competitors** are well-capitalised and their product strategy has synergies with yours, you are most likely going to see them move aggressively to take advantage of a crisis. They could start by poaching your team or going after your market share through aggressive expansion.

You might also need to take into account how nimble and agile your competitors are. Sometimes they might be a much bigger company with deeper pockets positioned to take over the market. Speed of execution can make all the difference in a crisis, and it might be a red herring if the competitor has no clue what being nimble and agile means.

Running a troubled business in a niche market might also result in your positioning yourself to be acquired by larger competitors. A crisis is a time when smaller players get acquired more aggressively by competitors with dry powder. It is also when private equity players are looking for cheaper distressed assets.

If you are well capitalised and are able to take the aggressor role, you should look around for weaker competitors (**defensive competitors**). If your competition is lacking in financial might as you enter a crisis, you have fewer problems, but it might also be the ideal time for you to get aggressive and ensure you have taken a substantial lead over them through the crisis. You might need to assess additional funding options.

In essence, your positioning in the market can be more effective if you have data about your competitors' position.

Funding

Funding is often the most stressful part for entrepreneurs. Even the best CEOs I know hate the process of fundraising. Before a crisis hits, it is useful for firms to plan their runway and understand their burn rates, areas of potential cost savings and, most importantly, ways to raise some quick capital if needed.

There are three types of financing that a start-up can go for: debt, grants and equity. It is important for start-ups to plug themselves into the ecosystem to ensure they know their financing options. I do not expect you to start pitching to investors when you see a crisis coming. However, you will need to know what realistic financing options are available for you. Following are some options you should collect data on:

Existing investors are the lowest-hanging fruit when you assess financing options. It is beneficial to keep them warm through regular communication and engagement to show them you are making good progress. It is even more important to show them you are in a position of strength if a crisis hits. To capitalise on the strength and run faster than your competitors, you might need them to top up their investments. Also, keep an eye on the *cap table** to ensure you are not diluting too much too soon.

Cap table refers to the list of shareholders and their stake in a firm.

Debt financing: I usually find management teams of start-ups very badly informed about their debt options. During a crisis, debt options are generally more available than equity. If you are a pre-revenue start-up, your chances of getting debt financing are still slim. However, if you have revenues to show, or time-bound contracts demonstrating future revenue, debt is an option you should not ignore. It is essential for you to assess who the right debt providers are for your needs and plan financing accordingly.

Grants: Entrepreneurs can take advantage of non-dilutive cash from grants. Often these grants are match funding that these organisations will do when you have some investors lined up. Despite that, grants are a very useful tool for keeping a start-up funded. This is especially true for early- and venture-stage start-ups, but perhaps not so useful for growth-stage start-ups.

Equity: Start-ups often forget some basics of the equity fundraising process. For instance, you might be a pre-revenue start-up with a very strong product and a team. It is important to know the type of investors who will have an appetite for such a deal. If you are looking for defensive capital for preservation and are desperate, remember you might get a very low valuation.

In essence, it is important to study the financing options you have and be prepared to move quickly if you must, once a crisis hits. As we come to the end of the pre-crisis data collection process, it is important to remember that crises often cause markets to pivot. This might accelerate certain business models while shutting doors on others.

> One of my portfolio firms Bibliu, which was digitising university libraries, had closed a $6.5 million round just before the COVID crisis hit us. Within the first four weeks of the lockdown, they had dozens of new requests from universities across the world to pilot their software with them. Thankfully, they had the capital to cope and were well positioned to take advantage of the situation.

It is important to evaluate where you are, what your strengths and weaknesses are and act once you have some idea of the direction where the crisis is driving the market.

Conclusion

I would not be surprised if you got here with the thought that this is a ridiculously depressing chapter. But you got here, and that is a good sign. There are successful days and there are days when we learn the hard way. We can read about the success stories of technology start-ups in the history of Microsoft, Apple, Amazon and many more. However, very few who study the collapse of a start-up due to a crisis reflect on the effects of a market crash and prepare their business accordingly.

In this chapter, we saw the different market crises since the 1980s. We learned several pointers from all of them. However, if there was one common fundamental pattern, it is that irrational exuberance precedes a crash. It is only human to want more, but sometimes it can be a mindless want. That hurts our decision-making capability, leading to bad investments. As money flows into such non-performing assets, the financial system starts creaking.

If there is too much easy money flowing into capital markets, it results in mindless consumption and artificially inflated valuations of businesses. An economy that is built on those two can be viewed as a building with a weak foundation. It doesn't need a strong tremor to bring it down. Therefore, it is essential to understand the causes and effects of recessions and how we respond to them.

Chapter 1, about the capital pyramid, and this chapter, about recessions, provide an understanding of how macroeconomic activities affect start-ups. In this chapter, we touched on some initial assessments you can perform across teams, products, competition and financing if you spot signs of a crisis. During the data-collection stage, it is also important to note that there are two primary dimensions at play here. One is internal data about your firm and the other is market data. Please see Figure 2.9 for a chapter summary.

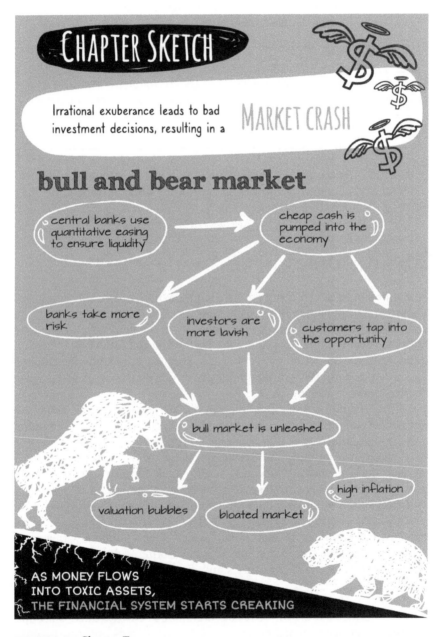

FIGURE 2.9 Chapter Two

The internal data that you have collected now might not change significantly as you enter the crisis. However, the external market data, and how you then perceive your internal data as the market shifts through the recession, can change significantly. It is important to remember that, at this stage, the focus is just data collection and not actions or decisions based on the data.

A team member who might be a misfit before a crisis might suddenly become a critical resource depending on how the market shifts. On a similar note, a competitor who is a small player might suddenly hit product-market fit and grow quickly. You might also see competitors go out of business during a crisis. Therefore, before making a decision based on internal data, you will need external market data, which is what we will start focussing on in the subsequent chapters.

The rest of the chapters in this book will walk you through the steps that an entrepreneur should take after a crisis has hits.

CHAPTER 3

Be Your Own Shrink

The fault ... is not in our stars,

But in our ourselves ...

William Shakespeare Julius Caesar

Introduction

In summer 2018, we went on a family vacation to Washington, DC. We stayed at my brother-in-law's place at Fairfax, Virginia. We had five families with kids staying there under one roof for more than five days. Tired of coping with the energy levels of the kids, we decided to try some outdoor activity. The choice was to go on a hike to the Great Falls, which offered a hiking trail that ran parallel to the flow of water.

It was a sunny day and I was pretty thrilled with the scenic water flow near us. During our hike, I took a little diversion from the rest of the family because I wanted to get closer to the water. In my excitement, I hadn't realised how steep the fall I managed to traverse was. I got to the water, enjoyed the experience, took some pictures and spent a few quiet minutes there. It was time to join the family on the main hike track.

I looked up and saw that I had a vertical climb to get back to them. I started worrying that the sun would set before I got back to my family. My wife was up there with our two- and five-year-old daughters. I would get a royal slap on my wrist for attempting such a foolish adventure if I didn't get there on time or if I got injured doing so.

I convinced myself that I should stop worrying and just focus on the next step. I started moving without looking too far ahead. Honestly, it wasn't that hard an exercise as the next step was mostly straightforward. Except in a couple of places where the climb was steep and slippery, it was only a short leap here and there. Soon, I found myself with the family. The physical effort I had to take to get up there was relatively modest in comparison to the mental efforts to overcome the panic and the inertia to act.

Once I got to the top, I looked back to where I had climbed up from and, funnily enough, I felt I had done something amazing. Therefore, if you find yourself in a hole, philosophically or practically, the only way is upwards. The simple thing to do is to not look too far ahead and just take the next step. That's what the rest of this book is about.

Crisis Is Here

Let's not fool ourselves: no amount of preparation can get you ready for a crisis. However, we have done our best to help with the process. We have so far discussed the capital pyramid, given a walkthrough of the crises of the modern technology era and discussed ways we can see trends that could typically precede a crisis. We also discussed briefly the information-gathering process from your ecosystem and the internal data collection required to prepare for a crisis.

Therefore, let's just accept that crisis is here and we must just deal with it. It is now time to move into the crisis and start exploring ways of finding your feet initially. To set the context for this section of the chapter, let us now assume you are at a point where the crisis has hit and the markets are tanking across the world. It's 23 March 2020 as the Dow Jones has crashed to 18,500 from 29,000 just a few days ago.

The world has gone crazy. Central banks are announcing crisis packages to avoid complete capital markets meltdown. Your suppliers and clients are going to have a tough few months. Your firm is looking up to you to lead it from the front. Let us start breaking things down as to what needs to be done.

PLEASE NOTE: There are several techniques I discuss in this chapter that can help with stress. However, I am not a professional psychiatrist or counselor, and I am not offering professional advice. The purpose of this chapter is to highlight the options entrepreneurs have to prepare themselves mentally in times of crisis. The techniques that I discuss as being effective for me or for people I know might not necessarily work for all.

Put on Your Seat Belt First

The importance of an entrepreneur's mental health cannot be underestimated, but it is often the most ignored aspect of an entrepreneur's attributes. A stable mindset is essential during normal market periods, but it is critical as things get tougher. As the leader of the pack it is the responsibility of CEOs to ensure they are in the best shape of mind to take on the crisis.

> *'Knowing yourself is the beginning of all wisdom'.*
> *Aristotle*

Understanding oneself through introspection and self-evaluation is a critical ingredient of an effective leader. This is of the highest importance, especially during a crisis. But self-awareness can often be a counterintuitive subject for a start-up CEO. Most top CEOs I have worked with have big egos. They are often too clever for their own good. I genuinely don't mean this in a negative light. Many of them do well because of these big egos and their resolve to prove the naysayers wrong.

It is their defiant nature that often gives them the strength and the grit to create new products, markets and go big on their vision. CEOs of start-ups get there because of their optimistic disposition for their business and the unflinching self-confidence with which they run the show. Their vision and the ability to thrash criticisms with conviction make them effective leaders who can take their businesses to new levels. However, they have to curb some of these natural instincts during times of a crisis.

It is important to prioritise preservation ahead of acceleration, growth and world conquest when the world is in a crisis. In order to make that mental switch, CEOs need to become self-aware and look at themselves. It is a hard task to keep their natural instincts in check and respect the context of the macro landscape that they will be operating in, at least in the short term.

My actual definition of 'radical self-inquiry' is the process by which the masks that we wear are skillfully and compassionately removed so that there's no place left to hide.

First, stop bullshitting yourself.

So here's a simple little thing that I do a lot. I would stand up in front of a group of CEOs and I'd say, 'Who here is brave enough to admit that they have no damn clue as to what they're doing? Who here is brave enough to admit that they're terrified?'

Everybody laughs.

I am puncturing the mask that we wear that says, 'I'm the only one who's struggling'.

If 87.9% of startups fail in the first two years, nobody is crushing it.

Jerry Colonna
Author of Reboot: Leadership and the Art of Growing Up (HarperCollins) and co-founder of the executive coaching firm, Reboot.io

> In tough times, leaders really need to put on their oxygen mask first because they need to stop to look at what's going on and potentially change the direction in which they're going.
> This is especially important when they are in that fight-or-flight mode. They're really not doing anyone any favours by showing up in a state of panic as a leader. That's the time to seek help.
>
> A trend has started in the Bay Area and I've noticed it in London, too. Some investors have been allocating a certain amount of the investment towards well-being and mental health of the entrepreneurs. So, if a certain amount is allocated like a separate bucket to use for these founders' well-being, they shouldn't feel like they're wasting investors' money.
>
> One other point to note is that mental condition is like dehydration. Once you're thirsty, you're already dehydrated. By the time you feel the sense of burnout, you're probably already there.
> I think the trick with that is to find the red light before the line. What are your symptoms that make you feel like things are too much, your judgements are not in the right place or your decision-making doesn't feel robust. Learning that about yourself, learning about proven techniques for you to reduce the stress at that point and finding the right support infrastructure is what it takes to keep on top of mental health issues. They don't need to be chronic to [negatively] affect your productivity and quality decision-making.
>
> **Yifhat Arnstein**
> Executive coach

Before entrepreneurs start evaluating how to run their business, they need to have a firm footing on where they stand mentally. If leaders lack clarity during a crisis, their decision-making capability will be badly affected. Some CEOs and business leaders I have had the pleasure of working with thrive during a crisis. A crisis brings out the best in them. Yet, it is often prudent to take stock internally (in your head) before jumping into action.

The Emotional Gym

Being a CEO can often feel lonely; therefore, be honest with yourself about where you are mentally. It is absolutely fine to be super-stressed for yourself and your firm during this time. There is no need to feel like a superhero. It is only human to have a breakdown during tough times. I remember listening to a Bloomberg documentary on Elon Musk, where he confessed about crying through nights and waking up to wet pillows. It happens to the best and the most persevering entrepreneurs. However, the important thing is to assess and accept where you are mentally and reach out for help if needed.

I think there's always going to be a range of personalities who are entrepreneurs. I think that founders need to be very resilient and optimistic to get through a lot of the rejection that comes with being them. But to be a leader, you need to have that ability to be insightful and aware. You're not just charging forward, but listening, paying attention and potentially being vulnerable.

Often I find that if I am able to establish the right connection with an entrepreneur, all guards are down. Once in that mode, I usually don't hit any of the defense mechanisms.

Yifhat Arnstein
Executive coach

Most of us seem to understand the importance of physical health much more than mental health. We are absolutely fine to go to the gym and exercise even when we haven't had fitness issues. But when it comes to mental health, most people do not attend to it until there is a sickness such as depression, anxiety or panic attack. The mind is akin to muscles that need looking after regularly as a 'business-as-usual' process. However, most of us react to mental health issues, rather than proactively dealing with them. It is not some technical debt that can be put aside and attended to later.

I must talk about an incident in a firm that I worked with in the past. A year after I got involved with this firm, I received a WhatsApp message from the COO that the CEO had committed suicide. Apparently, the founding team had known that the CEO had depression issues almost a year previously. Yet there were no disclosures to the board or to the investors until the fatality occurred.

It is hard for me to fathom the amount of pressure the CEO must have gone through to take his own life. However, if the founders of the firm took proactive measures, there might have been a better way of solving this challenging scenario. I must admit, it is not an easy problem to solve.

As investors or board members of a firm hit by such an issue, we can demand transparency. However, as a founding member of a firm, it is understandable to fear being asked to step down if the person revealed that his or her mental health is not where it should be. Therefore, it is reasonable that founders typically want to keep it quiet. But founders must realise that by not reaching out for help, they may be subjecting themselves to the same situations that got them into that worrying mental state.

Therefore, here are some suggestions:

- The founding team other than the person going through this issue must take ownership of this challenge and create transparency at least to the board of the firm.

- The board must first understand the severity of the issue. They must demand a professional assessment of the condition.
- If the prognosis is bad, then the right decision for both the CEO and the firm is for the CEO to step down, or step back at least until the CEO gets better.
- If the condition is not bad, then the board could allow the CEO to continue and perhaps offer support until treatment is completed successfully.
- The management team must step up to support the CEO and agree on a more frequent reporting mechanism to the board until things are better.

In essence, transparency, accompanied by objective and humane decision-making, is key to dealing with mental issues.

A request to the VC community: we have responsibilities to make money for our LPs. But that must also take into consideration humanitarian boundaries that we should respect. VC investors who have close LP oversight might have challenges in supporting a founder going through such mental health issues. In such a scenario, the VC investor must clearly articulate to the LP the issues that the portfolio firm is facing due to the CEO's condition. LPs could receive frequent updates on the situation as well. Transparency is the best policy in such situations, and remember, bad news travels fast anyways.

Let us now come back to the self-assessment that a CEO must go through. For CEOs seeking help, it doesn't have to come from outside necessarily. In his book, Reboot: Leadership and the Art of Growing Up, Jerry Colonna discusses the importance of not just focussing on resilience but also on equanimity. Resilience and grit are often highlighted as the attributes that mark the best CEOs. However, resilience with equanimity is what really makes you stand out when life throws a curveball at you.

We all have the ability to dig deep within ourselves and galvanise strength to face the challenges that lie ahead. However, most of us don't know how to tap into those abilities. Therefore, it might be good to talk to peer CEOs who might have gone through similar challenges, investors whom you trust, mentors and/or take professional help if necessary. Creating a support system to help us through the journey can make all the difference.

True grit is more than the capacity to grin and bear it.
To understand true grit, we need to understand false grit.
False grit is brittle. It's the sense that we are nothing if we can't
take a punch. In fact, we define 'taking a punch' as the ability to
not feel pain when we are punched.

False grit is dangerous. It feeds a stubbornness that, in turn, can
feed delusion. We mistake the tendency to delude ourselves that
our relationship will improve, our companies will succeed, if only
we double down on our old patterns, grip the steering wheel until
our knuckles whiten, and bear down. Stubbornness is not the
hallmark of the warrior. Leaders who persist out of
stubbornness, believing themselves to be gritty, are at best
delusional and, at worst, reckless. False grit awakens the Crow.

One of its implicit messages is that we should persist to prove that we aren't as
unworthy as the Crow claims. Yet a second implicit message is that if we feel like shit
after being punched in the face, it must mean that we are shit. The only way to escape
the grip of false grit is to recognize its falsity.

True grit is kind. True grit is persistent. True grit persists not in holding on to false
beliefs against all evidence but in believing in one's inherent lovability and worthiness. True
grit is the leader believing in the team's purpose, its capacity to overcome obstacles, and
the relevancy of the cause. True grit acknowledges the potential of failure, embraces
the fear of disappointment, and rallies the team to reach and try, regardless of the
potential of loss. True grit, the capacity to stick with something to the end, stems from
knowing oneself well enough to be able to forgive oneself.

To have inquired deeply and steadily enough to find the deep sense of purpose that is
beyond a personal mission statement. In that knowing of oneself, one is then able to stand
as a single warrior amid a community of brokenhearted fellow leaders. We see true grit
in the lovingkindness of compassionate leaders, those who embody the Buddhist principle
of bodhicitta and strive to be of service to others. I feel the truth of that and yet I
battle my own obstacles. How do you serve others when your heart is pained and your
warrior is terrified?

Jerry Colonna
Author of Reboot: Leadership and the Art of Growing Up (HarperCollins)
and co-founder of the executive coaching firm, Reboot.io

I think if you don't express vulnerability, that's when you really are
creating this black swan event for yourself in life. So you have to
have outlets. For a long time I thought that the mind was an infallible
thing in the sense that it's hard to beat that if you always think
you're strong. That was the biggest mistake I made.

I failed several times and every time I failed, I kept taking on the
stress, physically and mentally. I was strong enough to handle it for
a while, and then boom, it just crashed. Now, I've become very
proactive about that. I have a very good sense of what I can
control versus what I cannot control. I understood how much
physical health was actually tied to mental health because of the
kind of chemicals that your mind produce when you actually work
out. I have got a very strict work-out regime now.

I have a lot of my friends in Silicon Valley who are now founders.
They were generally active, but the moment they founded a
company, they stopped taking care of their physical health.
The challenge is that, that will eventually start affecting their mental
health. Being a founder means you have to respect your physical
and mental health more, not less. You are your biggest asset.

Akshay Sharma
CTO at Doc.ai

Organisational Emotional Fitness

One of the ways of preparing oneself for the task of taking on a crisis is to get into a whole-brain state. During times of stress, there are high levels of cortisol produced in our body, which can lead to a brain shutdown, resulting in bad decisions. You do not need to get a panic attack every day to start focussing on your mental health. You might just be reacting to triggers unlike before, in ways that could be starting to surprise you. Being in a good state of mind just enables you to deal with such triggers in a healthy way.

You will need to be in a place mentally where you are able to analytically break down the challenge ahead and make quick decisions. Yet, some of these actions might have to be done with empathy in times of a crisis. Therefore, it is essential to ensure that you are in a 'whole brain' state before any key decisions are made as a response to a crisis. The left half of the brain, which is analytical, needs to work with the right half of the brain, which is empathetic and creative.

Getting your creative side of the brain activated is essential. This exercise is important for a firm dealing with a crisis, especially for key decision makers. A crisis is a time when empathy needs to be demonstrated at all levels of your organisation. People need to trust each other to communicate transparently, especially during tough times. Get engaged in playful groups and fun routines that can help the entire workforce. Activating the creative side of the organisation's brain can help during times of crisis.

We have frequent Ludo matches, pool games, all virtually. We also had a cooking competition that we did a few weeks ago. We took help from performance coaches to really understand how we engage employees and create a sense of community.

It's very easy for our workers to panic from both a professional and personal life perspective. Therefore, we had to get creative to keep the environment fun and jovial.

Sachin Jaiswal
CEO of Niki AI

As the founder of the firm, you can see yourself as its parent. The children in a family get inspired and affected by the behaviour of the parent. That is true in a firm, too. In order to get your team to a healthy state of mind, you must be in a healthy frame of mind. That then translates well into connecting with your team, being authentic, transparent and empathetic so you can understand the emotions on the ground.

Coming back to mental health, there are several techniques to get into a whole-brain state of mind before taking on business challenges. This book is not about recommending yoga over meditation or mindfulness, or running over a Peloton session. All of us have ways we recharge ourselves physically and mentally. Several CEOs I work with have had to get into a routine at home as soon as the COVID lockdown came into force. A healthy morning routine involving either a workout session, a walk or a yoga session, helped them clear their minds before taking on the challenges of the day.

You can't have ambitions to climb mountains with poor abs. I meditate regularly and have practiced a form of Zen for over 15 years. I do free classes every month for entry-level people.

Once a month, I have a team meeting, which we call 'failure of the month'. We all share our failures, especially me, because I have so many of them. The biggest failure of the month actually gets a lunch voucher. So, everybody is dying to say what they screwed up that month. That's amazing. I love that we can celebrate failure in the company.

Joyeeta Das
CEO of Gyana

I find that I am at my best when I have a good workout routine, ideally with my personal trainer, alongside a healthy diet. I have also had the good fortune of learning a new technique called Psych-K to stay in a whole-brain state of mind while making difficult decisions. There are other modalities that could work, but it is critical that we are at our best before we get into action. All our faculties need to be aligned to take on the challenge ahead.

Once you have evaluated your mental abilities and are in a position to influence the firm's mental fitness, it is time for an assessment of where your aptitude and passions lie.

You and Your Business: A 3D Model

Crisis often brings out the best in people. Those who take it on and embrace it become pioneers who go on to lead their firms to new glories. Crisis can also bring out honesty and a real understanding of purpose in life amongst entrepreneurs. It doesn't necessarily mean you have been a liar all along. But in the busy-ness of building a business, you might have gotten too close to it and forgotten the reasons why you started it in the first place. In times like this, I typically suggest going back to a simple framework for evaluation, which starts with three simple questions:

- Are you still passionate about the business?
- Do you think you have the skills to drive the business forward?
- Are you still a relevant leader in a crisis-hit world?

Let us now look at each of these questions in greater detail

Passion Think through the reasons why you started the business in the first place. Think through how you got the business to where it is today. Without fear or self-doubt, see if you are still passionate about the journey forward. If your business is what wakes you up and makes you look forward to the day ahead, then that's where your heart is. That's the biggest self-validation you can have to move to the next step.

Skills I must admit, it's harder to answer the skill question than digging deep to see if you are passionate about the business. However, as the leader of a business, you should know your circle of competence. You have built competence in certain subject areas over the years and that is worth considering in these times. If the skills required to lead the firm are still within your circle of competence, you should be fine.

Even the best CEOs I know have some levels of self-doubt about their abilities to take their firm through a crisis. In such times, it is important to be objective and assess where the gaps in the skill levels are. Do not let the voice of self-doubt overcome your desire to lead the firm if you are qualified from a skills perspective.

We have a culture where there is no point at which you should feel vulnerable and sad and feel like giving up. You're always raring to go as an entrepreneur. This is simply not possible. It's not true for any human being. We wake up some days and, like everybody else, we have bad days. Of course, we have to get through it.

But it's not true that you don't have wonderful days and you don't feel like a failure. And there's nothing wrong with feeling that; it's just part of being human. But the culture we operate in glorifies that you have to be so rough and tough. If you're vulnerable, then you're not considered a good leader.

We're looking for founders who go on no matter what, but that is really what causes several mental health issues in the end.

Joyeeta Das
CEO of Gyana

The objective assessment will need to be in terms of where you are lacking as a leader of the pack. If you have been a visionary, yet have struggled with commercial negotiations in the past, you might want to consider identifying someone in your organisation who could step up to support you with the commercials. Remember, a crisis will demand renegotiations with several stakeholders.

You might be someone who is commercially savvy, yet operationally not in the detail. In that scenario, you might want to get the best operational person in the organisation to step up to support you through decision-making at a more granular level. Yet, these decisions will need to be preceded by your understanding of what you are not good at. Your mentors should be able to help you with the exercise of understanding gaps in skills.

After the assessment, if you feel that your skill levels can be complemented by another member in your firm or someone or something that can be quickly onboarded, then there is not much to worry about. If your passion levels are high enough, and the skills needed aren't too far away from what it takes to lead the business forward, you should move on to the next step.

Demand   The third dimension is assessing the trust that key stakeholders have in your ability to lead the firm through the crisis. The key stakeholders that you might want to talk to are your cofounders, the management team, the board and major investors. In this context, the assessment will have to be made from the perspective of your management, board and key investors to determine if they still feel you have it in you to take the firm forward.

In most scenarios, a crisis is not a time for a change in leadership. However, some of these stakeholders might have had second thoughts about your leadership abilities even in good times, before the crisis hit. Therefore, it is only natural that they might want you to step down. Your leadership skills might also be doubted if your firm needs to go into preservation mode in the eyes of your key stakeholders, and your instincts are still pushing for growth.

In a scenario where your approach is at loggerheads with that of the rest of the key stakeholders, you must engage with them and understand their concerns. If you cleared the passion and skills assessment tests, this shouldn't be a hard exercise. It is just as important to establish the trust amongst your core stakeholders that you are the person to lead the firm.

Step Away

You also might find that you are not as passionate about the business anymore. This is typically when the firm has moved on from the course that you charted for it when you initially founded it. It could also be that the board and the markets are driving the business in a new direction which you're not too keen on. In such scenarios, it can be hard to find the passion to commit to a course of continual problem-solving that a crisis would warrant.

It could be that you are still on course with your vision for the business. But perhaps even before the crisis hit, you have been asking yourself and the people you trust if you were the best person to lead the firm. You either felt that your skills were perfect for a start-up, but for a scale-up and growth stage business you were starting to be convinced that you weren't the right person.

It is difficult for you to lead the firm through a crisis if you are not convinced of your ability to do so. It is only fair that you hand over the responsibility to the next best person to lead the firm. But please do so carefully. It might be a well-known fact within the firm that you are considering a change in leadership, but the markets are still looking to you as the leader. Therefore, do not shock the market and the firm by mistiming your move away from leading the firm. It might be better to get your firm to a position of relative strength before you step down as CEO.

For instance, when Tom Blomfield of Monzo, decided to step down from his role as the CEO, it did shock us all. He was the poster child of London fintech. It was announced at the peak of the COVID crisis during the third week of May in 2020. The firm had announced several cost reduction measures, including laying off 295 staff. It came a few months after competitor Revolut had closed a $500 million funding round and a couple of weeks before Starling Bank closed a $40 million from existing investors.

The move was logical, because Tom's successor was announced as TS Anil, who was a banker. It would take an experienced banker to run the bank that Monzo had evolved into from a technology startup in 2018. However, the peak of a crisis was perhaps not the best time for this transition if it was purely operational.

In another instance, Magic Leap's CEO Rony Abovitz announced that he was stepping down as CEO towards the end of May 2020. He had made cost-cutting measures at the firm by laying off over 1,000 staff. He had also agreed to a pivot in their strategy from being a consumer device business to an enterprise device business. But, most critically, the firm had closed a further $350 million in funding to embark on the journey through the crisis.

It might have been a bad time to leave as the CEO of the firm, but at least the firm was taken to a position of strength before the announcement was made.

It might therefore be the best thing for the firm and yourself if you stayed honest and planned a course of action to step down. However, if after the assessment, you still feel confident about taking on the crisis, it's time to take the bull by its horns.

Switch Off or Snooze

Two important things that entrepreneurs often overlook are family time and sleep. I am guilty of that as much as anyone. However, it is important to switch off from work from time to time. Sometimes, a little distance from problems in hand will make them look smaller and help arrive at solutions faster. For me, spending time with my family is important because it obviously fills the house with joy and laughter and keeps the family happier and closer.

I also find that family time gives me a sense of perspective when I look at work-related problems. I am less desperate to solve them and that puts me in a position of strength mentally so I can take problems on with relative ease. That sense of perspective can be all you need to solve work problems.

A day trader friend of mine believes in switching off from work and follows that religiously. When he gets into two bad trades on a day, he stops making any more decisions for the day. He just shuts down the setup for the day and has some quality family time and comes back with a clearer mind the next day. He attributes his success as a day trader to a clear mind when he starts making decisions.

Switching off from action completely might not be an option for entrepreneurs preparing to navigate their firm through a crisis. Alternatively, taking periodic breaks can be a refreshing process while you are problem-solving.

The other secret ingredient for a balanced mind is sleep. How many times have we gone to bed stressed and woken up lighter? A good night's sleep can often be the medicine that can bring clarity of thought. Despite sleep being such a help, I find entrepreneurs giving up on that the most. The best entrepreneurs know when they are at their best and when they need to switch off and retire for the day.

The challenge with sleep is that it has a vicious cycle relationship with stress. A stressed mind that is racing fast keeps us from sleep. When this becomes a regular habit, it can lead to insomnia and further stress. There are several ways to break this cycle and get some quality sleep.

I ask questions about how things are with different aspects of your life and we get to a place where we understand what's feeling good and what's not feeling good. A framework that I use to help this conversation is called the 'wheel of life'.

It's basically a wheel that has eight segments, or however many segments you need, but usually eight. Each segment has a different label, depending on what your life consists of. This might be health, fitness, career, family, friendships, relationships, money, holidays, travel or any areas of passion you may want to have. You then rate each one of these segments on the wheel.

You fill in on a scale of zero to low to high, depending on how satisfied you are. This is not about how much effort you put into each segment. You might do no health and fitness, but you might be totally satisfied with that. Just focus on your instinctive satisfaction scores in that segment.

At the end of the process, you'll see that most people look at that and go, 'Ah!, I'm putting a lot of energy into my work and I'm really satisfied with it at the moment and I'm really unsatisfied with my family'. Then the conversation is, maybe you need to put some more energy into family life. This is a good assessment tool to framework when you feel down and do not know why.

Natasha Chatur, personal coach

One of my colleagues who had sleeping problems used to come to work in a really bad state. Often we would just see him entering work or hear him on the phone during a call and we would know he hasn't slept well. I suggested he should try hypnotherapy videos on YouTube. My favourite is Michael Sealey's hypnotherapy videos, which I listen to often. After he started listening to Michael Sealey's hypnotherapy sessions, he said he slept much better.

There are other techniques, such as simple breathing exercises, mindfulness and progressive relaxation that can all improve sleep quality. Please note that it is not professional medical advice that I am offering here. I am just pointing out different techniques that an entrepreneur can benefit from. Some of these techniques can work wonders while some might not really make any difference.

Once the introspection part is over and you have got to a calm and composed state of mind, the next steps are to ensure that you have bounced off some of your key thought processes with someone you respect. Most of us have mentors, advisors or a support system to discuss ideas and get feedback from. This process is more important during a crisis. It could be an advisor of your firm, a friend from your founders' network, an investor or just a family member. A mentor can go a long way to help you in chaos.

Mentoring

Mentoring can make a tremendous difference when you are looking for clarity during times of stress. I have always taken inputs from selected people at work or from family or friends, depending on the problem I am solving. The person I choose is someone who does not have vested interest or strong views in the problem domain. A mentor with vested interest could provide biased inputs and that could cost you precious time and resources during a crisis.

I also don't go to people who would just blindly support my ways of thinking. You will need someone to be critical when you want to make tough decisions. The fact that you might be grilled during a discussion with your mentor will make you analyse the problem more thoroughly before taking it to your mentor. At the end of such a grueling discussion, you should be clearer about what you intend to do.

You might have a few mentors whom you always fall back on. You would do well if you made sure that your mentors were in the right state of mind while they advise you. I remember a discussion when a start-up CEO was asking for advice from three of his investors about a possible quick fundraise as a crisis hit. One of the investors asked him to go for a down round without evaluating all the financing options they had on the table.

The investor clearly wanted a bigger slice of the firm for a cheaper price. However, he had failed to recognise that the company was in good shape because their revenues were sticky and the market they were serving was stable despite the slowdown. I had to pull the CEO aside and tell him he must evaluate cash flows, perform scenario analysis and ensure all other funding options were exhausted before going for a desperate down round.

There are other avenues of support. Some investors have started a support network of CEOs for their portfolio firms during the COVID crisis. This brings CEOs together (virtually), allowing them to share their experiences. This activity can be extremely helpful when you are looking for creative ideas to take on the challenge ahead.

In essence, it is essential to know whom to take inputs from during a crisis and which are the right ones to act on. However, a good mentor's role can't be exaggerated in difficult times. If nothing else, a mentor can be someone whom you can share your deepest concerns with, without fear of being judged. That alone could make a major difference during tough times. At this stage, however, let your mentor know that you will need time from that person as you navigate your firm through the crisis.

Executive Coaching

I can almost hear you saying 'here you go' at the sight of this topic. I must admit, I am not a big fan of executive coaching. I believe that experience coaches us better than education. However, the right person, who understands organisational behaviour and has extensive experience in psychology, can help with several aspects of your leadership traits.

Following are some of the benefits of executive coaching:

- Improved self-awareness
- Empathetic leadership
- Better time management
- Enhanced people skills

An entrepreneur needs the right balance among work, life, vacation, exercise, food and sleep at all times, but especially during a crisis. However, if you are an early stage start-up and are looking for a Series A, perhaps you are not taking enough salary to pay the crazy hour rates that a coach could charge. A good mentor would still be an excellent option in that case. Try to find someone with whom you can discuss your plans and from whom you can take advice. Ideally this person should not be operationally involved in your business.

Now that you have gone through an exercise of introspection, refreshed yourself and taken some input from your mentor or support system, it's time to charm a few stakeholders.

Connect and Inspire

A CEO's first role during a crisis is being the CIO (chief inspiration officer). When I look at a team of cofounders, the CEO should be the one who can storytell and paint his or her vision in rich colours. Inspiring doesn't have to be limited just to the team. In times such as this, it is important to be able to inspire a wider group of stakeholders across the organisation, partners, vendors, suppliers and investors.

The Team: It is important to first connect with your team. You might not have your plan of action to take on the crisis yet, but speak to your team frankly and with authenticity about the challenges ahead. Be genuine because trust breeds loyalty. Tell them where you stand as an individual first and then give them an overview of the health of the business. Remember, the data collection you did on competitors, product and funding before the crisis hit? Use that data to show them you have it in you to sail through the storm.

It is not just enough to send an organisation-wide email from your desk and expect your team to jump on the ship with you. More details on a crisis communication architecture is in Chapter 4. Crisis is a time when you should make yourself more available to your whole team and kill red tape and bureaucracy. Organise an informal town hall or a Zoom chat with a theme to lighten the mood.

Get creative with ways to connect emotionally with the team and show them you are as affected by the situation as they are, and you are more committed than ever for their sake and for the firm's sake. Humanise the situation as much as you can. But also be honest. If you are based in one large floor of an open desk office, just climb on top of a desk and shout out to your team. Gestures such as these make you more informal, human and approachable. Show your team that you are going to take on the crisis and you have it in you as a CEO and as a firm.

There might be questions from your employees about cost-cutting measures. It is important that you anticipate that, and answer those questions with a sense of conviction. The answer could be that, after an evaluation of cash flows and discussion with the board, there will be an announcement shortly on ways to navigate the situation. Give your team ways they can approach you if they are stressed. Choose someone on your team who can deal with grievances on a regular basis.

Those who go through shit together, stick together.

Investors: Remember, you are going to be in the inspiring mode for some time. Once you have connected with the team the focus needs to move to investors. Connect with your investors so that they know you are up for the job and can trust you with their monies. Never get into an investor conversation and deliver bad news straightaway. Even in the toughest times, there are always reasons for hope and cheer. Talk to them about these things before starting your sighs, huffs and puffs.

Reasonable investors generally understand running a business during a crisis and know that it is not going to be easy sailing. Therefore, they are not expecting you to deliver a lot of positive news. However, show them that the business is as healthy as it can be. Be genuine and authentic, not salesy. Speak with conviction even when you are delivering news about the pile of crap you find yourself in. Offer to connect with them more regularly, such as once in a fortnight or so, and do not wait for your quarterly board meetings to give them updates.

If you are fortunate like my portfolio firm BibliU, which is benefiting from the digitalisation during the COVID crisis, you have a strong positioning when you talk to your investors. Ensure that at the end of the discussion with investors, you fill them with confidence about your commitment towards the business. However, make sure you inform them that you will need their support if the business hits cash flow challenges.

Existing investors will typically be your early backers in a crisis. Therefore, make sure you set that expectation without sounding desperate. If you have to go back to them for investments during the crisis, it should be an easier discussion. Having the backing of existing investors during a crisis is also the litmus test that potential investors with dry powder are looking for.

Conclusion

This chapter was all about you, the entrepreneur. You've got to inspire yourself before inspiring others who look up to you to lead them. The first step is about how mentally attuned you need to be to take on a crisis. It starts with self-assessment and self-awareness.

We touched on how important it is for the organisation to be emotionally fit in such times. At every level in the organisation, people should be willing to communicate with transparency and empathy. This can only happen if they feel inspired by the leadership team of the organisation and trust them in leading the firm out of the crisis.

Once you have understood and accepted where you are emotionally, it is important to assess your ability and passion to take your firm through the crisis. We discuss a 3D model that can help you do so. At every stage of the process, you might have to get engaged in honest and transparent conversations with yourself and with your key stakeholders. The next step is about ensuring you have emotional and mental support on an ongoing basis.

The support could be in the form of a mentor, executive coach, family time or just a hobby that will help you take your mind off work. In essence, once you have understood where you stand and have had a discussion with your mentor or your advisor, it is then time to act. You are yet to understand more about the crisis and make any decisions, but before getting to that stage, ensure you have the full backing of your team and your advisors. Please see Figure 3.1 for a summary of the takeaways from this chapter.

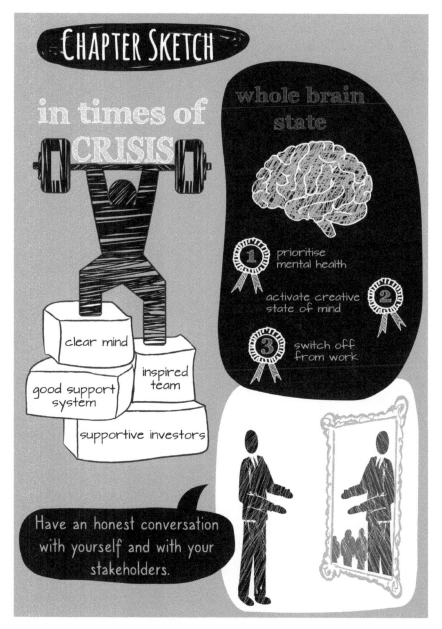

FIGURE 3.1 Chapter Three Sketch

It is extremely important you prioritise your mental health ahead of taking on a crisis. From investors' perspectives, it is essential that they are supportive if they find a struggling entrepreneur in such times. A humane approach could help the entrepreneur, the firm and can result in better returns in due course for the investor. Objective, transparent and informed decision making is essential during such times.

With a clear head, a good support system, an inspired team and supportive investors, you should now be ready to take on the crisis. The strategies to do so are laid out in the following chapters of this book.

CHAPTER 4

The Surgical Strike

I must be cruel only to be kind.

— William Shakespeare, Hamlet

Introduction

I landed in the UK in autumn 2005 for an assignment with GE Capital. Over the course of the next 15 years, I have had the opportunity of living and working in the great city of London. I have worked in teams that had Europeans, Russians, Americans, Indians and Australians. Save New York, it is hard to see the diversity and variety we get to see in London anywhere else in the world.

I know several of my British friends have not just been tolerant but also proud of the diverse nature of the workplace and social set-up in and around this great city. However, all that changed in 2016. As the referendum tipped in favour of Brexit and populist regimes thrived across the globe, we felt the world was moving towards a new normal. The markets in Europe took a hit at the news of Brexit.

What followed was nothing short of a political disaster in the UK for three long years. The UK was in a political turmoil that led to economic uncertainty. Several overseas investor friends I spoke to, between 2016 and 2020, agreed that the fundamentals of the UK economy were strong but market sentiment was weak. We needed a decisive leader to get the country out of this crisis. We got it with Boris Johnson, who was precisely that.

I didn't vote for the conservatives nor for a Boris leadership during the 2019 elections. However, I was glad when he was voted to lead the country out of the Brexit deadlock. I am not a Boris supporter, but he was perhaps the best person for the time and he got us through the first major hurdle of the Brexit nightmare.

This is precisely what we need in business leaders during a crisis. You may be right, you may be wrong, but you must be decisive. If you wait for data points to show up to validate your decisions, it might be too late. The same can be said of Jacinda Ardern, the prime minister of New Zealand, and Angela Merkel of Germany in the way they have led their countries through the COVID-19 crisis.

These leaders have been quite clear about their priorities in protecting lives over economies and enforcing lockdowns and initiating economic packages to support households and businesses. However, my favourite in the list of leaders who stood out during this crisis has been K. K. Shailaja, the health minister of the State of Kerala in India.

Kerala is a state in South India with 35 million people. Under the leadership of Shailaja, the state had the first COVID rapid response meeting as early as 24 January 2020. The 14 districts of the state had medical officers assigned to oversee on-the-ground activities. The public was quickly educated on the measures against the virus. A strict regime came into place to track and trace infected persons and treat them appropriately. At the time of writing this chapter, the state had about 1,200 cases and nine deaths.

To put this into perspective, Kerala's population density is 2,200 people per square mile. New Zealand has 46 and Germany 623 people living in a square mile. At the time of writing this chapter, Germany had about 184,000 infected people and New Zealand had about 1,500 cases. A comparison between Kerala and the other states in India will bring to light the effectiveness of crisis management in the state. By comparison, states such as Maharashtra and Tamil Nadu (my home state) have recorded 12 and 8 times the number of infected people, respectively.

Through the course of the COVID crisis, all of us have seen enough such numbers. Therefore, I apologise for bombarding you with more of them. However, the way the state of Kerala and Shailaja have handled the crisis is a case study for the top b-schools and businesses of the world to document and learn from.

The idea of walking you through good crisis management stories across the world is to help you with the rest of the chapter. Crisis management requires both sides of our brains working closely with each other. That is particularly true for this chapter because you might have to plan and execute a surgical strike in the interest of your business. The decision-making process has to be cold and objective, but the execution must be humane.

The models defined in this chapter and the next few chapters are not prescriptive. They are meant to help you think through your business in the context of a crisis and arrive at a solution. Market crises do not homogeneously affect all businesses in a bad way. Businesses can benefit from a crisis, some of them see a temporary slowdown, while others take a very bad hit. Let us delve into this a little bit before getting into the planning and execution of remedial actions for the business.

The Startup Bell Curve

Most experienced investors and entrepreneurs who have seen a crisis or two would tell you that quick and decisive action, early in a crisis, helps in a big way. There are also other schools of thought around scenario planning and taking action dependent on how the crisis unravels. Nevertheless, all of them would agree that inaction and keeping the business going in business-as-usual mode is very rarely the solution.

Before planning a course of action, it might help to understand the effect recessions can have on start-ups. That would help position yourself through the rest of the book and identify logical next steps.

Recessions have different ways of affecting start-ups depending on their sectors of focus and business models. There are three key categories that start-ups hit by recessions fall under.

- Business models that have become irrelevant or even start seeing negative revenues
- Slowdown of revenues while business models remain relevant
- Acceleration of revenues with business models taking off due to sudden changes in market fundamentals

For instance, some travel start-ups went into a negative revenue state during the COVID crisis. Loyalty startups focussing on restaurants, pubs and coffee shops were terribly hit by the crisis as their revenues plunged due to almost no transactions happening at these retail outlets. They might not have become completely irrelevant as businesses, but they might have to evaluate their market relevance until the crisis comes to a close.

Another small percentage of businesses would emerge as a silver lining to the crisis and see an acceleration of their business models. For instance, many education technology (EdTech) and communication companies saw their revenues take off as soon as the COVID crisis hit. Zoom saw a 169% increase in revenues, beating their annual forecast by Q2 2020.

If you imagined the distribution of startups hit by a crisis as a bell curve, the two categories of irrelevant and super-relevant businesses form the tail of the curve (see Figure 4.1). The majority of start-ups fall somewhere in between the two tails of the bell curve. These start-ups in the centre of the distribution typically see a fall in growth and revenues, but they would still be relevant. Sales cycles might be longer, but clients would still be interested yet cautious.

In the next section we look at a three-phased approach to dealing with a crisis. The first-order optimisation stage is applicable to all three types of firms in the bell curve, because it helps them stay lean and mean. The second-order optimisation is more applicable for the firms that need to reevaluate their strategic response in a crisis. The third optimisation applies to firms that need to examine the crisis to stay relevant and reinvent themselves. We discuss third-order optimisation and pivoting in Chapter 8. Let us now look at the 3D plan of action.

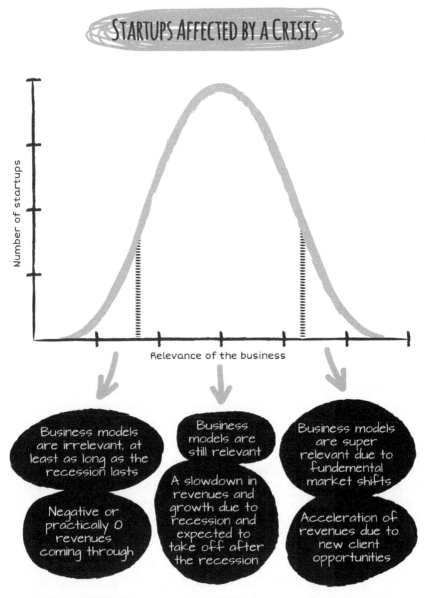

FIGURE 4.1 Crisis Bell Curve

A 3D Plan of Action

We will need to take a three-pronged approach to respond to a crisis. The initial step, called first order optimisation, involves taking tactical measures to preserve the firm through the crisis. We then move on to the second-order planning and execution, where we look at strategic ways of tweaking and course correcting the business. Last, the third-order planning involves data collection, planning, realignment and, if needed, pivoting the business to position it for what lies ahead.

Survive: First-Order Optimisation

This is the first step in the planning and execution process and involves the immediate preparation of the business to sustain the challenges of a recession. As you switch into preservation mode for the business, it is not just about cost-cutting recklessly; understanding the purpose of the business, your vision for the business and what got you there is also necessary. The data collection we discussed in Chapter 3 will come in handy during this phase.

Once you have a clear view of what you see as the core of your business, you then need to plan ways to make progress with that, while cutting costs on non-core activities and markets. The first-order plan is typically executed within the initial days of the crisis. You will also need a clearly defined communication architecture for smooth execution of management decisions. These are the focus areas for this chapter.

Normalise: Second-Order Optimisation

Once you have met the immediate and high-priority needs of the business, understood the core focus areas and adjusted the cost structures, the next step is to focus on the strategy for the medium term. The first-order planning would have given you a lot more freedom and latitude in planning and executing the next steps. The cash flow pressures should be alleviated and the leadership team should have the ability to define a context of operations for their focus areas of the business.

As a result, the second-order optimisation involves understanding the following changes in light of a market driven by the crisis:

- Change in infrastructure
- Change in customer behaviour
- Change in the relevance of business models

It is important to understand these fundamental changes to plan a course of action for the business. For instance, after the 2008 crisis customers were so unhappy with Wall Street banks that they wanted innovative ways of interfacing with financial services. That led to fintech companies.

On a similar note, after the dot-com bubble the internet acted as the infrastructure layer to support the growth of social media and internet-based companies such as Amazon, Facebook and Alibaba. The payments infrastructure developed by governments and regulators in countries such as Singapore and India allowed digital payments to grow quickly as soon as the COVID crisis hit.

With shifts in customer behaviour and infrastructure, the second-order planning and execution become critical for the strategic direction of the firm. We will focus on this in the next few chapters. Second-order optimisation is more strategic and will take longer to execute than first-order planning. As a result, you will need more data points to support your decisions, unlike first-order optimisation. The second-order plan of action will need a few weeks of research and discussions before being put in place.

Thrive: Third-Order Optimisation

The third-order plan is important because a crisis often throws a curveball to disrupt existing markets and opens new opportunities. Third-order optimisation is about looking beyond for a new normal. It is an exercise in exploring unknown unknowns. It is also important to take away some habits that you need to stick to during good times that you learnt during a crisis.

This step might not be relevant for all businesses in a crisis. If you are running a business that has come to a grinding halt due to a market disruption, this is certainly an exercise worth going through. This is also a stage where you know your existing business model is almost obsolete and must identify ways of reinventing yourself.

This process is often easier for early-stage start-ups than for matured firms. It can be an extremely time-consuming and high-risk exercise in larger businesses. However, it has been done in the past even within big businesses. Therefore, with the right leadership, vision, research and planning, it is possible to execute this step effectively.

Now that we have briefly touched on all three stages of optimisation, it's time to deep dive into first-order planning and execution.

First-Order Optimisation

When the house is on fire, you do not look to save your wallpaper. The focus will be on protecting lives, then essentials, and finally the structural elements of the house to keep life moving without any major obstacles. That is precisely what you should focus on when a crisis hits your business. In Chapter 2, you performed data collection to understand where your business was. That information, combined with the diagnostics that you will perform in this chapter, will help you with decisions later in this chapter.

If I must simplify the outcome, you need to protect your core business and people while preserving cash. If your business has become irrelevant due to the crisis, then focus on cash flow preservation for now while you reinvent yourself.

Before the COVID wave hit us, our workforce was largely based in California and Canada. We didn't necessarily have the cultural DNA to be efficient with a 'remote first' workforce. However, within a month we figured it out. It's not hard, except that context sharing and information passing becomes harder.

We are an AI software company, so you can technically work from anywhere. However, scaling culture virtually was a hard problem. As a CTO with more than 60 people working for me, it's a lot more difficult to conceptualise and put an operating model in practice to get the right cultural alignment across the firm. It meant having very little centralised decision-making and moving towards distributed decision-making. We identified leaders across different parts of the company who have high agency to make decisions. In the past, these leaders felt that they had to run things by me. They now know they no longer have to do that. I'm only there to give them feedback.

Akshay Sharma
CTO at Doc.ai

The first thing we did was to reassure all our employees and made sure they were comfortable and not anxious. They were provided all the tools and technology to work from wherever they were working. We then focussed on our clients who had challenges getting back to business and ensured project priorities were discussed and well communicated.

Navin Gupta
Managing Director of South Asia and MENA at Ripple

One assumption of this chapter is that you have identified and achieved business continuity wherever you can. During the first two weeks of lockdown, several businesses accelerated the process of getting their employees to work from home. When this is possible, a business can continue, and you can start getting back to the first-order optimisation process after that.

Cashflow planning and taking measures to extend your runway in an optimal fashion is one of the primary objectives of this chapter. Let us now look at why cashflow management is so critical.

CashFlow Is Oxygen

A few days back I was having a cynical discussion with a VC friend. During good times we prioritise growth over profitability, and during bad times we focus on cash flow over profitability. Is profitability out of fashion then? Both of us knew that businesses that fancied their chance during a crisis will need to go back to the first principles of doing business. One of the basic tenets of doing business is testing and ensuring the viability of the business model and the ability to turn profits. Yet, it was an interesting question to reflect on.

A more pertinent question, at a time when a business is trying to keep its head above water, is how to ensure there is enough cash flow to keep the business running. That's a tricky question because it is hard to time the bottom of a crisis. Therefore, calculating the amount of cash flow that would take you safely to the end of the crisis is hard. Remember, a crisis typically lasts longer than we anticipate. Therefore, the first thing to do is to create enough cash flow for as long as you possibly can.

You might be a business with revenues of £500,000 coming into the bank account in three months, but that is not going to pay your employees' salaries at the end of this month. Revenues are an indication of the clients' appetite for your products and services. Cashflow, however, is an indication of the health of liquidity and the operational agility of your business. It is also worth noting that during a crisis you might see a collapse in revenues. Even contractual revenues might not show up, if your clients want to renegotiate terms.

Many founders underestimate the value of good housekeeping. Having their accounting financials in order and understanding accounts receivables and payables are often considered boring. Working capital management is considered un-sexy. They're probably not going to make you a unicorn, but that can definitely kill you if not attended to. We've spent a lot of time helping firms through that. As cash has become (even more) king, focus has been to get the house in order.

Carmen Alfonso Rico
Partner at Samaipata VC

Therefore, it is essential to have a cashflow projection modelled even during good times to ensure you are always financially provided for. There shouldn't be any liquidity mismatch between short-term outgoing and long-term incoming cashflow. If there are any mismatches, suitable financing options must be planned in order to fill the gaps in cash flows. Alternatively, the flow of outgoing or incoming cash must be tweaked to ensure there are no nasty surprises.

This exercise becomes more critical during times of crisis. As mentioned, keep in mind that a crisis always lasts longer than we expect. Therefore, it is essential to plan a cut down of outgoing cash as aggressively as possible. Let us now discuss performing some diagnostics on your business.

Soul Searching

This process is about performing diagnostics across different aspects of your business to identify core and non-core areas. If you had spotted structural issues with the economy even before the crisis hit, you might have performed some data collection as discussed in Chapter 2. That data would help make quick decisions. If you had not done that, it is still not too late to perform some diagnostics on your business.

Running diagnostics to execute the first-order plan should keep more than cost-cutting in mind, such as the following:

- Understanding the core areas of your business
- Understanding core markets that you want to serve
- Spotting opportunities to improve cost structures
- Identifying product areas that are directly relevant to core business and revenues
- Identifying suppliers and vendors for cost optimisation and renegotiations
- Identifying areas of marketing that are still relevant
- Identifying critical team members to execute your strategy through the crisis

Despite it being the last item on this list, team is, in fact, the most important of all. People are your biggest asset. Treat your people well, and they will take care of your business.

While running through the diagnostics (see Figure 4.2), it is important to keep the objective in mind. Be critical, but recognise biases that surface during the diagnostic process.

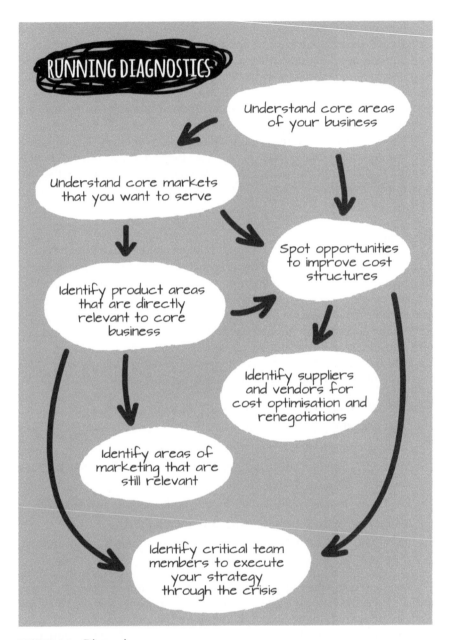

FIGURE 4.2 Diagnosis

What's the Heart of Your Business? The diagnostics process is to ensure you do not make any haphazard decisions and have a clear understanding of why you are making certain decisions. The first step in doing so is to zoom in on what the core of your business is. That will need to be aligned with your/your board's vision for the business.

If you enjoyed an increase in revenues in your core business lines as a result of the crisis, then you are amongst the lucky minority. The crisis moved the market in your favour and accelerated product relevance. But if you are in the majority, who saw a fall in revenues and felt cash flow pressures due to the crisis, then determining your core business is important.

Ask yourself why you started the business and what the problem you were trying to solve was. Every founding team has a vision that it wants to hold on to despite all odds. This is the vision that helps you persist during the worst days of your start-up journey. Understanding that will help you identify the part of your business you must protect.

It is quite possible that what you consider as the core business is not bringing you revenues yet. It might be that you have found an ancillary revenue opportunity to fund your core business. In that case, it becomes even more critical that you hold on to the revenue opportunities to protect your core business in the long run.

VC investors will cringe at this advice, because focus is everything in a VC investor's eyes. If you have a core business, focussing on it ruthlessly until you find 'product-market fit' and growing it from that point forward is the VC style of going about it. I agree with that approach if your start-up can scale only through VC funding and growth-based strategies.

One of my portfolio firms Gyana managed to sell their non-core product Neera through the COVID crisis to protect their core product Vayu, a NoCode data science platform. NoCode data science platforms allow users to perform analysis using algorithms without having to write a line of code. This is typically what VC-funded businesses do. They know their core focus and double down on it in spite of the crisis.

In stark contrast, when I spoke to David Brear, the CEO of 11FS, I received a slightly different viewpoint. 11FS is a digital transformation challenger consultancy that grew at an amazing pace from 2017. In 2019 they established 11FS Foundry with a vision to build a core banking platform for the digital era.

In David's view, although the services business had yielded the majority of his revenues in the short- and medium-term, 11FS Foundry is where he sees the long-term business opportunity. Therefore, he felt it was essential to keep the lights on for both these business lines despite the challenges that the crisis had thrown at them. I personally believe that the digital wave that the COVID crisis triggered might in all probability bring more opportunities for 11FS Foundry in the short term as well.

You get the picture though. This is a time where you need to preserve your core business, and it begins with knowing what it is, and more importantly, why it is. It might well be that your core business model is completely irrelevant during the crisis, as we discussed earlier in this chapter. In that case, you might still want to cut costs and go through the third-order planning process to identify next steps. More on that in future chapters.

Where Are You Relevant?   In your quest to run a tight ship through the crisis, one of the questions you need to ask yourself is in what markets your products and services are the most relevant. Let's say you have done well in London with your product and have recently rolled it out in Manchester. As part of the optimisation process, it is worth evaluating if you want to keep investing in Manchester, a nascent market for your product.

On the same note, if you have several product lines, it is essential to understand which ones are worth pursuing. *Contribution margin** is a tool that can help you understand which markets and products are viable during a crisis.

Contribution margin is a product's price minus all associated variable costs, resulting in the incremental profit earned for each unit sold. The formula is as follows:

Contribution Margin = Product revenue generated
– product variable costs / Product revenue generated

If you have scaled across several markets, there are going to be a few markets where your product has a lot more traction than others. This is typically measured by the contribution margin. This tool shows if your revenues in specific markets are high enough to pay off your variable and fixed costs. During times of crisis, this metric becomes important to help focus on the right things.

Let's say that you have decided to cut down variable costs associated with selling a product; you will still be incurring fixed costs such as office space and management salaries. Your contribution margin must be high enough to cover these fixed costs. Otherwise, you will be loss making.

Going back to identifying your core markets and products: even in good times, you must know the markets that have healthy contribution margins. An ideal contribution margin will be close to 100%, and most healthy businesses have contribution margins ranging between 60% to 100%. This will also help identify the markets and products you could double down on during a crisis and perhaps stop expanding into markets where your contribution margins are not high enough. The same methodology can be used to assess where a product is worth pursuing during such times.

Is Your Cost Structure Optimal? Following on from the analysis of the core focus areas for the business, products and markets, let us look at the importance of an optimal cost structure. In all the interviews I have done for the book, one consistent theme that has emerged is that businesses should increase and accelerate incoming cash and decrease and slow down outgoing cash. It sounds pretty simple and straightforward.

But what if your cost structure doesn't lend itself to making quick nimble changes to manage cashflows? What if your business model is more value-driven rather than cost-driven? It might be worth understanding the differences between value-driven and cash-driven business models.

Businesses that rely on low-cost structures, process automation and outsourcing are typically cost-driven. Businesses are value-driven when their core proposition relies on personalised services. For instance, luxury products and services can fall under this category. In a value-driven business, it might not necessarily be possible to apply some of the commonly known cost-cutting measures, such as automation or outsourcing.

Evaluating cost structure during the first-order optimisation process is meant to be performed ideally within the first two weeks of entering into a crisis. It might not be possible to revamp your entire cost structure for the first-order planning and execution exercise. However, it is worth understanding the importance of having efficient cost structures at all times, not just during a crisis.

One tool to stay on top of costs efficiently is the operating leverage of your business. Generally, operating leverage is lower when your fixed costs are lower. When a business has a high operating leverage, it helps during sales growth to increase profitability. This is because the incremental cost of sale is minimal. However, a high fixed-cost base makes them less agile during periods of declining sales.

The reverse is also true. When firms have a low fixed-cost base, they have lower operating leverage. However, with a high variable-cost base, as sales happen, the cost of sales also increases. Therefore, their profitability is flatter than in a high fixed-cost base business. But they are also relatively stable during times of falling sales, because their cost base reduces with reducing sales.

During my discussion with Simba Rusike, the CFO of Assurance IQ, he mentioned how critical the cost structure was for the success of the firm. Assurance IQ was acquired by Prudential for $3.8 billion after three years of operation. Their cost structure and data science capabilities made them the growth engine that Prudential was keen to tap into.

Having a variable cost model allows you to adjust quite fast. You don't have the cost overhead that you have to deal with before making a course correction. A variable cost approach just allows us to pivot into different opportunities, hypothesis test it, accelerate growth if it worked and kill the opportunity if it didn't. Keeping a light-cost footprint will help during a crisis, where adaptability is the way to survive.

Simba Rusike
CFO at Assurance IQ

After the COVID crisis hit us, I spoke to several CEOs across the world to understand how they dealt with the crisis. I have seen two broad types of firm deal with the crisis well. One set had efficient cost structures and effectively low fixed costs. Therefore, they were able to quickly respond by reducing costs and keeping the business afloat. The other set continually tested the viability of their business as they expanded; therefore, these businesses have been able to get to profitability if they wanted to.

Both these aspects are not mutually exclusive. They highlight that going back to first principles of doing business can help preserve your firm during tough times. It involves keeping costs low and managing higher profit margins. Keeping it that simple would help a good proportion of businesses face a crisis. Yet, this might not be easily achievable if your business model relies on growth first.

For instance, if you are creating a marketplace that needs onboarding critical mass of the supply and demand side to demonstrate network effect, then growth typically must come first. That is a proper VC approach, and unless you have already raised some funds just before the crisis or demonstrated network effect to excite your investors, you might struggle to raise further funding to keep the business afloat.

Also, as a VC-backed firm, your fixed costs might already be quite low. It is worth understanding the ratios that you need to track to ensure you are cost efficient. It might be as simple as the cost of acquisition (CAC) per customer and lifetime value (LTV) of customers. A ratio between the two can be compared with your peers.

More unconventional ratios/metrics can be between investments/revenues or (sales + marketing costs)/revenues and even the time it takes from the point of incurring marketing costs to the point of receiving the revenues. Some of these metrics will need to be specific to the business models you have and even the industries that you operate in. In essence, identifying the metrics that help you manage the cost efficiency of your business is critical.

Let us now look at the process of scenario planning that you should go through to understand the cash flow needs of the firm.

Scenario Planning

Once you have completed the diagnostics process, you will need to create scenarios and plan how you would cope through the crisis. It is quite difficult to spot a crisis coming at you, but it is equally hard to know how long it will last. Therefore, look at the cash flow position of the firm and understand your runway.

If it is March 2020 and you expect that the crisis will last until June 2021, try to model scenarios that would take you to December 2021. Model scenarios for when the crisis comes to an end sooner or later. Study the nature of the crisis and learn from history. For instance, if a pandemic caused the crisis, it might last 18 to 24 months. If it is a structural crisis that caused a recession, it might take a few quarters to recover.

In all these different scenarios model the following variables:

- Cash flows
- Revenues
- Churn
- Investment milestones

Based on the current performance of your firm and how the initial days of the crisis affected your business, project these numbers. Be conservative. Reach an agreement with your board and management team on all the assumptions behind these scenarios across these variables. Once you have agreed on the assumptions, based on what you and your key stakeholders feel, agree on which scenario is most likely to materialise.

Make sure you have enough money in the bank to survive. That's the number one goal. If you haven't done a fundraising round recently, then you probably want to figure out a way to stretch cash. Just make sure you're thinking about how to preserve cash as much as you're thinking about everything else. Our advice is that you must plan to get through all of 2020. In an ideal world, you should also plan to get through as much of 2021 as possible, because you don't know how the market is going to behave. If the market wakes up and things go back to normal you are in a good position, but it's better to be prepared for the bad scenarios and be able to survive.

Hussein Kanji
Founder of Hoxton Ventures

Our first priority was just making sure that our existing portfolio had everything it needed to weather the storm. We assessed that on a case-by-case basis, because each company is different. The different needs of each company, the different co-investors and how deep their pockets were, were all factors we took into account. Across the board, we started with rethinking the business plan, understanding where some savings can be made, how we could make resources more efficient and what other hypotheses we need to tweak.

Manuel Silva Martinez
General Partner at Mouro Capital

That should tell you how much cash you need to preserve or raise to ensure the business is protected through the crisis. This will then need to be reviewed through the lens of the diagnostics process you went through in the previous section. Bring the scenarios and the diagnostics together to see where the alignments and misalignments are. If your cost-cutting measures are perfectly aligned, and seem viable with your vision of the business, then it's a relatively easier decision.

In the following section we have put together a simple framework to help you with your decision-making.

The Soul versus Value Quadrant

Objective and ruthless decision-making is essential if you want to get through a market slowdown. Remember, you are going through this process because you are not one of the fortunate few whose business has taken off after the crisis hit. The decision-making process on where you will save costs and how, will need to be made across two key dimensions:

- How core is the business/product/market to your firm?
- How much value is it currently bringing to the firm?

The simple quadrant in Figure 4.3 should help you with the prioritisation process.

This figure will help you assess how core a product or a business line is to your firm versus how much value it is bringing to the table. Take a short- or medium-term view on the value aspect because you are in a recession and are looking at ways to preserve cash. The framework uses a generic term *value* here, but that can be replaced by *revenues, cash flows, growth* or even *brand equity* in some instances.

Let me briefly go through the quadrant now using product lines for ease of discussion and to get the easy decisions out of the way first.

High Value/Core: When a product line is core to your business and is a high-value proposition, press the pedal on it. Be laser-focussed on delivering

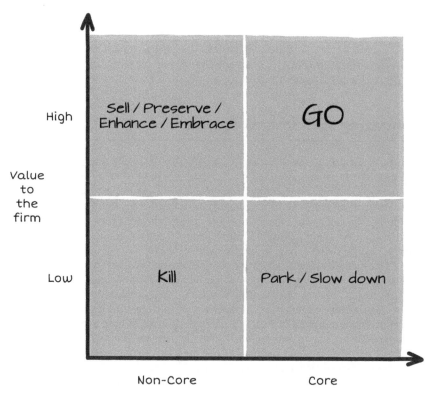

FIGURE 4.3   Soul versus Value Quadrant

that through the recession. This is the easiest decision quadrant in the framework.

Low Value/Non-Core: When a product line is non-core to your business and is still a low value proposition, kill it. It might be a difficult decision if you see value coming in the near future; however, this is not a time for speculation or wishful thinking. Be ruthless.

High Value/Non-Core: This is the most interesting part of the quadrant, and I have seen different approaches to this. My instant reaction is to sell that product line to improve cash flow. This might give you a couple of quarters of runway, which could be massively helpful to focus on your core business. I mentioned my portfolio firm Gyana selling their non-core product line to preserve and grow their core product line through the crisis. However, Gyana had the luxury of cash flow as they had closed a funding round just before COVID hit and managed their cash flows quite well in response to the crisis.

However, there are other approaches to deal with this particular quadrant. You might choose to preserve the non-core product line in light of the growth or revenues you are seeing from it. You might end up enhancing this product line through the recession as you get more customer traction. As a result, this might end up becoming core over a period of time, which means you have effectively embraced this as key to your business. In all these instances, the key outcome must be cash flow preservation.

An Amazing Turnaround: FrontM

My portfolio firm FrontM is a technology platform that provides connectivity applications to remote locations. Its core business lines were airlines, helping them to reap ancillary revenues from passengers on board. The firm was also looking at some maritime connectivity cases before COVID happened. Although we had no cash flow issues, due to strong investor backing and funding from government grants, we were having challenges generating revenues from the airline clients even before the crisis happened.

Once COVID hit and all airline client discussions stalled, we had to start looking for revenue opportunities within maritime. The versatile application platform that the team had built enabled us to roll out health-care applications for maritime customers within weeks. Our existing relationships with our satellite communication clients helped shorten the sales cycle. The firm saw revenues within a quarter and are now looking to expand into maritime aggressively. Expanding into maritime has helped them extend their runway into 2021 and become less dependent on investments.

The plan is still to raise funds for growth; however, they will sustain and grow even without external capital.

Focussing on the non-core product line can sometimes feel like selling your soul to the devil. I have seen many CEOs crib about that in the past and many run out of motivation for the business as a result. However, the risk of not exploiting the revenue opportunity from the non-core business is that the business might cease to exist. If you choose to go with the non-core product line, you must agree on checkpoints with the board to assess when there will be life pumped into the core product lines that you really believe in.

And so you dangle a carrot (the hope of returning to the heart of your business) to keep you focussed on the non-core areas of the business. You might want to see your non-core product line as a means to an end. As these product lines make more revenues, you increase the chance of achieving your vision for your core product line.

Low Value/Core: This is an easy decision in the context of the crisis but emotionally hard for entrepreneurs. You might want to park your passions for the time being and focus on revenue generation before you get back to the heart and soul of your business. You might also take a less binary approach if you are not that cash-strapped to keep the core areas of the business alive through the crisis. However, that needs to be clearly discussed and agreed with the board to ensure there are no cash flow concerns.

The immediate thing that most boards and CEOs startups think about is, 'What's my cash position and how long does it last?'

In late March 2020, some firms expected a turnaround in a quarter; some felt it would be three quarters. Depending on their point of view, most people created different scenarios in terms of how deep this crisis would be. With a view of the cash position at the end of the year 2020, our portfolio firms performed scenario analysis. They figured out in different scenarios what they needed to do with their expense rate, revenue projections and cash collection ability. They also factored in churn rates that they may have in the customer base across these scenarios.

The second thing that we thought about was the vertical they were in. Some verticals have been more immune to the crisis, whereas verticals such as travel have been affected hard. From a consumer perspective, businesses that could be categorised as a discretionary spend category have been much more affected by the crisis.

In the enterprise software world, there's a lot of direct sales that happened. There is relationship building, pipeline building and deal closings that need personal interaction. With the lockdown, however, all that has changed. Sales teams are now building relationships with clients over Zoom. We are yet to see how well that works. I would take a conservative approach to sales projections across these businesses.

Arvind Purushotham
Head of ventures at Citi

Cold Decisions, Humane Execution

We have understood the core focus of the business across markets and products. We have discussed the importance of keeping an optimal cost structure. We went through a framework to help determine what stays and what goes. Now you need to focus on applying this strategic thinking to cost decisions on the ground. Although I recommend making more aggressive cost-cutting than your cashflows indicate, you might have reasons to go softer. However, the earlier and the larger the cost savings are during a crisis, the better it is for the business.

Decision-making must be objective if you are looking to get to a good position to take on the second-order optimisation stage. However, despite an objective and unemotional decision-making process, the communication and the execution of it must be humane. The CEO of the firm plays an important role in developing the communication architecture of the firm during times of crisis.

It is very affirming if you can make it through tough times, and if you can survive through a storm, you make it out on the other side pretty lean and mean. This is why people say great companies are built in times of crisis and it is absolutely true. The main surprise from the dot com burst was how long and painful that crisis was; no one predicted that.

So you learn that you are way better off taking action early in the face of uncertainty - it is easier to rebuild from a sound base than to constantly adjust spend on the way down because you made the wrong assumptions. Experienced operators and VCs will say 'make the deep cuts early' because we know nothing destroys company morale more surely than gradual rounds of layoffs.

Fred Destin
Founder of Stride VC

Surgical strike of cost-cutting measures can be 'sandwiched' between humane communication. Firstly, manage expectations with clear messaging. Then, follow up with the cost-cutting measures. Lastly, communicate to boost the teams' morale. Communication that precedes the cost-cutting measures will need to be about setting expectations on the status quo, which is to soften the blow. The communication post-execution will need to be about improving morale and providing context to the team.

Let us look at the communication architecture options that you can deploy through the first-order optimisation process.

Communication Architecture The first-order optimisation is the point at which effective communication architecture helps with organisational morale. It is also essential to have the right narrative across all your key stakeholders. If you are a young start-up with agile communication set up like daily standups, you might want to have short bursts of information delivered to your people regularly. However, if you are a larger scale-up with a couple of hundred employees, you might adopt more formal communication methods.

I may be speaking in a bubble. In Silicon Valley, I don't think there's a shortage of capital. There may be a pandemic, but for good companies, good ideas and good teams, there has never been a dearth of money. We were able to secure our position well before the pandemic hit us. We knew growth was happening. Being a healthcare company, the pandemic just accelerated our growth, which means that all our product lines are actually revenue positive.

Our challenge is less about capital and cash flow, and more about hiring the right talent. In Palo Alto, we compete with Google, Facebook and Apple for talent. We provide a sense of ownership of great ideas to our talent force, which is harder for these big firms to do. We also are cognizant that people making a career choice based on just monetary compensation may not be the right fit for us anyways.

Having said that, my number one challenge right now is that I'm not able to hire fast enough. It's not that I can't hire, but I have to hire somebody who fits the ethos of our culture and fabric. Identifying that through Zoom is extremely hard. Therefore, when it used to take a couple of long coffee shop meetings, it now takes several Zoom calls to understand the potential hire before offering him or her a role.

Akshay Sharma
CTO at Boca

Authenticity: The Team   In either case, the right amount of communication, at the right time, with authentic and genuine information must be provided to keep the organisation's morale up. Overfeeding employees with information can be a distraction and not communicating regularly might result in a nervous workforce. There might have to be a mix of formal and informal modes of communication depending on the mood of the organisation, too.

In starting a quick, objective and targeted cost-cutting activity, information flow can be unidirectional. Management can communicate the impact of the crisis on the firm and measures you are taking to combat the crisis to the employees. Therefore, when it comes to making tough decisions, it might not come as too much of a surprise to your people and doesn't lead to too many questions.

Most stakeholders in business, for good reason, understand that if you do your job right, as a crisis manager, you're going to have to make some difficult choices. Trust is a key commodity that businesses rely on. Whether you are engaging with your team, customers, investors or suppliers as a crisis manager, your fundamental mantra must be about maintaining high levels of trust.

This is true even in good times, but during a crisis you are starting from a position of disadvantage in trust across these stakeholders. Therefore, your strategy and execution must focus on the most important commodity that you need — trust. Once you have that, the rest become much easier.

Nicola Persico
Professor at Kellogg school of Management

Transparency: Investors Consider your investors when you plan your communication architecture for the first-order optimisation process. Investors need to understand your plans for the business in the short- and medium-term. As the crisis throws new challenges, you must proactively reach out to investors and update them on the challenges you face, the opportunities ahead and your decisions on how you want to steer the business forward.

It is important to communicate your strategies to your investors. It is perhaps more important to communicate bad news to them promptly during these times. Transparency is the best way to ensure you receive their support and advise. Do not wait for your monthly or quarterly board or investor update. Investors are generally happy to take time, listen to you and offer advice and help for the journey you are embarking on.

We sit on the board of a lot of companies and we encourage our companies to deliver bad news faster. As the COVID crisis began, we started doing weekly calls with all companies. With some companies, it was happening two or three times a week depending on the gravity of the situation. At one point, we were running two board meetings a day ; We don't even know what a quarterly board meeting is anymore since we have board huddles all the time now.

So, with companies we work at daily and weekly engagement level. With LPs, we have more proactive communication. We have several large global institutional investors in our LP base. They have seen several crises in the past and haven't really panicked yet. Still, we have made ourselves available to both our startups and LPs and ensure there is transparency at all levels.

Ganesh Rengaswamy
Partner at Quona Capital

Optimism: Clients and Suppliers With clients and suppliers, take a more tactful approach to communicating. Showing vulnerability and telling clients how bad your cashflow position is, might not be the best way to hold on to them. Be a little bit more upbeat with clients without falsifying information. With these two sets of stakeholders, get the best person in your team to work with you in engaging with them regularly. You typically have certain members of your team who have the best-trusted relationships with these external stakeholders. Get them involved in communication.

A detailed stakeholder map and a corresponding communication technique and tone can help bring clarity. On each of those legs of communication you might have to draw out a schedule and assign it to the best person to send that out. Get a group in charge of communications within and outside the organisation and make sure they are in line with the tone and semantics agreed on for the narrative with the stakeholder.

Empathetic Optimism: Social Media You also might want to decide if you want to engage on social media and what the tone of engagement would be. During a crisis such as COVID, even if your business is performing well due to the rise of digitalisation, you might want to play it down and show some empathy to the affected. However, you should also demonstrate that you are contributing to society and to your clients (if you are), in all possible ways. A lack of empathy on social media can come back to hurt your reputation.

Once you have understood your organisation and agreed on a frequency and mode of communication through the first-order optimisation process, it's time to evaluate the commercial relationships that you have with your partners, clients and vendors. The following sections will detail the steps to take.

Clients: Increase Incoming The first step is to see if you can increase cash flows in the form of revenues. Be mindful of the focus areas for the business while negotiating with your clients. Keep clients who are in your focus areas closer to you at this time. Also focus your conversations with clients on the following avenues.

Expansion: Discuss if clients have more opportunities within their business lines for your products. You should do this even during normal business periods. However, if you have a good relationship with a client, he or she might either extend your business or top up with a new product or service. This can be extremely beneficial during tough times.

If you are running a consumer business, look at how you can tap better into your existing user base without having to spend too much on acquisition costs.

One of the startups I invested in had a huge under utilised consumer base and only 2% of it was monetized. So, one of the main objectives was to increase the 2% to 25%. That alone, without growing the user base, would improve visibility and viability for the next investment round.

On the flip side, there's one firm that I work with that basically was picture perfect for this crisis. But the focus for them wasn't crazy growth, because the community itself was growing organically. They had to solve the problem of how to increase user time on the application. The current crisis has helped expand the community, but how do we ensure it is not fake adoption? You create value within the product and increase the value created.

David Fogel
Cofounder of Alma Angels, ADV, and Israel Tech Parliament

Some of our B2B companies have been devising tactics on how to retain customers. We look at how to reduce customer churn and ensure that the product is more easily integrated and onboarded by users. We are effectively trying to minimize friction at every point of sale. Those are the aspects of enterprise products that we've been speaking to founders about.

Kelvin Au
Head of venture at Founders Factory

Quicker Payments: Renegotiate payment terms to see if you can receive some cash (receivables) earlier than previously agreed. This can help alleviate some of the immediate cash flow challenges that you might face. Remember, every little action helps.

Pricing Models: Renegotiate pricing models, especially if the revenues are purely transaction or usage based. The number of transactions or the use of your platform might fall drastically through a crisis. If clients are paying you a transaction commission, then you might see that trending to zero.

Hedge your risks by renegotiating the pricing model with your clients. Ask for a minimum fixed payment that the client could make in exchange for lower transaction or usage fees. This would mean you will receive a small revenue even if there were no transactions on your platform.

We're encouraging our portfolio firms to do two things. One is to increase the cash runway to 18–24 months. It's not possible for every business that we've invested in to do that, but we are encouraging companies to think about that as the first step.

The second thing is to work out how they can achieve the same level of growth within the constraints of the landscape. They can't go into hibernation from a growth perspective. We're encouraging them to think of efficient ways to build that growth.

For some companies that have got a long payback period, for example, that might be doing more B2B partnerships in which you take a lower gross margin but take some upfront cash. We're looking at another business where they were going to build out expensive infrastructure that would have given them a gross margin improvement, but it had a high capital cost. They are now revisiting the plan and thinking more about how to do that without that infrastructure investment. So what we're really encouraging people to do is think about increased focus on efficiency, without giving up on the ambition of scale.

Camilla Dolan
Founding partner at Eka Ventures

Pricing model negotiations should be based on the churn modelling exercise you did through scenario planning. If you do not have scenario models with the best, neutral and worst-case scenarios of customer churn, you might not be able to perform pricing changes that are contextual and meaningful.

Suppliers and Vendors: Decrease Outgoing

Be objective in your assessment of vendors and suppliers. If a supplier or vendor does not fall in your area of focus that you identified in the diagnostics process, add them to the list of terminations. Be benevolent with these stakeholders by agreeing on a gradual ramp-down of the engagement, rather than immediate termination. However, this book is not about running charities, so let me cut to the chase. If you do not need a vendor in your core areas of business, you shouldn't let them burden your cash flows.

Force majeure is one of the main things we learn in law school. But in contrast, they don't have that as a mandatory clause in the business environment. It is actually quite staggering that people just take it for granted, because force majeure by its very nature doesn't occur very often. Make sure there's always a way out, and that there aren't any onerous or unilateral termination provisions. This means that during an unforeseen event, it is possible to negotiate termination provisions and make sure that any contracts you breach do not have punitive consequences.

There's always something you can do strictly by the letter of the law, but, ultimately, it is still about the relationship. That's usually the baseline. Your relationship with your landlord, your vendor, your supplier is fundamental in you being able to negotiate your contract and being able to have flex in your contract.

Victor Chang
Legal counsel at Curve

Also consider discussing a new payment structure with the vendors and suppliers you badly need to keep the business going. Instead of a monthly payment plan, negotiate a quarterly or a half-yearly payment plan if this is acceptable. However, in dire times, I would terminate non-core vendors and suppliers aggressively to ensure those who really matter are kept happy.

It is in your best interest to keep the suppliers that matter to the running of your business paid on time as they would be under cash flow pressures as well. Therefore, keep the money flowing to those who matter to your business during this time. This might sound cruel, but a crisis is a time when you are looking to survive: it is ok to be cold in decision-making.

Once you have made decisions about your vendors and suppliers, about who will or will not be continued, figure out how to deliver the news. The COVID crisis has seen some mindless firing of people and suppliers through very short and rude Zoom calls. That attitude will come back to hurt you if you are a small or mid-sized player, and cause you reputational damage if you are a big player. If you can't hold on to a supplier, at least hold on to their goodwill.

It is now time to evaluate cost-cutting options internally.

The Firm: Align Culture In Chapter 2, we did an evaluation of where the firm was and who was critical to the operational capabilities of the firm. That information will help us with evaluating cost-cutting options within the firm.

Following are some obvious choices of cost-cutting during dire times. But the objective is perhaps more than that. When it comes to internal costs, the outcome should be about creating a cost-conscious culture within the firm. As the leader, it is important to show the team that you are taking serious cost-cutting measures. This can quickly lead to an avalanche of voluntary cost-saving suggestions from the team.

Consider brainstorming with the team on how you can cut costs creatively. The best idea wins a reward! Gamifying cost-cutting can yield excellent results both culturally and monetarily. Yet, as the leader of the firm, you should be leading this from the front. If you preach without practising, your team will take it only as seriously as you do. Let us now look at some cost-cutting options.

Office Space: In a world where the workforce is becoming truly global, office rent is one of the areas I would look to cut costs. In the post-COVID world, I wouldn't be surprised if offices are used more like a conference area for critical meetings, board discussions and workshops. I truly hope that organisations will see the benefits of letting staff members work from home. This cost-saving is an obvious choice.

Management Salaries: If you have a management team and a board that is getting paid way above the rest of the team, it is worth revisiting their compensation structures. This is a time when the management teams should step up to such initiatives and offer to give up a slice of their short-term compensation in the interest of the business.

We started with the management team taking a pay cut. We then asked for volunteers in the company who would take a 10% pay cut, especially those who are in the upper bands of pay. People came forward, and lots of them volunteered.

I then held a workshop with the team and discussed ways we could cut down costs in creative ways and the impact that would have on their day-to-day work. In the workshop we had several ideas. People were honest and were happy to cut down on subscriptions, cloud services and so on.

As we emerged out of the first phase of lockdown, we saw that people had changed their way of work to the new cost base. We rewarded the best suggestions on cost optimization with Amazon vouchers to celebrate it and ensure that they felt it was a team sport.

To help team morale, we had a regular newsletter that consolidated statistics about places where the teams' parents are from. We proactively monitored the situation for them.

Joyeeta Das
CEO of Gyana

Marketing: We have identified core business lines, products and markets through the diagnostics process. It's worth going through a detailed breakdown of the costs associated with these non-core business lines, products and markets. If you have been spending on marketing the non-core parts of your business, you might want to cut those down. Often, it might not make sense to spend on marketing certain products that are irrelevant during a crisis and they might be low-hanging fruit too. In other scenarios, just as a crisis kicks off, markets might pivot towards a product that no longer needs too much marketing.

For instance, pharmatech platforms that deliver pharmaceuticals to your doorstep grew without any marketing spend even during the initial days of the crisis. However, they are in a minority of businesses that benefitted from the crisis. If you are not one of the fortunate ones, it might still make sense to ramp down on marketing spend to understand where the market is heading as the crisis unravels. This will help position your firm accordingly through the second-order optimisation process we will describe in future chapters.

Operations and Technology: If you have an outsourced operational process that is no longer relevant or core to your first-order optimisation process, that should go, or at least pause. While making operational and technology cost-cutting, it is critical to assess if you are adding any major operational risks to the firm. Make sure the board and the management team are aware of the risks and are happy to assume the risks of the operations function that is going to be paused or culled.

Supply chains that are serving the non-core areas of your business can be areas of saving as well. In essence, follow the diagnostics data and make quick and easy decisions. Technology costs could come down if your infrastructure and costs associated with it fall as product usage goes down. Your technology team might have costs like cloud subscriptions that they may not necessarily need. Look for areas where small-value, large-volume cost can be cut.

Team: Handle with Care   Of all the decisions you might have to make, letting your people go will be the hardest. Before resorting to redundancy, consider a few creative options:

- See if the management team have taken a salary cut.
- See if the senior management team is willing to take a salary cut. The alternative could be that they might lose a good part of their team.
- See if you can roll out a wrapper percentage cut in people's pay instead of laying off employees.
- Evaluate government support such as furlough pay.

If you have done all that and still are falling short of the cost-cutting you need to do, as agreed by the board, then look to lay off employees. In places such as Silicon Valley, letting go of people is not considered a major issue. Both employees and employers understand the handshake mechanism and are always cognisant of the implications. However, in other parts of the world, laying off employees can come with reputational and legal implications.

In Chapter 3 we looked at identifying the poor performers and the outliers in the organisation. Poor performers are those who are working on critical projects, loyal to the firm but lack the quality expected by the organisation. Outliers are those who are good quality, but lack the passion for the business and are expected to leave the firm anyway.

It is worth evaluating your pool of employees again in the light of the crisis and the focus areas drafted for the firm. Employees who are most vulnerable in this process are the low performers in the non-core areas of the business. This is followed by the low performers in the core areas of business and then the outliers. Before you make the final list of employees you would let go, consider talking to the outliers on their willingness to leave the organisation voluntarily.

If you had adopted an effective communication methodology, employees must already have a sense of what the management considers to be the focus areas for the short term. If you have a clear performance management process in place, they will also know where their performance ranked across their business unit or organisation. Therefore, a layoff might not come as a surprise.

As you are announcing the layoffs pretty early in the crisis, the market still might be hiring for talent. Therefore, there is a good chance that the employees you choose to let go could find a job quite quickly before the crisis takes off. Sachin Jaiswal at Niki.AI, a firm where Ratan Tata is an investor, had to let go of a third of their workforce due to the COVID crisis. However, he mentioned that more than 50% of those people got placed within the following four weeks.

The furlough process was horrific. Especially when we always try to live by a 'no man or woman left behind' principle. The processes are hard and the scars will definitely stay with them and us for a long time.

David Brear
Founder and group CEO of 11:FS

In one of my previous firms, I had a situation where one part of my team had two engineers. I was in the unfortunate position of letting go of one of them. I assessed them both with my performance criteria, picked one and let go of him. Literally 45 days later, the second person resigned. I was livid. I lost a lot of respect for that person, because I could have saved the other person's job if I had known this person was going to leave anyways, right?

From then on, I always talk to people to discuss if they were planning on quitting anyways and if they would like to be on the 'list'. That'll end up saving somebody else's job. Therefore, if there is a volunteer, we have offered a month's salary extra in the severance package.

Kunal Mittal
Chief product officer at FrontM

The decision to let go of people, and who, has to be scientific, methodical and quick. However, the delivery of the news has to be as humane as possible. Try to deliver the news within a day, if possible, without staggering the layoffs over a period of time. This helps the survivors to take relief in the fact that the worst is behind them and they have to get going with the job in hand. If the crisis deepens and you have to make further cuts in a few months, at least they will understand that it was beyond the firm's control.

The delivery of bad news should be as personalised as possible. Try to split the delivery of the news to your employees across the management team and senior managers. Provide a forum for exceptional circumstances to be discussed as a quick follow-up. Always try and help these employees to find a job within firms you have relationships with. Suppliers, vendors, clients and peer groups of start-ups can all be excellent places to suggest. However, also beware of competitors who might want your employees to learn about the operational details of your firm.

There are different ways firms approach cost savings with their work-force. Some take a blanket salary cut approach, some lay off in one swing, and some lay off in iterations. However, the objective behind it is to create a runway for as long as possible with the least amount of operational and reputational risk. The art is to ensure you hurt as few people and families as possible in the process. Let us now go through a few experiences of CEOs across the world and their thoughts on the first-order optimisation process.

It's like pulling off a plaster. It was quite easy to do arithmetic on the cost cutting, but the really hard bit was the human layering of that. We had another problem, which was that almost the day that the full lockdown got announced in India, the government announced a moratorium on loans. What that meant was a huge amount of work to do across technology and operations. So, we were not going to have any kind of lockdown or relaxation as a team. However, at the same time, we needed to tell this team, 'You're not going to get any bonuses and your salary is going to be reduced. You can't buy that house you've been dreaming of and you can't have that child that you were planning to'. These were literally the kind of conversations we were having.

How do you motivate people to do extra human work in a really anxiety-inducing situation and take away their financial comfort? A lot of founders were saying stuff like, 'Why don't we cut the salary for three months?' I'd say, 'But how do you know what's gonna happen in three months? What are you gonna do if your team asks you how you know what's gonna happen in three months? Because they're not going to trust you if you don't give them a genuine answer'. We had to tell our team that their salaries were going down by 40% and we didn't know when they would get it back, but they'd have to trust us and have to work 150%. That was the hardest bit.

As somebody who's very comfortable with risk, I think the biggest test for me was in a very risky, frightening environment to reassure my team but not lie to them, give them the truth and tell them that I don't know what the future holds. The founding team took a salary cut. We also looked at the top earners in the organisation and said, 'You can choose to forfeit 50% of your salary, but save your team from layoffs'. The alternative was that they can do the layoffs. Unanimously, they wanted to take the hit and save their teams.

We did a special town hall where we had people that ranged from earning a couple of hundred dollars a month to the super senior guy and told them it's shitty out there, but stick with us. We came up with a structure and a message.

'All pandemics have phase one, phase two, phase three. We're in phase one and it's hell, and this is how hellish it's going to be, but it will end. The worst is going to be phase two, which is going to be the unlock, and all the confusion and chaos. I can't tell you when it's going to end but it's gonna be horrible. So you have to have the stomach to get through that. Phase three is like, whoa! Everything's fine and life is good'.

The entire firm is now obsessed with this phase one, two and three, and it defines everything like our product road map. I think it helps them also understand the money situation because they know that phase one we're like, cut costs, you know, head down, phase two, just survive with less income, life's a bit shit, and then phase three, oh, I can earn money again. They get it but once we get there, life is good. We are all in this as a team.

Lizzie Chapman
CEO of ZestMoney

We went from active fundraising mode to cost-cutting mode overnight. A complete U-turn from a growth mindset to a survival mindset. In 10 days, we had a plan that came into effect and executed to the dot.

If there were any markets where contribution margins were not positive, we stopped catering to that market. Those were markets where we had invested for future growth but if they were not revenue generating, there was no point in continuing to fund growth in those markets with the hope that network effect was going to kick in. We did cut down on marketing spends that were going into the geographies where we were not really seeing positive contribution margins, which helped bring down marketing costs by 75%.

We looked at our office facilities and cut down rent by 30% at first, and then completely killed our office rent costs. We then looked at variable costs. We negotiated with each and every vendor to get better terms. We accelerated revenues by focussing on a couple of backward integrations like the ones with ITC. One of our most sought-after products (by consumers) was from ITC. We were able to increase our margins by 5% by directly integrating with them and getting rid of middlemen.

We had grown the team in anticipation of a fundraise. So, we had to cut down on 30% of the staff who were not in core functions of the business. We did one-on-one calls from 9 AM in the morning to 11 PM. It had to be done in one go, so people do not live in anxiety. At the end of the process, the four of us (founders) huddled together and we couldn't feel anything. We were just blank and tired.

As a CEO, I am also the communication architect of the firm. I had to provide honest and clear communication beforehand without sugarcoating it. We did evaluate other options, but we didn't know how long the crisis was going to last, and we had to make early and deep cut in costs.

After the cuts, the very next day we sat down with the leadership team and set a context of operation for each one of them. This helped team morale as each one of them had something to look forward to; it was so empowering. We were operating from a lean base, the team was excited, but most importantly, 50% of those we let go found another job in four weeks time.

Sachin Jaiswal
CEO of Niki AI

What Next?

That concludes the first-order optimisation process. You have understood the soul of your firm, you have looked at scenarios of cost cutting and executed measures in line with one of the scenarios. Keep taking stock on the health of the business and cash flows until the business landscape gets better.

The first-order optimisation should just give you the breathing space to steer the ship through the storm. In the process of cutting down outgoing cash and increasing the incoming cash, you have created the much-needed buffer time as you and your management team plan and execute more strategic steps. A crisis can shut some doors and open new ones, effectively changing the market landscape itself.

Therefore, you need to be in a state where you are worrying less about the immediate term and start focussing on the medium-term strategy of the firm. Some market trends become clear a few weeks into a crisis. The COVID crisis opened up opportunities for digital collaboration, health care, edtech and even cybersecurity. However, this wasn't obvious as soon as the crisis hit, because the whole world was just focussing on dealing with the pain.

A few weeks into the crisis, we were able to see these trends emerge. We are still not done with the COVID crisis at the time of writing this chapter. We are most certainly not done with understanding major market shifts and drifts due to this crisis. However, businesses that entered the crisis and stayed relevant despite a fall in revenues will have enough data points to strategise next steps. We will cover that in the second-order optimisation process.

Conclusion

Time and time again, the one input I have received from CEOs and VC investors who have sailed through a crisis is this:

'Act swiftly and decisively. Cut more aggressively than you can project'.

The earlier you spot the crisis and act, the better it is for all stakeholders involved. The team will have less cash flow pressure and clearer heads to execute more strategic measures. Let me quickly summarise where we have got to so far.

In previous chapters, we discussed the macro view of capital markets and went through the crises we have seen since the 1980s. We touched on some data collection on your business that could help when you see an overheated market or structural economic challenges emerging.

However, all that preparation might not be enough to predict that a crisis is coming, the time of it or help you respond to it. For instance, although there were sporadic signs of an overheated market before 2020, the COVID crisis was largely an event-driven crisis. Therefore, if you had been prepared for a crisis caused by structural issues in the economy, you might not have been entirely prepared for the speed at which we were hit by this event-driven crisis.

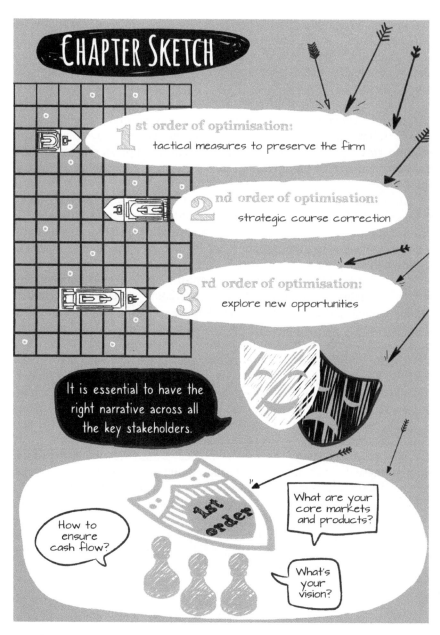

FIGURE 4.4   Chapter Four

In any case, once a crisis is here, the first step is to ensure that you are punching from a stable footing. The leaders of the organisation must be clear about their abilities and passion to drive the business forward. They should be able to establish a support system that they can rely on through the tough times.

That readiness will then prepare them for what we discussed in this chapter. Firms get hit in different ways by a crisis. Some of them become completely irrelevant, some get a big boost; and the majority stay relevant with a fall in growth and revenues. For all of them, the first step is to preserve the heart and soul of the organisation. See Figure 4.4 to capture the gist of this chapter.

Once leaders have identified the soul of their firm, it is then about managing cashflows to ensure the soul of the firm is preserved through the crisis. This can be possible by a good understanding of cost structures and focus on the business across products and markets. We discussed all of that at length in this chapter.

Then you need to execute a well-thought-through cash flow management strategy. Increase short-term cash by renegotiating with clients, tweaking pricing models and accelerating receivables. If you have suppliers and vendors looking for payments from you, negotiate on terms that will ease your cash flow. Be objective about your suppliers and vendors.

Finally, we talked about the people who make the firm what it is. We did touch on assessing the performance of your employees during the data collection described in Chapter 2. Many organisations do this as an annual or half-yearly exercise. These data, combined with the focus areas for the business as identified by the first-order optimisation, should help you make quick personnel decisions.

We also touched on the importance of communication architecture through these difficult times. A CEO should find ways not just to communicate but also to connect to employees with authenticity. That will reduce nervousness, breed trust and help you deliver bad news when you need to do so.

Once you have done all this within a span of a couple of weeks of the crisis taking shape, you should be in a good position to plan the second-order optimisation phase to reposition your firm. That's what we focus on in the next three chapters of this book.

CHAPTER 5

Check Your Mirrors

... it is a wise father that knows his own child.

William Shakespeare, *The Merchant of Venice*

Introduction

If Albert Einstein was the greatest scientific mind of the last century, Steve Jobs is certainly the greatest consumer connector of all time. It is hard to look past him when you are looking for 'how to connect to the customer'. I don't think I would queue up to buy any product at 5 am on a cold London morning in October. I did that for the iPhone, twice. I had to be the first at work who owned the latest model of the iPhone.

The role of a start-up can be simplified into two key activities: build a product and sell the product. Developing a product is often the easy bit. But when you are out there selling it, the penny drops. This is because entrepreneurs often struggle to connect with their users. When you create the connection, you are able to even change consumer behaviour in ways never seen before.

> '**Technology** alone is not enough – it's **technology** married with **liberal arts**, married with the humanities, that yields us the results that make our heart sing'.
> *Steve Jobs*

That was what Steve Jobs did to his customers. He connected with them and was able to create the reality distortion field like no other CEO has managed to do before or after him. Jeff Bezos took the obsession for the customer to a whole new level with Amazon. Jeff created the connection through execution as much as Steve did. However, Steve still stands out for his launch events and how well he delivered them and the brand equity he built by humanising technology. This chapter is about beginning the second-order optimisation, with consumer behaviour being the first key pillar of the optimisation process. Let us first go through an analogy to bring the concept to life.

Second-Order Optimisation

One good analogy is worth three hours of discussion.

Running a business can be compared to driving a car from one destination to another. The more I think about it, the more I am amazed at the number of similarities between the two. Therefore, I am going to use the analogy of a roadtrip to bring the second order optimisation process to life.

The second-order optimisation is a process through which you will assess your business in the context of three different dimensions and how they are evolving through the crisis. You will need to look at the capabilities of your firm through these three lenses.

- Infrastructure and its evolution through the crisis
- Market and consumer appetite changes through the crisis
- Business models that are relevant through the crisis

So, to come back to our analogy, let's say you are planning a road trip from London to Nice in the south of France. And, to enhance the analogy, let's also assume you are driving a Tesla. You should be able to plan your road trip across three activities:

- Check the map
- Check the car
- Check your mirrors

If you are doing the trip in a Tesla, you will want to check the route from London to Nice, charging stations along the way, channel crossing infrastructure and the quality of the roads you will be travelling on. The charging stations need to be spaced out adequately to ensure your car has enough charge for the trip.

In a business context, your roads are the infrastructure needed to run the business. Infrastructure for a business could be regulatory frameworks to support the business. It could also be technology infrastructure such as the cloud, processors, internet speeds needed to expand your business. Businesses also rely on ecosystem infrastructures such as good skills and funding sources.

The charging stations are funding rounds, the distance between charging stations is the runway your business has and the channel crossing infrastructure can be the regulatory and governance factors you might want to consider through the journey.

On a similar note, your car can be compared to your business model. Some cars go from 0 to 60 mph in under 5 seconds, others take longer. Some cars are just faster than others, some are more fuel efficient and others are better on rugged terrain. Business models can be seen in a similar vein. Some businesses take off quickly and get into revenue fast, while others have longer sales cycles. Some business models are cost-efficient, and some are more resilient than others during times of crisis.

Before you get the car moving, you check your mirrors and have a look around. This allows you to understand the traffic and hazards around you, so you can navigate your car accordingly. This assessment is analogous to the study of markets and consumer appetite for your products and services while running a business. This continuous checking of traffic and hazards is similar to an ongoing process of understanding consumer appetite, behaviour and market movements.

You might have clean roads, charging stations and a Tesla to drive, but if the roads are too clogged with cars, you won't be able to travel at an optimal speed. Therefore, you need all three dimensions to make a start-up successful. Infrastructure, business models and consumer behaviour need to be understood for the second-order optimisation of your business.

If you are a start-up that has executed the surgical strike described in Chapter 4, and you are looking for strategic positioning and direction, use this framework to identify a way forward. Chapters 5, 6 and 7 of this book focus on getting these three dimensions assessed for your business, and that is the second-order optimisation process.

Most crises bring new market forces and shifts. Failing to understand these forces might put your revenues at risk, in the medium term at least. Understanding the direction of the markets, new infrastructure changes and how business models evolve in line with them will also ensure you don't lose out on the opportunities a crisis brings to the table.

This chapter is all about customers and their behaviour. As we've said, developing a product is often the easy bit, selling it can be harder. And increasing sales sustainably over time is even harder. A crisis can change the way consumers behave. During the COVID lockdown, we saw that even people in their 70s started to use digital solutions like never before.

Let us start with an assumption that you have a proposition and a few capabilities built or at least a few capabilities in mind that you want to build. That will be the base for your hypothesis testing against different customer-related factors. This might have to be an ongoing process that can be set for a monthly or quarterly review, based on where you are in the crisis. You might have to create a consumer capability matrix that can guide you through the process.

Let us look at how you can assess changes in consumer behaviour through the crisis as part of the second-order optimisation process. Please note that all the following ideas and stories will help you think about how to understand consumer behaviour. However, they still need to be tested through iterative refinement to yield the right results in an accurate fashion.

The Who

The first step in understanding consumer appetite for your proposition is by asking yourself who your ideal customer is. It might help if you have an avatar of the customer clearly defined, depending on your business's capabilities. This is an important step because sometimes your understanding of the 'who' can be different from the actual customer. The market would show you the other 'who' you should take into account or point out that you have the wrong avatar of your customer.

Ask yourself which section of your user base really needs your product. Understand through empirical evidence if their behaviour has changed through the crisis. We will discuss different ways of collecting evidence later in the chapter. Let us take Zoom as an example. Before COVID happened, the typical customer for Zoom was a business that had distributed teams and wanted a digital method of communicating and collaborating. On the retail consumer end, customers were working professionals using the tool to communicate and collaborate.

Don't assume that your customers of yesterday are going to be your customers of today or tomorrow. Understanding churn is important but binding behaviours to service levels is critical, too. Because of all the work we've done in building ventures, I'm obsessed with A/B testing.

It might indicate that you should look to focus on other areas, because your market dynamics are changing. Another segment of customers or a service or product line might be suddenly more relevant. It could be an opportunity to look at an enhancement or another product or accelerate a product to market that you had in the back burner.

Nicole Anderson
Managing Partner at Redsand Ventures

However, as the COVID crisis hit, the daily active user base for Zoom increased from 10 million users to more than 200 million. Not all of them were paid subscribers to the app. However, the composition of the user base changed dramatically during the lockdown. Schools started using it for daily virtual classes. Personal trainers and yoga instructors used it for their training sessions. Families and friends used it to just start getting together. Use of Zoom across small businesses also exploded through the crisis.

The crisis helped achieve several years of digital transformation in under a few weeks. The Zoom application was solving a major problem for its users. We were all desperate to connect with each other. The sudden jump in user base was also made possible by good internet bandwidth and cloud infrastructure. There were times in March and April when we had difficulties in accessing Zoom recordings for a few days. There were also challenges in cybersecurity, but those were addressed as soon as they were identified.

In essence, the Zoom product team had a good problem to solve. Their user base had increased 20 times in a few weeks. However, their subscriptions might not have increased 20 times. Their challenge was to understand the needs of each segment of their user base, why those users were using the application and how they could effectively monetise this user base. Without that analysis, the 200 million users might not stay after the lockdown was eased.

Let us look at another example of an enterprise software company. Let's take for example a data analytics company selling software to mid- and large-tier companies. The customer in your eyes could be the chief technology officer (CTO) of the company. But in many cases, the actual customers of the software product are the users of the tool in a business that the CTO supports. Therefore, the product needs to be built in line with the business users' expectations.

However, you will still need to keep in mind quality control, disaster recovery, the longevity of customer support, pricing and other criteria a CTO might have for the product. But the actual user experience of the product will need to be crafted for the business users who will make a case for your product to the CTO. In recent times, we have seen an evolution of business-to-business (B2B) software firms using a B2C2B approach to taking their product to market. The B2C2B here stands for business to community to business.

In this mode of going to market, companies first focus on building a community of users for their product. This community typically provides constant feedback on the product that can help refine it. These communities can also bring businesses and enterprises they work for to the table. As a result, it becomes an easier sales process with the enterprises you are targeting.

Therefore, in the light of a crisis, it is important to revisit the definition of your core consumer to identify doors that are opening and those that are closing. Having a clear definition of each of your user profiles is essential. But what is perhaps more important is creating a mind map of why the customers use your products and services. Staying on top of the 'Why' through the crisis will help you make essential course corrections as you create your product road map. Let us now discuss the 'Why' of your customer base.

The Why

When I was at PwC, we used to look for firms in trouble, either reputationally or with their regulators. It is often easier to win a client who is in deep trouble or pain and needs help: they are more likely to use your product or services. Where there is no fire, there is no money. This is also precisely why a crisis can be a great time to start a business. The right business, solving a chronic issue that the target consumer base has, can sell like hot cakes even during a crisis.

This point is also stressed by the MEDDIC framework, which is widely used by sales professionals for enterprise sales. It asks the following questions.

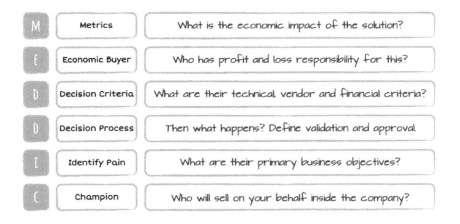

M	Metrics	What is the economic impact of the solution?
E	Economic Buyer	Who has profit and loss responsibility for this?
D	Decision Criteria	What are their technical, vendor and financial criteria?
D	Decision Process	Then what happens? Define validation and approval.
I	Identify Pain	What are their primary business objectives?
C	Champion	Who will sell on your behalf inside the company?

This chapter doesn't focus on how to do sales, but there is a line in the MEDDIC approach about 'identifying pain'. That is a key point to focus on, especially during a crisis. Crises have the ability to exacerbate cracks in social and economic setups. Every crack that opens up during a crisis could be an opportunity for your capabilities to fill.

The sales methodology MEDDIC was born out of the Parametric Technology Corporation (PTC) in the 1980s. It focusses on customer pain being a key driver of the sales strategy. During a crisis, a methodology such as MEDDIC can differentiate you from your competitors. Here you are focussing on the customers' pain and on the wins for the customer.

Emma Maslen
Executive Coach and Founder of Inspire·em

Going back to the Zoom example, asking a why about their core capability can help address if the massive changes in the who for their product really matters. Let us take a few user groups that have started using Zoom since the lockdown began.

Users Older Than 60: They have come to Zoom to communicate with their family and friends. They are a user segment that would not be inclined to become paid subscribers of the product. They might also be the first to stop using the app once the lockdowns are eased. They are perhaps a user segment where revenues will be the lowest. We'll look at how such a consumer base can be monetised in the section 'The How'.

Schools and Students: Several schools started using Zoom for their virtual classes. They are a segment that might be inclined to become paying customers depending on the length of their sessions. This is also true for personal trainers and yoga teachers who use Zoom. However, there might be a slight behavioural difference between these two user groups. As schools reopen across the world, Zoom subscriptions will go down. However, yoga and personal coaches might find the virtual delivery of sessions more convenient and scalable. If their customers also find it more convenient and effective, the usage with these user groups will last.

Small and Medium-sized Enterprises (SME): Several startups and SMEs moved to Zoom for collaborative working through the lockdown. They were mostly paid subscribers of the application. And, most of them figured out how to operate in the lockdown before long. Many startups I have spoken to also confirmed that they worked from home and used Zoom as the norm; personal meetings were the exception. Therefore, this will be the stickiest user group from a revenue perspective, even after the lockdowns.

This is not an exhaustive analysis of the Zoom consumer base. The examples were used to bring the analysis process to life. All these behavioural predictions are my hypotheses based on why people are using the Zoom app. My hypothesis could be proven wrong during testing, but you should follow such a process with your customer analysis.

We can use a similar approach to enterprise software assessment, too. Let me go back to our portfolio company BibliU, who have created a digital library platform for universities. Just after the COVID lockdown was imposed in Q1 2020, their sales pipeline had 60 new pilot requests from institutions across the world to onboard their platform. Students would return to universities in due course; however, it would give BibliU enough time to have penetration across several organisations in the world.

Pre-COVID, most companies were trying to get into fintech. Banks and insurance firms didn't have a choice but to undergo digital transformation to stay relevant. But lifestyle businesses and technology players such as Amazon, Google and Apple were teased into fintech. Since COVID, this behaviour has slightly pivoted towards healthcare. Most companies are now wanting to be in the healthcare value chain. The reason for that is any company that has access to a large consumer base sees an opportunity to become a distribution platform for health.

Especially when you can start moving healthcare onto a smartphone, leveraging an existing consumer base becomes a no-brainer. For instance, Apple is significantly investing in healthcare technologies including watch and wearables. In fact, those are now like building clinically validated models using the data that they have from their users.

Akshay Sharma
CTO at Doceri

Educational institutions are also quite sticky customers because they do not change their technology platforms very often. Therefore, once they have a foot in and students and staff start using their application on a day-to-day basis, it would be hard to change the behaviour and move away from a digital library experience.

There are still a few who still prefer paper turns over mouse clicks, but a big portion of BibliU's consumer base of students and staff would be onboard from a behavioural perspective. That, along with the technological agility of educational institutions, could create a virtuous cycle that helps further adoption and penetration for the company.

We have covered two dimensions: namely, the 'Who' and the 'Why' to understand the consumer during a crisis. It might be worth creating a matrix that maps capabilities against customer segments. The matrix should be colour-coded based on the level of need and stickiness of the customer. A sticky customer segment could be tagged as green, a customer segment where the evolution in behaviour is still in progress towards the sticky side would be amber, and where you think the customer segment is not sticky could be red.

One of the benefits of fintech is that you get very quick, very cheap micro data points that you can use to spot behavioural trends. Are users beginning to order more from home, has the transaction value increased, has their average order size gone down by 60%, and so on? That gives me a sense of what their disposable income could be. It might not be a perfect correlation because it might be a need, but these data points are invaluable.

We then ask ourselves if the behaviour patterns are going to be sustained or if it is a point in time behaviour. We do A/B testing with our hypothesis. In several parts of emerging markets where we have invested, people are doing more e-commerce. I don't anticipate they'll go back to old ways. Remember MPesa in Kenya, which was born out of a crisis?

In Kenya, it was the constitutional crisis in 2007 that forced people to use digital payments and they never went back. We have evidence from past crises that show that these behaviours get pretty sticky because people see the benefits of these new behaviours.

Monica Brand Angel
Cofounder at Quona Capital

The colour-coding effectively indicates the level of need the customer segment has for your product. The greater the need combined with transformation in behaviour the more you can move a customer segment from red to green.

Need Matrix	Customer Segment 1	Customer Segment 2	Customer Segment 3
Capability 1			
Capability 2			
Capability 3			

To avoid subjectivity, give a needs score to each of these capabilities per customer segment. Once you have identified the needs scores, the next step is to identify expected value across these segments.

The How Much

The qualitative assessment of consumer behaviour based on their need for your product should be complemented by a quantitative assessment. Although the qualitative assessment focusses on customer needs, the quantitative assessment must focus on the value that tapping into a customer segment would deliver to the firm.

Value assessment of product capability should be based on market research data against specific customer segments. Market data should be augmented with use and growth data based on your experience with that customer segment so far. Therefore, consider using the following three parameters:

- Market size
- Growth rate
- Usage rate

You might not have all this data when you start this analysis on your product capabilities. Market data might be available, however, growth and usage data might be too nascent. How you get better growth and use information is covered in the next section. Once you have these three dimensions of data, you will need to use them to create a simple quadrant to help prioritise your focus. This quadrant might evolve during and after the crisis.

Develop a process to keep updating this information. If you notice any marked changes in the behaviour of the customers, it will show in the growth and usage data. That will inform decisions on course corrections where needed.

Value

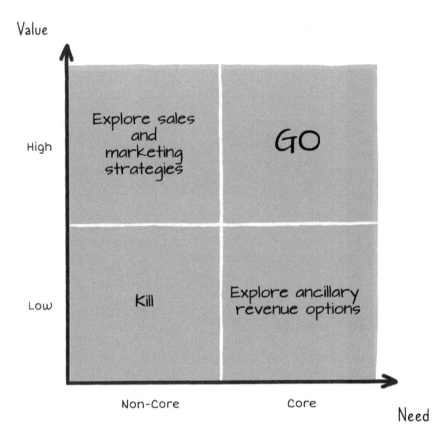

Here is a simple framework to help prioritise your capabilities based on the need for them during and after a crisis and how much value addition the need will bring to the business. I often find it an easy conversation to press the 'Go!' and 'Kill!' buttons in our strategy discussions with entrepreneurs. It is really when either the need is high without enough value or when the value is high without a need it becomes hard to convince CEOs on a clear way forward.

Let us discuss these quadrants in a bit more detail.

Low Value and Low Need: You could have spent a lot of time and effort building a particular product line. But if the market is telling you that there is neither a need for it nor any money in it, you should listen. This is typically an easy decision unless this is the only capability you have as a firm. Kill it!

High Value and High Need: This is like the BibliU example in which there is a high demand for your edtech platform from universities and there is good money involved as well. This is often when your product sales happen without a penny being spent on marketing. Beef up your sales and delivery team, ensure operations and technology are suitably resourced for the ride. Go!

High Need and Low Value: This is perhaps the quadrant where I find entrepreneurs struggle to move with conviction. The market continuously tells them that there is a need for their product, but often they find very little value in these opportunities – a promising pipeline on paper or big growth numbers, yet very little revenue to show.

Startups need to be really focussed on their target market. You need to be really clear about what you are, what problems you are solving for, and who your client is. It's not about focussing on 50 or 100 customers; it's probably best to focus on the top 10 (in a B2B scenario).

Every week keep engaging with five of them, and the next five in the next week, and keep rotating. It's all about engagement. You cannot go and focus on a massive portfolio and hope and pray that things are going to stick. It's also about validation. The firms that will succeed are the ones that are looking around, continuously evaluating their positioning and adapting quickly.

Sabine VanderLinden
Cofounder at Alchemy Crew

One way to address this challenge is to look for ancillary revenue streams, but these streams typically happen once you have established growth. Therefore, this must be prioritised below your high-need and high-value capabilities, especially if you are resource constrained.

I have seen instances in which teams have chosen to keep certain capabilities that fall in this quadrant to demonstrate the social or environmental impact side of their business. Businesses that take a growth-first approach might keep this quadrant, with a view to monetising the growth in the future. However, when you are under cash flow pressures, the capital required to keep this quadrant alive might not be sustainable.

If the only capability you have as a firm falls under this quadrant, innovate ways to be extremely cost-efficient and continuously test the market to transition the capability from a low-value proposition to a high-value one. The focus must be to work with customers to understand what it takes to make it a high-value proposition.

High Value and Low Need: The first name that comes to mind when I think of this quadrant is Steve Jobs. He was a master at branding a luxury as a want, a want as a need and a need as an obsession. Touch screens were around even before Apple launched their iPhones. However, customers didn't really see a need for them. Since the launch of the iPhone in 2007, customer behaviour has evolved so much that they might have to go through a digital detox to stay away from these devices.

Often a product capability is perceived as a low need because there hasn't been an intuitively designed product or the product suite hasn't evolved enough. It might mean that there are a few steps the product suite has to take before the product's capability is viewed as a need. For instance, 10 years back if Google Chromecast had been launched without a mature smart tv and an Android ecosystem, I would have brushed it aside. However, as smart televisions became more common and Android more sophisticated, customers realised that the next logical product evolution would be casting the video from a mobile device to a television screen.

If you find your capabilities are low need, create a clear growth strategy that aligns and informs the product strategy. With the customer at heart, a well-defined product strategy can create markets that previously hadn't existed. More ideas on how a customer can be brought onboard in a frictionless journey will be covered in the next section. As customer demand increases for these low-need capabilities, they can be moved into the high-need, high-value quadrant.

The How

A good product team makes the process of assessing and delivering to customer expectations a series of data-driven experiments. Customer centricity is embedded into the DNA of the firm from the early days so that even operational activities revolve around that basis. However, there have been instances when an entrepreneur pitching to us has no idea of how to substantiate that their product would be in demand.

'Are customers using your product and why'? is a question every entrepreneur should seek to find scientific answers to. It must be a data-driven exercise so that there is no ambiguity that your product is indeed used. Let us look at a few ways of how to understand customers better and ensure your product is relevant for the target market.

Ask Them

During the iPhone launch in 2007, Steve Jobs revealed that he had shown the iPhone's music (iPod) application to an insider who hadn't seen the interface before. The music app was packed with features for those times: playlists, artists, albums, widescreen videos, cover flow and so many other amazing features that were never possible on a phone before then. As Steve finished the demo, the insider noted how much he enjoyed the scrolling through songs with a swipe: 'You had me at scrolling'.

The best and the most authentic form of feedback is received when you talk to your customers. Be it a B2C or a B2B solution you have launched, you need to engage closely with your customers to understand if the solution addresses their needs. I remember a firm I invested in that acquired several small businesses as clients within six months of us investing in them. When I met them for a strategy discussion after six months of closing the round, they had good acquisition numbers.

However, when we double-clicked into the numbers, we realised that they didn't have the transaction volumes and sizes that they expected. In fact, those figures were practically close to zero. We understood that, despite having onboarded a good number of small businesses, their platform wasn't being used by the end customers who are transacting with the small businesses. They weren't receiving feedback that would help them improve customer experience.

We worked with them and agreed on an engagement model and KPIs that would help track progress. They started aligning operations and customer support on these KPIs and soon found transaction volumes increase. Within three months of getting this feedback process in place, they had demonstrated good growth in transactions. One quarter later, they had monthly recurring revenues in the five digits. They have gone on to become one of my most successful investments to date.

If your product really addresses a customer need, your marketing costs come down too. Therefore, it is important to ensure there is a continuous feedback loop. Feedback could be anything from just a thumbs-up or a thumbs-down button, a review request, a survey, a call with your customer service team, complaints data or even a social media discussion. But it needs to be a fundamental element that drives your product road map.

Get Them

There are several ways to find your customers, get them hooked and keep them hooked without churning. There is no silver bullet that gets you customers overnight. However, it typically involves two key attributes: distribution and product. Understanding your customers and the customer segment helps funnel down your distribution channels.

The purpose of this section is not to walk you through every single distribution channel, but it might be useful to understand the options you have and get creative from there. This is a short list of distribution methods to engage with and acquire customers.

- Offline events
- Virtual events

- Search engine optimisation
- Voice engine optimisation
- PR through traditional media
- Content marketing
- Social media advertising
- Referrals
- Traditional sales through relationships
- Community development
- Email newsletters

All these channels could be used to acquire customers and build brand equity if you do them right. However, depending on the type of customers you want to target, you may need to choose the right channels and measure success against them. The process of choosing the right channels needs to be data driven. You may use multiple channels, but it is best to identify the core distribution channel and a few supporting channels.

Once you have measured and understood that the channels are getting you results, then it is about scaling up from there. There may be a scenario in which none of these channels really gets you results. However, in the process of trying them you would glean precious data about customer behaviour and uptake of your product. You may have to make another attempt at identifying the best distribution channels with a slightly different approach in engaging with your customer base.

If none of the attempts really takes off, it is time to revisit your product or pricing or both.

Understand Them

There are some aspects of your product that you can improve by asking your customers, but several dimensions of your product need to evolve based on the subtle feedback from customer behaviour. For instance, in their initial days, LinkedIn had a button that allowed a user to invite their contacts to the app. Through continuous trial and error, the LinkedIn product team noticed that the colour of this button had an impact on the user.

A red button had better results because it made users click on it and send invitations out. The redder the button was, the better the results were. However, they didn't ask the customers about this. Their user acquisition numbers and usage analytics showed them this particular behaviour. Therefore, your product team needs to have data analytics on customer behaviour to be able to understand what is driving acquisition, churn, stickiness and usage. It's not just about what your customers say, it's also about what they do.

The fundamental principle in these challenging times is to build greater empathy and stronger customer relationships. It's an obvious statement but a very hard differentiation to execute, especially in a crisis. For instance, in the current context even the sales teams in lending portfolio companies are being trained on responsible customer outreach and collections in order to support the performance of loan book in a customer empathetic way. Where some consumer lenders are being blasted on social media right now for unscrupulous customer practices, our portfolio company Zest Money has been lauded for its customer supportive approach.

Creating a reputation and culture within the firm that makes customer focus second nature is a major differentiator during a crisis.

Ganesh Rengaswamy
Partner at Quona Capital

There are several ways that can be employed to understand customer behaviour. Sentiment analysis can tell you broadly if users are happy with the product or not. However, constant A/B testing is essential if you need to have a deep understanding of which parts of your product needs tweaking. A/B testing can be done per customer segment to have targeted feedback for the product team to act on.

A/B testing is not a new concept. It was used in agriculture in the 1950s to test effectiveness of fertilisers on certain crops and soils. It was used in clinical trials in the 1960s. Since the 1990s, the marketing world has adopted A/B testing to track the success of campaigns. In the software space, though, it enables us to check if functionality or a simple feature has yielded the expected results.

During my discussion with Simba Rusike, the CFO of Assurance IQ that was acquired by Prudential, he mentioned that data science was pretty integral to business model development and product road maps in their organisation. Data-based understanding of customer behaviour needs to be integrated into operations, marketing and product development at an early stage. Once that is achieved, understanding customer behaviour becomes second nature and even mundane.

You now have a view of what your core capabilities are based on the value-versus-need quadrant. You have set up a data-driven approach understanding and capturing customer feedback on an ongoing basis. This will help define and refine your product and business model. However, one of the key aspects of delivering value to customers is dealing with touchpoints.

Our focus was very much about making sure that the GDP per capita in Pakistan is not out of sync with what opportunity we were trying to capture. The best example I can share of that is of Bykea. It's our portfolio company with a motorbike platform. They were breaking even prior to COVID in Karachi on razor-thin margins.

The beauty of it is that there are so many bikes in the country and there's really a minimum marginal cost of using them. In fact, if you want to buy a five-year-old bike, it's $150. You can pay that back by working three weeks on the bike. So the business was always built with extreme focus on cost efficiency.

Rabeel Warraich
General Partner at Sarmayacar

After defining the 'How?' and the 'How much?' of understanding customer reactions to your capabilities, think about how well you execute your product. This can be as much a qualitative exercise as it is quantitative. However, the focus must be on reducing the number of touchpoints and providing a seamless and frictionless customer experience.

Often these terms are used for B2C products, but it is equally important for B2B rollouts as well. Before going to the B2B aspects of touchpoint management, let us look at an example of how user onboarding is affected by touchpoints.

Figure 5.1 captures the number of times a customer clicks to open a bank account with fintechs such as Revolut, Starling and Monzo compared to incumbent high street banks. These fintechs have shown how frictionless user journeys can help onboard millions of customers in a relatively short period of time.

It is true that these fintechs are yet to demonstrate their ability to increase the lifetime value of these users and that their growth story results in a viable business model. But onboarding millions of users the way these firms have gets them to a

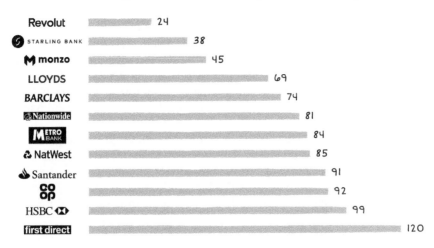

FIGURE 5.1   Number of Clicks to Create an Account *Source: Data from builtfor-mars.co.uk.*

pole position. They still need to drive through the race to win it, which means they need a viable business model that scales and taps into the acquired customer pool.

The fact that people wanted more easy-to-use and transparent banks post 2008 was definitely a trust issue. I think another interesting factor was iPhone coming in. It changed the perspective of the world with regards to the capabilities of apps. People expect seamless engagement and minimum number of clicks in a B2C product. Those are the same people who end up working in enterprises.

Therefore, what you see is that, that ease of use has become an expectation for enterprise software. In the last three to four years, B2B users have started to expect transparent and easy-to-use products that reduce complexity.

David Fogel
Co-founder of Alma Angels, ADV, and Israel Tech Parliament

Although a frictionless customer journey with minimal touchpoints can help you acquire customers, you need to have a clear value proposition to ensure you don't end up with a high churn rate. Often, I see a start-up acquiring a huge consumer base but not making the most of it. Especially through a crisis, when the cost of acquiring customers can be high, it is critical to tap into the existing customer base.

As mentioned, minimising touchpoints is equally important for B2B businesses as well. If you have a software offering for enterprises and if your integration process with the client is intrusive, that might increase your distance to revenue even if you manage to sell quickly. It is therefore important to see how you can make deployment and integration as seamless and simple as possible.

Where your product needs on-premise integration within the client's systems, explore options of contractually derisking potential deployment issues. A paid prototype could be an excellent way to get into a firm and slowly expand from a low-cost base. You could also build a community of users who can get you clients. In the process, the community can help you overcome the infrastructure and procurement hurdles you are likely to face through the sales process.

Behaviour versus Value

Although customer behaviour is what we get to understand through the data and research we perform, customer values are often what drive those behaviours. Therefore, it is not just important to capture changes to the superficial behaviours of customers but also to double-click into how customers' values are evolving if not pivoting.

An EY report on sustainable investing (**https://www.ey.com/Publication/vwLUAssets/ey-sustainable-investing-the-millennial-investor-gl/$FILE/ey-sustainable-investing-the-millennial-investor.pdf**) highlights that millennials are inheriting more than \$US30 trillion in wealth. Their investment values are increasingly aligned with socially and environmentally friendly opportunities. This is driving growth in environmental, social and governance (ESG) investment opportunities since 2012. The fact that these trends are starting to emerge after the 2008 banking crisis might be more of a causation than just a correlation.

On a similar note, several customer behaviour trends are starting to reflect their underlying values. Supporting small local businesses instead of large capital market–backed businesses, the rise of Shariah/Islamic finance, preferring businesses that have better data privacy controls are all some examples of how customer trends can be driven by values. However, unlike behaviours that can be captured as a moment in time exercise, capturing changing values will need a larger data set. Yet, businesses need to stay on top of how these values are evolving to ensure they align their products and services accordingly.

Let us now look at Fred Destin's decision and the reasons he backed Zoopla, the real estate listing website, during the 2008 crisis.

The beauty of the Zoopla business was that the operating leverage was high and we had recurring revenues. We were able to build traffic fairly cheaply and our engineering team was lean and excellent. They did a lot with six or seven people. We naturally had a beast that should be very price resilient. The only variable cost was marketing and we could tune that up or down so that we didn't start losing too much revenue.

We did have the risk of losing a large proportion of our real estate agent clients to our competitor Rightmove. The competitor could have taken advantage of the crisis to come and crush us. But Zoopla had two advantages: Rightmove was a public company and they were not price aggressive. They were doing monopoly pricing and were quite happy to do so. Rightmove never had to use price to compete because they had scale and volume. So, you had a dominant player charging premium price and no interest in destroying their own margins and probably couldn't without getting killed by the public markets.

Then, on the other side, we had a bunch of incumbents, primarily publishers, who were bleeding much harder than we were in the crisis. That was due to much higher fixed costs. As with all these crises, if you're a nimble startup, it's really an opportunity for you. I think we design organisations that thrive in chaos. That's the definition of a startup. Whenever there's a market dislocation, we actually tend to do really well provided we don't die.

In the case of Zoopla the objective was to get funded. We got two term sheets, went with one and the investor pulled out two days before the closing. I went to my partnership and I said, I wanted to invest £3 million into Zoopla. We weren't a big fund, so it was quite a big commitment. I fundamentally believed in the founder and I felt we could crush the competition. It was a heated discussion and I think at some point, I really pounded the table and said, 'I will put my career on the line behind this investment'.

We ended up basically doing it solo. Shortly after that, we got investments from Octopus, and then there was no looking back. I think that's one of the few moments when I put my career on the line, because that's what I'm paid to do. I'm paid to have opinions.

Fred Destin
Founder at Stride VC

Finally, see Figure 5.2 for a chapter sketch to summarise the gist of this chapter.

FIGURE 5.2   Chapter Five Sketch

Conclusion

In the second-order optimisation process, customer behaviour is one of the three key pillars. We used the analogy of a road trip at the start of this chapter. If you look at your mirrors only at the start of the journey but not throughout, you risk having a major incident. This means, you have to stay on top of customer behaviour and market appetite at all times.

We went through the process of staying on top of customer behaviour. It is important to identify the customer segment clearly before aiming to serve them. We then looked at analysing why they are your customers and what is in it for them. Once you are able to identify these two issues, then it becomes easier to align customers with capabilities.

We looked at frameworks that exist to help identify how big a pain you are solving for the customer and prioritising your capabilities based on the pain they are addressing. It is also equally essential to understand the value your capabilities add to the business. We looked at a simple framework to assess capabilities based on the needs of the customer and the value they add to the business.

The capabilities you prioritise through the crisis will ideally be the ones that are needed by the customer but are also equally commercially viable. If the revenues possibilities are low for a need, then we will need to assess ways of making ancillary revenues. In essence, it is important to ensure that a particular pain point is big enough that a customer pays for a solution directly or indirectly.

We have seen several products through the years that created new markets through clever ways of transforming customer behaviour. In time, products that were initially seen as wants soon became the needs of a customer. However, products that didn't have great customer experiences have not lasted long. Therefore, it is not just important to identify key capabilities based on the customer behaviour analysis and value frameworks we discussed but also to meet the needs in a user-friendly way.

It is also critical, especially during a crisis, to tap into the existing customer base as much as possible. An acquired customer base that is untapped is a wasted opportunity. In essence, it's very hard to go wrong if you have your customers at the heart of your firm. Make customer-centricity second nature at all levels in the organisation. That will ensure that the products built through the crisis get traction.

The next chapter is about the infrastructure pillar of second-order optimisation. Once you have understood your customer, you will need to look around you to assess if you had the infrastructure needed to run the business. It is a fundamental factor that will decide how fast you can grow.

CHAPTER 6

Map the Trip

Uneasy lies the head that wears a crown.

William Shakespeare, King Henry IV

Introduction

In 2011 I was doing my PG Diploma at Said Business School, University of Oxford. We had a diverse set of students making up the cohort. Diversity across age, gender and nationalities really helped the classroom experience. One of the more senior people in the class was an investment manager from San Francisco. I felt he didn't need a b-school to learn global business.

He had a general management degree from Harvard Business School and had done a few more modular courses from Yale and UCLA. During our third module of the course, we had to walk from one campus to another and I got into a casual chat with him. He asked me what I planned to do after the course. I said I had two potential courses to take. One was a masters in finance or a masters in financial engineering.

However, I confessed to him that I was split between the two. He gave me an analogy to help me decide between the two courses, and it has stayed with me since. He said that if I wanted to be the person who understands the wiring, circuitry and all the technical 'stuff' that happens to identify the speed of a car and show it on the display, do the financial engineering degree. Instead, if I wanted to be the person looking at the speedometer, watching at the road, and wanting to steer the car in the right direction, do the masters in finance.

It was an excellent insight, and it helped me understand where I wanted to be in my career. I did the masters in finance degree and it was largely thanks to that two minutes of conversation. In Chapter 5 we discussed an analogy of a road trip to running a startup through a crisis. We will now build on that further to discuss the relevance of understanding the infrastructure pillar of second-order optimisation.

We touched on how infrastructure (the roads), consumer behaviour (traffic) and the business model (car) all need to be aligned to ensure you can complete the road trip successfully. We then focussed on consumer behaviour, the first pillar of the second-order optimisation process. This chapter focusses on the infrastructure aspects of second-order optimisation. Through the examples we provide, you will be able to see why an understanding of infrastructure is critical to getting your medium- and long-term strategies right.

Infrastructure

The infrastructure pillar of second-order optimisation is analogous to having good roads, strong connectivity, charging stations and petrol pumps during a road trip. A lack of good roads will reduce the speed of travel. Without enough fuel at right intervals you might not be able to complete your journey. Similarly, for a technology startup to thrive, it needs the right infrastructure support.

We love the number three, if you haven't already noticed. Most of the structures we have developed for this book use three dimensions or three categories. Infrastructure is not going to be different. We will study three key aspects of the infrastructure dependencies for a startup to succeed:

- Policy infrastructure
- Technology infrastructure
- Ecosystem infrastructure

Let us go through each one of these and understand how they have positively or negatively affected businesses.

Policy Infrastructure

We discussed in Chapter 1 how regulators and central banks sit at the top of the capital pyramid. They are responsible for making sure that the economy is in good shape and there is liquidity flowing through the system. However, in recent times policy makers have been driving not just economic policy but also innovation policy. In some countries policy makers have even laid the rails that the technology startups can use to accelerate the expansion of their products and services.

Regulations are critical and often they are part and parcel of the business model. Let me explain why. A business idea can often exploit a regulatory gray area. There is a regulation that on each piece says that Uber cannot operate as it does. But then Uber thinks that there's margin for maneuver there, that it's a regulatory gray area.

That's precisely because other incumbents think they've got it covered with regulation, but sometimes they haven't. In the US, you call a phone number and you get a taxi cab where you want. If you're in the suburbs, you have to reserve it, because there are not enough cabs. These incumbents thought that this model and the regulations protected them. They thought that if you wanted to become a new taxi company, you have to go through the same process, that you have to have the same regulation on drivers that everybody else has. We've got the phone number that everybody has a little refrigerator wall and Uber doesn't.

Uber came in and chose to disrupt the regulation with their business model. Uber's business was going to take drivers who are not licensed, who are not certified, whose cars are not checked. All things that the Limousine Commission said couldn't be done. That's what I mean when I talk about regulatory gray area.

Nicola Persico
Professor at the Kellogg School of Management

As a technology startup, you must be aware of the policy that either you are waiting for or are wary of. It can make and break businesses and business models. During the Brexit negotiations, for instance, fintech firms in the UK were worried about how seamless the passporting of their licences would be in Europe after Brexit. If they wouldn't be allowed to passport their license, they would need to go through painful regulatory hurdles to do business with Europe.

As soon as COVID hit us, the Indian government announced a moratorium on loans. That meant we had a huge amount of work to do. It's hard to explain how much tech and ops work had to be done to conform, it was just so much work to do. We were not going to have any kind of lockdown or relaxation as a team.

Lizzie Chapman
CEO at ZestMoney

Therefore, it is essential for startups to map out their capabilities across the regulatory landscape and understand which one of their capabilities has the highest potential or risk because of changing regulations. I come across startups that are solving an interesting problem but have no idea what the regulatory implications on their business are.

The first thing you deal with is the crisis. The second thing you deal with is why it occurred. Between 2008 to 2010 people were fixing the economic disaster by getting liquidity moving around the system, creating stimulus packages and generally getting the economy going again.

Once we came out the other side, we were like, what was the problem there? How do we make sure we learn from it, create competition and move systematic risk away from big incumbent organisations? How do we set a different bar? As innovators started thinking along those lines, the regulators kicked the whole thing off. Ten years later fintech in London is such a rich community in terms of innovation, talent, funding and regulatory infrastructure.

David Brear
CEO at 11FS

Some regulators have taken a collaborative approach with the innovation ecosystem to help firms get clearer on their regulatory risks. They run sandboxes to put these startups through an evaluation process, tweak their approach and in doing so clear their regulatory hurdles. This has been seen largely with the financial services industry. The other industries that have regulatory oversight are the health care and the pharma industries.

In pharmaceuticals, for instance, the process of getting a drug to the market is filled with challenges. Clinical trials can slow down the process and often kill the chance of getting the drug to the market. This process takes several years and costs billions of dollars. The cost of getting a drug to the market can be anywhere between $314 million to $2.8 billion as per a recent study.[1]

In the case of pharmaceuticals, though, the regulatory hurdles have become an opportunity for startups to exploit. In recent years, there have been several startups that have been using advanced technologies to accelerate the drug discovery process. Let us now look at a few instances where regulations have positively or negatively affected the innovation landscape.

Payment Services Directive (PSD 2) PSD 2 as it is famously known in Europe is a regulation introduced by the European Banking Authority. It came into force in early 2018 and was intended to ensure that banking customers were in charge of their transaction data. PSD 2 provided the ability for third-party providers to use customers data, with their approval, to offer them innovative solutions. This has led to a new paradigm called 'open banking', which puts the customer at the heart of financial services.

This meant banks had to open up customer transactions to these third-party solutions if the customers wanted the services of these third parties. This put the banks in their place and ensured that the customers were the real owners of their data and that the banks can't claim ownership.

[1]https://jamanetwork.com/journals/jama/article-abstract/2762311

As a result of PSD 2, there has been a whole suite of new ways for customers to access financial services. Customers can now aggregate transactions across all their different financial products and services, such as deposit accounts, savings accounts, mortgages and credit cards. It has also created a bigger opportunity for personal finance management applications to provide more insightful suggestions for customers to manage their money.

Although data ownership and privacy has been a much debated topic in recent years, several parts of the world have approached it differently. That has also affected how well startups have been able to leverage customer data to provide better products and services. For a technology startup in London that is even remotely related to financial services, it is critical that they understand the implications of the open banking wave. PSD 2 has been a beneficial regulatory move that will continue to define European fintech business models for years to come.

The average bank deals with 128,000 regulations, according to Bank of America, and that's just in the US. If you're a global bank you deal with regulatory change every 12 minutes, according to Thomson Reuters. One country somewhere in the world will change a regulation every 12 minutes in financial services. If that regulation is 30,000 words, it's no wonder that no one wants to get into banking because it's just a pain in the backside.

Therefore, if you are a startup operating in the fintech space, you would need to be very well plugged into the regulatory landscape.

Chris Skinner
Author and Board Member at IFS

Blockchain and Cryptocurrencies

In October 2008, Satoshi Nakamoto launched a paper on Bitcoin and the framework behind it called Blockchain. That was timed perfectly because the Lehman Brothers collapse had happened only a month previously, and trust on Wall Street banks was at a historic low. As innovators and customers were looking for better alternatives for value exchange, Bitcoin hit a chord. The current financial system and the capital markets were viewed as too centralised and controlled by a powerful few.

That gave rise to not just a technological and financial paradigm, but also a social one: decentralisation. The following few years saw the term Blockchain rise to the top of coolest jargons. The world has seen several technology terms such *AI, internet* and *quantum computing,* but none of them took off as quickly as Blockchain did.

Thanks to Ethereum, which evolved following the Bitcoin boom, a development community started to come together across the world to create applications that would be stores of value. Applications were set up as ecosystems that had value exchanged in cryptocurrencies. These ecosystems were projected to become economies that would hold and increase in value as customers used the application more and more.

However, what hadn't been factored into all this was how governance would be managed, how policy would be set and, in times of crisis, how price volatility would be managed for these cryptocurrencies. Historically, most of these key issues were dealt with by the regulators or central banks across the world. But in the case of a decentralised value exchange system that relied on its network to offer decentralised governance, no one had a real answer.

In 2017, the Blockchain bubble burst after several billions of dollars were lost due to greed and no authority was qualified or prepared to accredit these value networks. This led to a Blockchain winter that saw several cryptocurrencies lose their market capitalisation by 90+% by early 2018. What once used to be jargon to attract investors soon became something investors and the ecosystem became cautious of.

Technology paradigms are often in different stages of evolution. For instance, in Blockchain, despite all the hypes, we're still at the infrastructure stage. Whereas, if you look at payments, most organisations are now abstracted from the infrastructure layer. Many fintechs don't even know how Visa and Mastercard work.

Therefore, as a startup, understand what your position is within the stack. What will make or break you over the next 18 months. Find out how much runway you have to get there and then make decisions on how to position yourself based on the maturity of the technology and industry infrastructure.

David Fogel
Co-founder of Alma Angels, ADV, and Israel Tech Parliament

We still haven't figured out precisely how some of these governance challenges for cryptos would work. However, the Blockchain community have figured out some solutions through permissioned Blockchains for large enterprises to use for decentralised applications. This might be a slow and painful evolution of the technology coming of age, but it is an excellent example of innovation happening too fast while regulation and policy are left far behind.

In my eyes, cryptocurrencies can only become mainstream once the regulatory infrastructure and policy of these value networks are clearly defined.

India's Aadhaar In Q4 2016, India saw a sudden demonetisation drive led by Prime Minister Narendra Modi. The digitalisation of India's economy had begun by then. Innovation across the country was largely focussed on e-commerce, though. There were a few unicorn startups that had thrived through the e-commerce boom in the country, followed by the payments. However, digital payment was still in its infancy in the country.

Post-demonetisation happened in 2016, and the digital payments eco-system in the country grew at a tremendous pace. This was also catalysed by the Unified Payment Infrastructure (UPI) that the government devel-oped. The UPI acted as the rails to build for the payment infrastructure in the country. The UPI now supports more than $1.2 billion worth of transactions per month.

Two other key infrastructure upgrades happened at a massive scale in the country since 2016. A national identity card called Aadhaar was launched. It has now become the primary identification mechanism for 1.3 billion peo-ple in the country. An economic identity is the fundamental building block needed before onboarding your people into the financial system. The Aadhaar initiative has provided just that. It is far from perfect, yet it is a baby step in the right direction that offers the infrastructure needed to build banking and insurance services for rural India.

The Aadhaar initiative was well supported by the mobile internet infra-structure rolled out by Reliance Jio. Figure 6.1 shows the past and expected increase in internet users in India.

As Figure 6.1 shows, close to 300 million people have come on to the internet in India since 2016. Very much like the mobile internet penetration followed by the mobile payments platform M-Pesa in Africa, India has seen a rise of payments and fintech startup success stories such as Paytm, PhonePe and Google Pay. Paytm received funding from Softbank, Ant Financial and Berkshire Hathaway to support their growth story. PhonePe has been more of a spinoff from Walmart's acquisition of Flipkart.

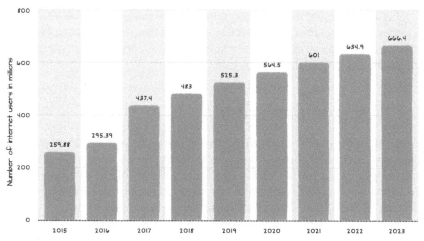

FIGURE 6.1 Number of Internet Users in India from 2015 to 2018 with a Forecast until 2023 (in Millions)

Source: https://www.statista.com/statistics/255146/number-of-internet-users-in-india/

Payment booms have been a good start for fintech innovation in India. That is now being followed by insurtech, lending and other clusters of innovative financial services providers. The UPI infrastructure combined with Aadhaar, followed by mobile internet, are key factors that have led to this rise of fintech opportunities in India.

Drug Discovery Drug discovery is the process that pharma companies go through to ensure efficacy of a drug before it can be launched commercially. This is different from the other examples we have discussed so far in this chapter. Pharma companies across the world spend billions of dollars in getting a drug to the market. The drug goes through stringent clinical trials and regulatory hurdles before it can make money for the pharma firms.

The process of getting a drug to market can often take over 10 years. This is partly due to the regulatory burdens but also because of the inability of today's technology to simulate the interactions between the drug and the affected cell. As a result, this limitation has become an opportunity for technology startups to solve. Firms using machine learning on classical computers are working on creating digital simulations of these drug interactions.

In doing so, the theoretical testing of the efficacy of the drugs is expedited with greater accuracy. In more recent times, quantum technologies are being explored to solve the drug discovery problem more effectively. This is precisely where the interaction between innovation and regulation are different with the pharma industry.

In this industry, the limitations that have been partly caused by regulatory hurdles are opportunities for technology firms to solve. Firms that do it effectively are typically chased by VC investors across the world.

Let us now close the discussion on how the policy aspect of infrastructure can help innovation. I hope it's amply clear that the interaction between policy and innovation can't be ignored by entrepreneurs when they view their capabilities in light of the crisis.

Technology Infrastructure

In the 1950s the development of transistors replaced expensive vacuum tubes and made electronics cheaper. In the 1970s microprocessors brought down the cost of CPUs, leading to the era of computers. This was followed in the 1990s by the introduction of GPUs (graphics processing units), which kept Moore's law alive and supported the technology paradigms we are seeing today.

For the purpose of this discussion, let us go back to the dot-com boom and bust period. Those were times when computers had started to become more mainstream, yet the internet was still nascent. The survivors of the dot-com bubble burst and the firms that were founded after the bubble were internet businesses such as Amazon, Google, Facebook and Twitter. All their business models and growth were based on the infrastructure layer called the internet. Without the internet infrastructure starting to become more mainstream, these businesses couldn't have risen to where they are today.

Jeff Bezos, the CEO of Amazon, quit his Wall Street job and decided to sell books on the internet because he believed in the potential growth opportunities that the infrastructure allowed for the business model. This is also true for the other tech giants whose revenue models relied on advertising revenues from internet users. As firms such as Amazon and Google became more mainstream, they eventually became the infrastructure or the distribution channels for businesses to thrive on.

Recently, an entrepreneur pitched to me and Max. He was building a decentralised traffic-regulating system for self-driving cars. We loved his vision and he had some patentable technology created, too. However, the automation involved in decentralising the traffic regulation process needs tonnes of data from self-driving cars to get to acceptable levels of accuracy. Unfortunately, the self-driving car ecosystem is still in a nascent stage, and his idea was perhaps too ahead of the infrastructure needed.

The importance of having a matured technology infrastructure layer is what we will discuss in the next section.

Rise of the Machines   The concepts of artificial intelligence and robotics have been around since L. Frank Baum created the Tin Man character in *The Wizard of Oz*. However, as science latched on to the concept, it took several decades of AI winters to see meaningful breakthroughs in this space. AI was thought to be a program that could just mimic human intelligence. This approach was soon found to be hard to achieve.

The rise of the internet and social media applications generated the quantum of data like never seen before. These data acted as one of the much-needed infrastructural elements for the rise of AI. Unlike human brains, machines learn through a data-intensive process. For instance, as kids learn to label things, helping them identify a car is a much simpler process. If kids then see a car on the TV or online, they are able to identify them. However, this level of cognitive capability for a machine takes much more data input.

The rise of social media coincided with the development of GPUs. They were initially developed by NVidia during the dot-com period. GPUs are much more efficient in identifying three-dimensional images. They can be four to five times faster than traditional CPUs in dealing with deep learning algorithms.

Vast quantities of text, images and other unstructured data were being generated while processing power was also improved by the GPUs. In line with Moore's law, the pace of growth in semiconductors has kept up with the increase in data volumes. As a result, AI and robotics found the much-needed infrastructural components to get out of their winters.

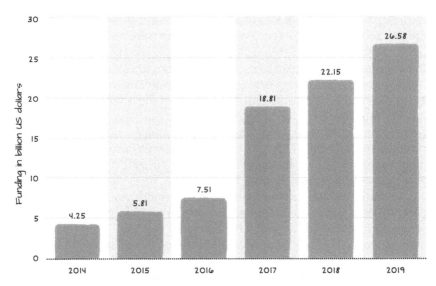

FIGURE 6.2 Funding of Artificial Intelligence (AI) Startup Companies World-wide from 2014 to 2019 (in $US Billion)

Source: https://www.statista.com/statistics/621468/worldwide-artificial-intelligence-startup-company-funding-by-year/

Figure 6.2 shows the amount of investment put into AI startups between 2014 and 2019. Investment is a much-needed component, but that typically needs to be preceded by other aspects of infrastructure, as seen with the AI boom.

AWS and Innovation   The launch of Amazon Web Services (AWS) in 2006 is a pivotal event in the evolution of the entire startup ecosystem. AWS is a special innovation in my eyes because it is arguably a major technology paradigm that didn't have any meaningful competition for seven years. The impact it had on the technology startup industry can hardly be exaggerated. The cost of infrastructure for startups fell massively, thanks to AWS.

Today we are so used to the AWS and Azure infrastructure that we take this setup for granted. Going back 15 years, technology businesses needed their own hardware infrastructure such as server capacity in storage and processing power to serve their customers. On-premise server infrastructure was so expensive that startups needed upfront funding to get their products and services off the ground. In comparison, today's startups can bootstrap quite effectively, thanks to the maturity of the current cloud infrastructure options.

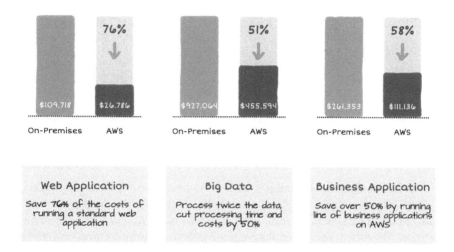

FIGURE 6.3 How Much Do AWS Customers Save?

Source: https://aws.amazon.com/economics/learn-more/#:~:text=AWS%20helps%20you%20save%20 more,by%20an%20average%20of%2028%25

The low cost of doing startup has most certainly improved the speed of innovation by removing a huge barrier to entry for those who want to start lean and mean (see Figure 6.3). Companies can launch products within weeks of identifying a problem and a solution, start refining their product and get to a point where they can go for funding after launch. That has been more of the norm for startups founded since AWS started.

Microsoft Azure might inch closer to AWS in terms of market share. It might take the lead in the cloud market, thanks to the might of Microsoft in the enterprise software market. But, in my eyes, AWS will remain the pioneer that changed the face of the startup world by laying such a fundamental infrastructure layer benefitting a generation of innovators.

Broadband and Video Genre   Some of us might remember the first time we used the internet. I was in university, and I remember emails taking a few seconds to load. Today my daughter has her schooling on Zoom and her piano classes on Skype. My six-year-old nephew has discovered a passion for drawing by looking at drawing videos on YouTube. The internet and broadband has become so much a part of our lives that I can discipline my kids saying I will switch off the internet if they don't behave.

Economies and ecosystems can boom once the underlying infrastructure is there. I moved back to Bangalore from the UK a year ago and COVID happened. People are getting used to working everything out from mobile. To give you an example, I would have never expected my father to be ordering his clothes from Flipkart. Even when he's going wrong with his sizes and fit he's just doubling down.

India's tier-1 and tier-2 city dwellers have mobile internet now. I lived in the UK for nine years, but Bangalore life is luxurious. I can live my life without stepping outside my door. People have pivoted really quickly. Amazon Prime quickly created an online grocery store. That's a huge market in India that they're exploiting. Food delivery apps have exploded to the nooks and corners of the country, essentially changing our lifestyles. I don't see us going back to the pre-COVID life anytime soon.

Chitresh Sharma
Former CEO at Swipi, Entrepreneur and Advisor

When YouTube was founded in 2005 and when Khan Academy was founded in 2008, the internet wasn't this fast or reliable. The advent of the smartphone in 2007 helped push the telecommunication industry forward in terms of internet speeds. Since then, the introduction of 4G and super-fast internet at home has changed the way we communicate, connect and seek entertainment.

The introduction of Netflix, Disney, Amazon Prime and so many other different streaming services has changed the way we entertain ourselves. The on-demand entertainment options and binge watching has become so popular that we are never short of options to spend time. However, these are avenues that we are able to exploit because of the internet infrastructure.

In 2015, these streaming services wouldn't have worked in my village in India. Today, broadband home internet and 4G services have made it accessible even in rural parts of the world. More recently the rise of TikTok has been another spectacular trend to view. With 1.5 billion downloads, the app has China and India as its biggest markets. Not the US or Europe. In India alone 323 million people used the app in 2019.

With 5G infrastructure being rolled out across the world, connectivity and entertainment options are only going to get better. A lack of infrastructure, however, doesn't necessarily have to stop you from moving forward. It can help you identify more capabilities you need to have within your product suite to fill the gaps in infrastructure and create a new market.

One particular instance of that kind of innovation was when YouTube wanted to serve through the TV. On top of the experience they offered through a mobile device, they wanted to move to the TV. This was because the average TV watcher tends to stick to a program for longer than the mobile YouTube watcher. However, the hurdle to delivering a seamless experience was the remote controls for TV. The remote control wasn't a good enough infrastructure to make the YouTube experience on TV as good as it is on the mobile.

They realised that they needed a technology that would project the mobile experience onto the TV screen at the click of a button, so they developed the

Chromecast capability. This is an excellent instance when the infrastructure gap led to further innovation. This example also links up quite well with user behaviour in response to certain products, which we will discuss in detail in Chapter 7.

We have now touched on how policy infrastructure and technology infrastructure can make or break a business and its capabilities. Let us now look at how ecosystem infrastructure can help with your business.

Ecosystem Infrastructure

The relevance and impact of the ecosystem on your business might have to be assessed through the crisis. In this instance, I refer to two key components that would affect the execution of your strategy: funding and talent. The flow of talent might change through a crisis, and so can investor appetites.

The former is often dependent on the latter in many VC communities. Many of my Bay Area friends tell me that there are four aspects that you need to get a pitching opportunity with a Silicon Valley VC investor:

- A Stanford degree
- Previous successes or failures as a startup person
- Experience as a product person in one of the tech giants
- Have gone through programs such as Y Combinator

That sounds insular on the surface, but there are sound reasons for that. Entrepreneurs who fall into at least one of these categories have a good idea about how to run a technology startup. Defining product strategies and executing them effectively is quite difficult when you are starting without any clue. If you have been through the process already in a previous setup, it improves your chances of success.

As a VC investor, we have to increase our probability of success in every possible way. Sticking to a strong ecosystem helps us get there more often than not. That is not to say that entrepreneurs outside of these criteria can't succeed. I have seen business minds who have had no b-school or top university education, but that is more of the exception than the example.

Talent Infrastructure Inclusion (or the lack of it) can be an issue in a setup where entrepreneurs with degrees from certain universities are preferred. But that comes with years of efforts in creating an ecosystem that has top technology and business institutions grooming the talent needed to keep the quality of innovation high. For instance, 10 years ago, the startup ecosystem in India was not as mature as it is today. VC investors had to look for entrepreneurs who had passed from IITs or IIMs, both considered premium institutions in the country.

As the ecosystem matured, and first-generation tech entrepreneurs helped the next generation hit the ground running, we see more inclusive investments happening across the country. There is still preference for graduates of the top schools; however, exceptions to that rule are becoming more common. A multi-generational approach is essential for maturity of a startup ecosystem that can take a more inclusive approach.

We were based in Palo Alto, therefore, we were largely looking for local talent. However, we had a diverse team with many immigrants. Many of our employees are from Canada, I am from India and our founders are from Belgium and France. Despite the diverse workforce, we have always been based in Palo Alto, therefore, all of us had to be locally based.

As COVID hit us, we quickly adapted our talent acquisition process. We have now expanded our search to across the US as we have all gone remote. We have started hiring from Boston for talent from MIT for instance. That has now opened up a bigger talent pool for us and better options for the students graduating from different parts of the country.

I see this trend becoming more of a norm as we emerge out of the crisis.

Akshay Sharma
CTO at Onc.ai

Recently, I was having a conversation with a life sciences tech startup involved in drug discovery using quantum computing methodologies. The startup is based in Europe and is keen to stay in the region because they have the best life sciences talent coming out of Cambridge and Oxford in the UK. However, the CEO felt that funding in the UK and Europe is more conservative than in the US.

Obviously, make sure that you're financially resilient, but equally make sure that you have the right diversity in the team. If you're a startup, particularly a fintech startup, where the team is incredibly young and visionary. You might be missing something, which is someone who's been on the block. Make sure you have a mentor or a gray-haired person who has been through a downturn. You may need to engage with regulatory bodies and government services and would need an experienced hand who understands what happens when recession hits. If you don't have that person on the leadership team, then you've got a major gap.

Chris Skinner
Author, speaker and fintech influencer

The startup needed quite a lot of capital to grow and Europe didn't have the risk appetite to serve his ambitions. Therefore, the CEO had to reach out to Silicon Valley's usual suspects to fund his business. He might have a challenging time choosing between Europe and Silicon Valley as his base because the firm's talent comes from Europe and funding is largely from Silicon Valley.

It might be worth noting that during times of crisis the talent ecosystem can have a lower appetite for risk and choose corporate roles over a riskier startup role. This is also a time when cash-rich blue chip players look to poach top talent from less mighty firms. The COVID crisis has thrown a spanner in the future of work mix. With remote working becoming more of the norm, developers in expensive hub cities have already moved to cheaper locations within their countries. This might eventually lead to cheaper team costs in the medium term at least.

Let us now look at how the funding landscape evolves.

Funding Infrastructure   The purpose of this section is not to talk about what a pitch deck should look like. If you are an entrepreneur reading this book, you must have access to enough material online that can give you that information. The focus of this section is to talk about the following aspects of funding:

- Understanding all funding options and how they affect each other
- Understanding that funding is not just about the quality of your investment proposal but also about trust
- Looking beyond just equity financing
- Approaching a funding round from a position of strength

Mixing It Up   We discussed in Chapter 2 the different types of funding that are available to an entrepreneur: equity, debt, convertible and grant funding. Depending on the traction you have achieved with your revenues and the stage at which your firm is, you might find some of these funding options better than the others.

Equity funding is the most common of these for technology startups. With early- and venture-stage firms, there are crowdfunding options too. Some growth-stage B2C firms such as Monzo in the UK have successfully completed crowdfunding campaigns in the last couple of years. This is largely to build brand awareness amongst its users. However, a big slice of these rounds have come from their large institutional investors.

In the UK the introduction of the enterprise investment scheme (EIS) has been highly successful in supporting early-stage ventures. From an investor standpoint, residential real estate is looking less and less attractive. As a result, investors are looking at other tax-efficient ways of deploying their funds.

EIS and SEIS have attracted angel money into the venture ecosystem, helping bridge a major funding gap. The ecosystem has matured drastically from a funding perspective in the last decade thanks to this piece of legislation.

Sarah Turner
CEO of Angel Academe

Among angels, micro VC investors, crowdfunding platforms and mainstream VC investors, you shouldn't have any lack of options when it comes to equity funding. However, do some research on how the feeder system works. Certain angel ecosystems have relationships with VC communities more than others. Similarly, some VC investors often co-invest or feed their deals into bigger VC investors. Therefore, understanding the dynamics across the investor community can help the financing road map.

We've actively helped founders get to the US markets, even in the COVID world. We've done a few deals in which we invested in firms and helped them get to the top-tier funds on the West Coast. We know that these funds are not going to make a decision overnight. We work out a mechanism to give these startups a million bucks to take all that pressure off, if the big name firm wants to then write a $2 million ticket and set the terms and the valuation, we'll just structure our investment as a note or a SAFE. SAFE stands for simple agreement for future equity and is similar to a convertible note, the difference is that SAFEs are not considered debt instruments, whereas convertibles notes are.

If you fail with the West Coast funds, because it's too early or they don't want to do it, then the startups can just come back to us and we'll top up and write the rest of the check. We'll give them all the flexibility and a way to get to a Sequoia or a Founders fund in the US without having to slow down operations.

Hussein Kanji
Hoxton Ventures

Debt funding is often ignored by startups. This is understandable in early stages of a firm when revenues are yet to arrive or when they are pretty low. However, as recurring revenues start coming in, debt funding is a good option. Firms that are in the public private sector partnership space should consider government-based debt funding. Some of these funds might be slow options, but they can come with very low cost of capital.

In a cut-throat VC-driven startup ecosystem, government funding can often be seen as meaningless, but these funds are handy when VC funding dries up during a market slowdown.

Before COVID, we were supporting around £6 billion of finance. We have added a further £62bn during COVID due to various capital facilities we have opened to protect the business ecosystem in the country. It's not £62 billion of our own balance sheet, but the amount we guarantee in loans.

For the venture space, we launched the future fund. We're doing CLNs (Convertible Loan Notes) to help out SMEs. When we launched it, it was meant to be a £250 Million programme. I think £770 million worth of capital is released already and the facility is still open.

A lot of our products are actually designed to be countercyclical with automatic buffers. As you get into more trouble during a crisis, we don't even have to know that it's happening, we will see an increase in demand because they're demand driven. So, if there's a crisis, if capital starts shrinking, we should automatically see an increase in our demand for our products and be able to respond effectively.

Alice Hu Wagner
Managing Director, at the British Business Bank

Grant is another option that often gets ignored by technology startups. Research and development funding by government agencies is often free cash that firms can tap into. R&D tax credits might not qualify as a funding option, but for technology startups, that is another avenue of cash flow.

A financing strategy developed with all these options in mind can be crisis proof. While doing so, try to understand thresholds across these options. Some grants might have thresholds on equity and debt funding already raised on both the positive and negative sides. For instance, certain grants might expect you to raise some equity before they can release the money. You might also lose eligibility for certain grants if you have in total raised beyond a certain threshold in equity or debt.

Now that we have looked at the different options, let us look at some of the softer considerations during fundraising. There are three key aspects that an entrepreneur looking to raise funds should focus on. The rule of thumb should be to create trust with the investor even before you have met them for the pitch.

- Quality of the pitch
- Familiarity with the investor
- Similarity with the investor

A good-quality investment proposal is obviously fundamental to successful financing of the firm. It involves thinking through the business model, understanding the market opportunities and challenges, ensuring team dynamics reflects during a pitch and addressing the investor's economic expectations. I am not going to tell you how to do that well. There is enough content online on creating a good pitch deck and preparing for a VC pitch.

Many say that cold messages don't work. In the age of LinkedIn, I don't believe that. I have hired an analyst and invested in an entrepreneur who both cold-pinged me on LinkedIn. However, make sure you study the investor before a cold approach. If you are planning to broadcast a cold message on LinkedIn or by email to investors, you don't deserve a response. Show some respect to the investor's time by making sure you are operating in a field of interest to the investors. Most reasonable investors will like it and should respond to that.

Entrepreneurs often ignore the fact that investors are human beings who are biased. We are not machines who make cold analytical investment decisions all the time. It's true that we strive to do so, but we all come with an intellectual and emotional package, and that invariably affects the investment decisions. Therefore, how do you tap into that to get a positive investment decision? That is precisely what we will cover in this section.

The Mere-Exposure Effect   You cannot ignore the importance of creating familiarity within investment circles, before the funding round. Familiarity breeds trust and there are so many ways of getting in front of the investor without the investor realising it. Social media is an excellent way to do so. You can track investor behaviour on LinkedIn, for instance, and create traction so that investors notice you.

The more they see your brand popping up on their feed, the more they will trust you when you get in front of them for a pitch. It's a way to create cognitive bias towards your business on a consistent basis. This psychological effect, called the 'mere exposure effect', makes people prefer you when they are familiar with you.

This is a technique that crowdfunding campaigns and even good marketing campaigns in general rely on. They believe in building up to the campaign to achieve the right results. In essence, all they are doing is creating a trusted lens through which the conversation can take place between them and the customer/client. You might not necessarily have to do marketing activities to attract investors. Even putting up a bit of good thought leadership content that pops up on the investor's feed can help in establishing trust. It is especially helpful if the content is good and acknowledged for good quality by credible people in that space.

In essence, try not to make the conversation with the investors cold. You might have received a warm introduction to the investor, but ensure you have researched them enough and have become a little familiar to them before the pitching event.

Similarity Bias We tend to trust those who have more in common with us. There is a lot of noise that the VC industry is discriminating. Especially investors in the West seem to like Caucasian males more than people of other races, colour and gender. But we are all born with bias, and when we deal in a trust-based transactional exercise, it makes us more comfortable to invest in people who have more in common with us.

Almost a year ago, I was pulled into a Twitter conversation where the topic was about diversity within VC portfolios. I had to talk about the importance of diversity and how that helps to arrive at a balanced decision. A balanced approach definitely helps during times of crisis, too. I got challenged in that conversation when someone asked me to talk about how diverse my portfolio was.

As a result, for the first time, I started listing the nationalities of entrepreneurs I had invested into. We had Europeans, Americans, Indians, Pakistanis, Malaysians, Australians, Scandinavians and Africans in our portfolio. I proudly claimed that I was not just doing the talking. The person who challenged me on the Twitter conversation went quiet. We were still low on gender ratio, as only 4 of our 19 investment firms had women founding members.

However, a more honest introspection followed. We had never discussed creating diversity in our portfolio as a strategic differentiation within our investment committee. Although I loved the fact that we had done something good inadvertently, I wanted to understand how it came naturally to us, whereas it was seen as an exceptional thing by the wider VC community. The answer was, 'I am an immigrant': our entire investment committee is formed of immigrants from Asia.

This made us very comfortable looking at an Egyptian entrepreneur doing fintech in the UK or a Malaysian entrepreneur doing ecommerce in Europe.

We didn't have to try hard. In some sense, we were biased, too, but we were biased towards the minorities who often got excluded, inadvertently making us look good. We now intend to do it more consciously; however, it is just an illustration of why entrepreneurs cannot ignore similarity while fundraising.

Look for investors who look like you, have similar educational backgrounds, even have similar tastes, hobbies or are fans of the same football club. Every little helps to establish trust. I do not condone the lack of inclusion by the investor communities. However, getting the diversity wiring into the heads of these cheque-signers is going to take a few decades. As more diverse founders get funded, there will be more people who are biased towards a more diverse pool of entrepreneurs to get the balance back. But until then, you have to play the game to ensure you win the funding needed to keep your firm going.

The Missing Link

We looked at the three key pillars of the second-order optimisation process: namely, infrastructure, consumer behaviour and business models. We covered the infrastructure aspect in this chapter. We discussed several examples to bring to life why the infrastructure elements across policy, technology, talent and capital are critical for a viable business model. However, it doesn't mean that businesses can't scale without those elements at all.

There have been instances when one or more of the infrastructure elements have been missing, and there is an exceedingly strong part of another infrastructural support that compensates for that. Alternatively, if either consumer behaviour is extremely supportive or if there is an innovative business model that helps with the acceleration, the lack of infrastructure can be overcome.

For instance, when Tesla started their journey in the electric car segment they didn't have two key elements. The first missing element was the charging point infrastructure and the second was satisfying evidence that electric cars could be a viable mass business model. Therefore, they started with the luxury car segment with the Roadster. The margins were higher with the Roadster and proved to the market that the business model could scale.

In launching the Roadster, Elon Musk demonstrated that the model could work. More important, he had enough proof of execution to access capital that helped make subsequent mainstream models and build the electric charging points. The Roadster was launched in 2008 and after Model S and X, the mass product Model 3 was launched in 2016. That had given Tesla almost a decade to prepare the infrastructure required for the mass electric car movement.

Fast forward 4 years: Tesla had 4 straight quarters of results and was due for an S&P inclusion. In July 2020 Tesla became the largest automobile manufacturer in the world after going past Toyota in market capitalisation. Despite all the allegations of rigging of accounts, I believe this is just the beginning of a revolution that Tesla has pioneered.

The key takeaway here is that, if one of the elements, namely infrastructure, consumer behaviour or business models, is missing, there is still hope. But it is harder, takes longer and will also need much more capital to make it all work. If you do not have the luxury of time or capital needed for the exploration and evidencing that Musk and his team went through, reevaluate the value proposition. This is especially true during a crisis, in which both time and capital are rare commodities. Let us now look at Figure 6.4, summarising the chapter's key takeaways.

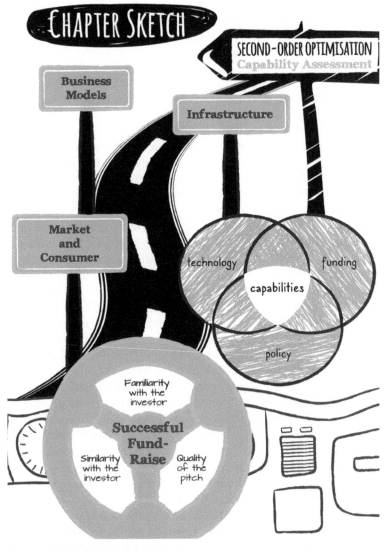

FIGURE 6.4 Chapter Six Sketch

Conclusion

This chapter discussed one of the three key aspects of second-order optimisation. A matured infrastructure layer is critical for startups to build their use cases on. When you are as big as Tesla, you can afford to create the entire electric vehicle charging infrastructure needed for your car network. When you are a Google, you can create a Chromecast to stop relying on a bad remote control infrastructure.

Of course, that is not possible for every startup. When you are already bootstrapping to deliver a product, it is hard enough just getting that across the line. If you do not have the necessary regulatory support, technology infrastructure support or financing available, you might struggle to get your idea off the ground. When you are in a crisis, it is even more important to leverage as much of the infrastructure layer as possible.

Often, you will find some infrastructure options are opened up during a crisis. Especially when there is a government or a regulatory agency involved, you might find new avenues opening up to support innovation in the form of technology and research grants, which can help your cashflows in the short term. However, it is important to stay on top of these trends.

A crisis is also a time when new trends emerge. For instance, the dot-com bubble gave rise to social media, and AI startups used that as a launch pad. We saw cloud and high-speed internet give rise to gaming and better connectivity applications, which have come in handy during the COVID lockdown. We also saw fintech rise from the 2008 crisis, which was supported by the smartphone infrastructure that became mainstream from 2007 with the iPhone.

We also find that crisis brings about changes in two other key dimensions: consumer behaviour and business models. We have seen a rise in marketplaces since the 2008 crisis. We have also seem consumer behaviour change since 2008, because consumers were frustrated with banks and looked for better financial services. That led to the rise of fintech. Consumer behaviour has changed again during the COVID crisis towards digitalisation and remote applications.

In the next chapter we will study the importance of understanding business model innovation. This will also be part of the second-order optimisation process.

CHAPTER 7

From Fiats to Ferraris

No profit grows where is no pleasure ta'en.

— William Shakespeare, The Taming of the Shrew

Introduction

When we looked at the preparation for the first-order optimisation, we stressed the importance of getting yourself to a good state of mind first. Once you are in a good frame of mind, it becomes a stable footing from which you can start delivering the first-order optimisation.

When it comes to the second-order optimisation and executing the strategies, the reverse is true. It is first important to understand external factors such as consumer behaviour, consumer values, policy and investment environment before arriving at a business model that can scale. In that sense, the business model is something that is largely under the control of the entrepreneur. The third pillar of the second-order optimisation process is the business model.

Over the past few decades, there has been no shortage of thought leadership content about business models. Peter Drucker defines a business model as what a business will and won't do. In my opinion, a good business model enables a firm to create value for itself in the process of creating value for its customers. The role of the management team is to ensure that the value created for the customers and for the firm is balanced.

If customers benefit disproportionately, shareholders might lose value and vice versa. However, if shareholder value is prioritised ahead of value addition to customers, the business model becomes unsustainable over a period of time. Therefore, the management team must ensure that this tug of war between customers' interest and shareholders' interest stays healthy at all times.

The right business model ensures that, in the process of creating value for customers, shareholder value is maximised. In this chapter, we will look at different business models, their risk profiles and how entrepreneurs can employ them during a crisis to help them sustain their businesses and emerge as winners.

In Chapter 5, we discussed the analogy of a road trip to describe the second-order optimisation process. One of the three aspects of the second-order optimisation process is the business model. In the road trip analogy, the business model can be said to be the car you choose to use. It is difficult to say in absolute terms that one car is better than another.

You might think driving a Ferrari is more 'cool' or driving a Bentley is more 'sophisticated' than driving a Fiat. But in the world of utility, a Ferrari might be a better car on an F1 track and a Fiat might be a better choice while driving through high streets with narrow parking spaces. Therefore, depending on the context, one car might be a better practical choice than the other. It is the same with business models.

For most of the chapters in this book we developed simple models that can help you think through your business. In most cases, they have been 3D models. However, in the case of business models, we might have to go one step further and have a 4D model. When you look at business models through the lens of this 4D model, it can help you assess the viability of the business model in your specific context.

The 4D Lens

For entrepreneurs, a business model defines how they choose to make money from their customers. There are several business models that have been around for years and new ones being developed as well. Business models evolve depending on how a firm chooses to approach its market and the stage that the business is at any point. Therefore, there is no business model that is perfect for all contexts, industries or stages of the business.

As soon as the COVID-19 crisis hit, we immediately did a triage of the sectors in our portfolio to assess where our companies were going to be hit hardest and where their solutions were going to be needed the most. So clearly, that brings us to the remote patient monitoring and telehealth solutions we have in our healthcare practice. We have quite a few education companies whose solutions are easily transferable or were originally used in some combination of virtual and in person contexts.

We also have several financial health solutions that are built to better enable consumers and small businesses to weather financial shocks with some measure of resilience. So, those three broad buckets are places where we knew companies needed to be prepared to meet the moment. They were going to be challenged to think about the right ways to expand their products to meet a bigger customer base, show up for their existing customers in ways that their teams might not have been challenged to do before and think about all of the means of adapting to the moment without compromising their original business model.

Victoria Fram
Managing director, VilCap Investments

Let us now go through at a 2 × 2 dimensional view of business models and how each of the different types of model rank across these dimensions.

Time: Longevity

The time dimension constitutes two factors: namely, longevity and velocity. Ideally, you want the product to hang in there for as long as possible and grow as fast as possible. In the process, you also want results in the shortest possible time. The business model you choose would need to balance both these factors of the time dimension.

Let us assume that you have understood your customers as discussed in Chapter 5 and have rolled out a product that they need. Longevity is about how long you will stay relevant for that client. If your customers need your product a few times every year, such as an enterprise software application to generate regulatory reports, your business model needs to be aligned with that. However, if your customer is likely to use your product several times a day, such as a communication or social media application, then that is a different beast altogether. Your business model needs to take these factors into account to ensure you create value for the business in line with customer use.

In doing so, your focus needs to be keeping the time taken to get to your targets as minimal as possible. That is defined by the velocity factor.

Time: Velocity

The velocity dimension is about the pace at which you can scale and hit your target KPIs. The KPIs could be either growth or revenues or both. If you are well funded and are taking an aggressive approach, your focus will lean towards growth. If you are in survival or preservation mode through the crisis, your focus will generally be revenue targets. Either way, your distance to these thresholds will have to be lowered by your business model.

It is important to understand and be able to measure the velocity with which your business can grow. Some business models lend themselves quite well to steroid growth and others might enable slower growth but have higher longevity or just be sticky. If you have enough capital to grow and have a sticky product, the focus could be all about high velocity.

However, if you are short of funds, take a slightly more conservative approach and look for depth within a limited customer base before pushing for growth. On the business model side, for instance, a recurring revenue stream might help with the short-term cashflows while you prepare for medium-term growth. As you grow, you might want to tweak your business model to tap into the growth numbers.

Space: Scale

The space dimension is about the scale (versatility) and weight (stickiness) of your business model. It could also be defined as the versatility that your product offers to your sales and revenue engines. You might have an enterprise customer relations management (CRM) application as your product. If you are able to penetrate your enterprise clients and start selling other products that have synergies with your CRM application, that will help you scale your presence within that organisation.

On a similar note, you might have a B2C application for motorbike sharing in South East Asia. Your application can have features such as payments added to it as your customer base increases. Rolling out a lifestyle product initially and then supplementing it with a fintech business model at scale has become a trend in emerging markets. Therefore, it is critical that you identify the scale you can achieve using your business model.

Again, as mentioned with the time dimension, your business model can be versatile to achieve both growth and/or revenue.

Space: Weight

The weight dimension identifies the stickiness you might want to achieve irrespective of the business model you choose. In a B2B context it really stands for how difficult it is for a client to replace your product. In a B2C context a lower churn rate means your product is sticky. Some business models are inherently stickier than others. Sometimes the industry and penetration of digital in the industry can also help achieve greater stickiness for your product amongst your customers.

For instance, one of my portfolio firms offers an AI-enabled virtual library platform to universities. Universities aren't the most digitised organisations. They take years, if not decades, to replace their software. Therefore, the platform they are building, we hope, will be quite a sticky product for their clientele. I can say the same about FrontM who are building a remote communication and collaboration platform for the maritime industry.

The banking system, for instance, was built for the paper distribution of value through buildings with humans. And now we're dealing with the data distribution of value through software and service. The new model is completely different. If you were built for a system of physicality and buildings with humans, how can you deal with the digital distribution through software and servers when that's an alien concept to your business model?

Chris Skinner
Author and Board Member at 11:FS

These two examples highlight that the industry you serve could add stickiness to your product. That is also the reason why we have used weight to refer to stickiness. In physics, your mass is constant, but your weight is different, depending on if you are on the surface of the earth or in space. In a similar sense, your stickiness differs based on the context of your business. The same product can be quite sticky in some markets and not so sticky in others.

For instance, QR codes have made quite a big impact in China and parts of India. Sixty-seven percent of Chinese people use their mobile phones to scan QR codes on a daily basis. Despite their simplicity in facilitating transactions and interactions, QR codes haven't quite taken off in the developed parts of the world.

Generally, business models with recurring revenues are typically seen as sticky and more resilient to economic cycles than others. Therefore, it is wise to employ the right business model based on the context in which the business is operating. Let us now discuss different business models in light of the 4D model and see how they rank across these dimensions.

The Business Model Barometer

At the beginning of my career in technology, I looked up to a solution architect and learnt a lot from him. He often said architecture is about knowing precisely where to compromise to achieve the goals of your solution. If you compromise the wrong factor, you will end up with a solution that doesn't address your functional or nonfunctional needs.

It is the same thing with business models. Depending on the industry you are operating in, the strengths and limitations of your product, the maturity of your customer base and your cashflow positions, you might have to compromise on certain aspects of your business model. A hardcore VC investor is going to push you to be a sexy Ferrari, but if your constraints mean you have to drive a Fiat for some time before swapping it over for a Ferrari, that would still work.

You should be agnostic about the business model you embrace, because if you do not strike the right balance between creating value for the firm versus creating value for the customer, you will not last. If you create too much value for the customer and very little for the firm, you might be tagged as an 'impact firm'. With all due respect to social impact businesses, their mission can be conflicting to what the capital markets expect of them. Therefore, even in a social impact business, consider creating a scalable and viable model for the shareholders.

If you are in a business that prioritises shareholder value ahead of customer value, explore ways of increasing the perceived customer value. This might derisk your firm from reputational issues and in the long run keep churn low. Here is a simple chart of how you should be striking a balance between the two key stakeholders for your business: shareholders and customers.

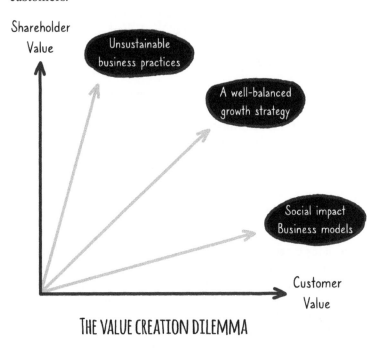

THE VALUE CREATION DILEMMA

In this section, we will look at different business models and how they rank across the different dimensions we described in the previous section. Our research has identified more than 30 different business models. For the purpose of simplicity, we will bucket them across three categories, which are based on their ability to generate revenue rather than growth.

For the benefit of those who are focussed on growth rather than revenue, I will highlight the growth potential of each category of business model. Please remember that there are no good or bad business models. Business models need to be used in the right context to ensure value is created for both the customer and the firm.

The classification of business models can be done based on the predictability of revenues:

- Contractually predictable
- Behaviourally predictable
- Hybrid

Contractually Predictable

Contractually predictable business models are those that can generate smoother revenues with higher levels of predictability. These business models are more predictable with cash flow generation than others because customers are tied into a contractual relationship with the firm. They are generally considered safer in times of a crisis when you are struggling to hold onto cash flows. Common terminology used in the investor world is 'recurring revenues' while referring to such business models. When you have recurring revenues, you have a higher probability of surviving through a crisis and convincing an investor during a market slowdown.

Enterprise Software   There are several business models that have relatively more predictable cash flows due to the contractual nature of the value generated from the customers to the firm. Enterprise technology is an example in which the startup sells a product to an enterprise. They would typically go through a not-so-pleasant sales cycle. Once they have impressed and have received approval from the business sponsor in the organisation, they typically go through a procurement process.

This is followed by a pilot process, in which the enterprise client tests if the product is fit for purpose. This process is sometimes paid, sometimes not. This is then followed by the strategic deployment of the product in the enterprise. The startup generally wins a licensing deal by this stage. The end-to-end process typically takes several months, if not years. If you are dealing with clients such as the UK's National Health Service (NHS), this can take years.

Let us look at the four dimensions we discussed in the previous section in the context of an enterprise technology business. The sales cycles are generally longer than a consumer business. Therefore, the distance to revenues or growth is longer. It is prudent to set expectations with your board about how soon you will start showing results. As you close more clients, the sales cycle is going to get shorter. Yet, in the beginning, it can be a pain and something that needs complete understanding from investors and the board.

The good thing with this business model is that because your sales cycles are longer, it can also be the barrier to entry for the competition. Clients are less likely to switch to a different product, and revenues have longevity. In VC terms, the lifetime value of a customer is higher with an enterprise software business.

We have touched on the time and stickiness dimensions. The enterprise software business model is certainly scalable; however, it might not be as quick and seamless as other business models. Every time you want to cross-sell products, you might have to go through onboarding and procurement processes. Integrating the software into your enterprise clients can also be intrusive and act as a barrier to scaling.

Therefore, the enterprise software business model offers scale, stickiness and longevity but compromises on velocity and pace of growth.

Software as a Service (SaaS)   The SaaS business model has become increasingly common among technology companies. With the advent of cloud infrastructure, the SaaS model offers the versatility of the cloud, a less-intrusive deployment strategy (when compared to enterprise software) and in many instances the stickiness and longevity of revenues.

There are some limitations with SaaS when the enterprise wants to host the software within its firewalls and infrastructure. This often happens in highly regulated environments such as financial services and health care. This can lead to a longer than usual onboarding and deployment process. Therefore, if you are choosing this business model, make sure you understand industry-specific implications of doing so.

On a general note, SaaS might not have the longevity that an enterprise software business does, because onboarding is simpler in the SaaS world. Therefore, displacing a product is relatively simpler, too. However, longevity in a SaaS model is better than transaction-based business models. SaaS businesses can grow faster than an enterprise software model because they are generally not as intrusive.

Let us take the Shopify example. They had about 10000 small business customers at the time of their Series A round in 2010. By 2019, they were growing at 10000 customers per week. Shopify had an SaaS subscription model and created a seamless customer experience to learn the platform. Their customers described the experience as 'minutes to learn and a lifetime to master'. Despite a subscription model, SMEs can be fickle customers because they are quite vulnerable to economic cycles. Therefore, Shopify made the platform sticky by offering a suite of applications developed by their community of developers.

Subscription   Even the mighty Amazon and Apple are exploring subscription models these days. Amazon offers a discounted price when we subscribe to some of the listed products, and Apple has launched Apple Music (and Apple One), which offers streaming services for a monthly subscription. A subscription business model typically charges a regular payment from the customer, thereby providing the business with a more predictable cash flow.

In recent years several e-commerce offerings have moved into a subscription model. Firms have started to sell nuts, coffee, toiletries and nutritional supplements using subscription models. The growth of Dollar Shave Club and their subsequent sale to Unilever for $1 billion and the story of Graze being bought out by Unilever for £150 million have attracted more attention and investments into the subscription space.

The subscription model has been employed in the B2C/D2C space; yet, a comparison to enterprise software or an SaaS business doesn't make sense. However, when risk appetites fall, the stickier revenue business models tend to be preferred by investors. Let us assess the subscription model across our four dimensions.

From a time perspective, in a B2C context, subscription models offer more longevity of revenues. The cost of acquiring these customers is also generally higher, and as a result the time it takes to grow is higher. It is possible to achieve scale in growth and revenues using this model as demonstrated by Unilever's acquisitions. The scale is going to be limited in a B2C context due to the nature of regular payments that the customers need to make. In essence, a subscription model derisks a plain vanilla B2C business, thanks to its stickiness.

There are white labelling, licensing and subscription-based models that fall into the contractually predictable category of business models. They all have similar risk profiles. They are slower to grow, slower to show results and have a higher cost to acquiring customers. Yet, they are more sustainable revenues, often stickier and offer a firmer footing when you are looking to scale.

Let us now look at behaviourally predictable models. Note that these are broad generalisations, and contractually predictable models will also need to understand consumer behaviour to scale. But they are inherently stickier and less reliant on constantly adjusting to consumer behaviour than behaviourally predictable models.

Behaviourally Predictable

These models do not tend to have a contractual obligation with the customer to continue a particular commercial relationship with the startup. In all honesty, I had to get creative with this particular category name because I didn't want to call it a 'sporadic', 'irregular' or a 'variable' revenue opportunity. This categorisation of business models cannot have a negative connotation because it can be relevant even in the middle of a crisis.

A sustainable business model is one that is close to the ebbs and the flows of its market. Your relevance is your sustainability; you can be relevant only if you truly do everything you can to understand where your various markets are in the continuum of response to what you take to market. This has to be embedded into the organisation's operating model.

Nicole Anderson
Managing Partner of Redsand Ventures

Behaviourally predictable business models can be seen as more growth-focussed, and in good times VC investors fall in love with them. Yet, they have their shortcomings when you assess them through a risk lens. With the advent of data science, these models can become more predictable from a behavioural standpoint. Therefore, understanding the behavioural patterns of your consumers is critical to making these models more viable. However, they are not generally considered as reliable for consistent flow of revenues during a crisis.

You might have gotten lucky if you are running a B2C business in health care using a transaction-based business model during COVID-19. But those are typically the exceptions. One interesting example in this category is the Aarogya Setu app launched in India to combat COVID-19, which is now the fastest app to hit 50 million users. Launched on 2 April 2020, this app had 50 million users in India by 15 April. To put things in perspective, the internet took four years to hit that milestone, whereas Facebook took 19 months and Pokémon Go took 19 days.

HOW LONG DOES IT TAKE TO HIT 50 MILLION USERS?

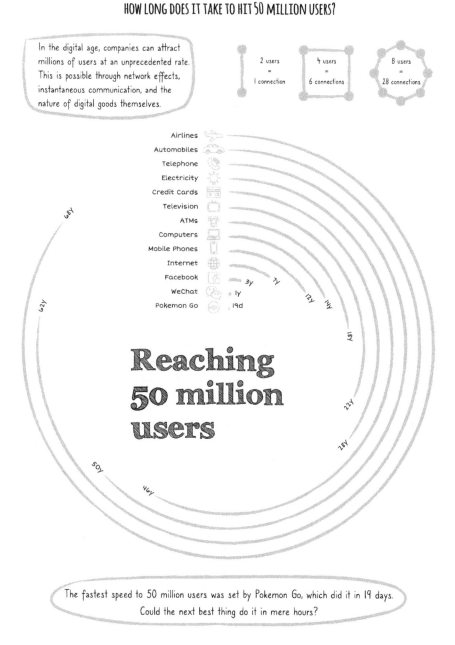

In the digital age, companies can attract millions of users at an unprecedented rate. This is possible through network effects, instantaneous communication, and the nature of digital goods themselves.

2 users = 1 connection

4 users = 6 connections

8 users = 28 connections

Airlines
Automobiles
Telephone
Electricity
Credit Cards
Television
ATMs
Computers
Mobile Phones
Internet
Facebook — 3y
WeChat — 1y
Pokemon Go — 19d

68y
62y
50y
46y
28y
22y
18y
14y
13y
7y

Reaching 50 million users

The fastest speed to 50 million users was set by Pokemon Go, which did it in 19 days. Could the next best thing do it in mere hours?

Let us look at a few examples that can be considered as behaviourally predictable models.

Advertising   If you are not paying for it, you are the product. This realisation amongst consumers happened in the last few years, especially after the Facebook and the Cambridge Analytica controversy broke out. Over the last decade, social media use has become habitual amongst consumers. Most of us look at our social media feeds even before we brush our teeth in the morning.

As consumers, we become dopamine addicts and in return, we give away our personal details, relationships, opinions, transactional activities and more for these firms to use. These technology firms, now giants, have monetised our data and continue to do so in the form of advertisements. The advertisement technology industry (adtech) has come on in leaps and bounds over the years.

Technology firms can now link the digital and the nondigital identity of a consumer. Consumer preferences are understood through their browsing history and presented as an advertisement at the best possible moment. Linking digital identities of consumers and their search details across devices such as laptops, smartphones, smart TVs and even smart speakers is underway. This already happens across applications on a smartphone.

With so much sophistication, the omnipresence of data is making the advertisement industry more powerful and consumers addicted and ignorant if not powerless. To get to this state of power these firms have had to take big slices of the market. This is primarily due to the data-hungry engines they use to predict and control consumer behaviour.

With a large consumer base comes large quantities of data. This data will help them predict consumer behaviour and monetise the behaviour and the data. This model works well when a firm has a large consumer base. However, without that ammunition, it is difficult to create a viable business model, especially during a crisis.

Looking at advertising as a business model, the time to get to a critical mass of consumers can be a big barrier. The consumer base can also come with a huge acquisition price tag, but once that barrier is overcome and data are generated from consumers, your predictive models start to get better and the scale that can be achieved is huge. Facebook and Google have demonstrated that the 'winner takes all' approach works.

The stickiness of this business model relies more on how well the firm stays on top of customer behaviour. There is a risk if consumer behaviour or values pivot or a crisis similar to the Cambridge Analytica incident occurs. Also, if you are not one of the winners, the advertisement business model might not be resilient during a crisis. Having said that, the forced 'digitalisation of everything' during COVID-19 has increased the number of people online and the advertisement revenues of the tech giants.

Let us look at the Pinterest example. During their Series A, Pinterest didn't have a clear business model and no revenues. They had a five-membered team, a fast-growing user base, which was at 1 million unique users and 20 million page visits. Their growth metrics attracted investments. They have since tapped the social ecommerce model in which about 1% of their user base created the content and the rest just used it. To keep the platform sticky, Pinterest's focus has been to keep their content creators happy.

By the close of 2019, Pinterest was the fourth largest social media platform in the US next to Facebook, Instagram and YouTube, although this statistic could have changed with the growth of TikTok. Yet, Pinterest hit over 80 million monthly active users in 2019 and $1.14 billion in revenues for the same year.

Transactional

Technically we can group many ecommerce businesses under a transactional business model. Businesses can have a moment in time approach to making a transaction happen and take a commission from these transactions. In the new age of data, these transactions can also be a data exchange instead of a money exchange.

In essence, when some form of value exchange happens, be it data or cash, your business makes money from these transactions. There are models that create firm value on either the number of transactions or use of their service by consumers. For the sake of simplicity, I am bundling these up with transactional models, because they are pretty similar from a behavioural perspective.

Our business simplistically is lending money, and we always say we're in the business of . . . making money. That's right, we lend money, we make money. So if you don't understand how money works, and how capital markets work, and how money gets priced, how can you do what we do? We sell a product that will always be in demand. There's never going to be any product market fit challenge in the business we run. Everything we do is about pricing risk.

Lizzie Chapman
CEO at ZestMoney

Much like the advertising business model, transactional models also have the risk of drying up transactions. If consumer appetite falls, or if the demand for a particular transactional service falls, revenues will be affected badly. When you are on the right side of the market, you will enjoy growth like many ecommerce businesses did as COVID-19 lockdowns rocked the world. The variable nature of revenues makes it essential for startups to stay on top of the behavioural transitions of consumers.

Startups with transactional business models will need to stay on top of consumer behaviour, but they also need to be agile in identifying course corrections if their market pivots. Quick understanding of how markets are evolving and an ability to tap into that can derisk variable revenues. Much like advertising, transactional businesses need to have data science as their backbone to be able to react quickly to consumer behaviour changes.

Let us look at the four factors to assess the transactional model now. Transactional models are typically efficient from a time perspective. However, the longevity of the model will really depend on how sticky the offering is. If customer behaviour has been well understood and tapped into, transactions can keep flowing through for a long time. Once the product-market fit is identified, growth can be achieved at a good pace provided you have the capital for customer acquisition.

Despite these features, a crisis can easily kill a transaction model if the business is on the wrong side of the market. Therefore, transactional models have to be derisked suitably with a strong data science approach, agile team, low cost base and an ability to add a stickier business model. On that note, let us now look at hybrid business models.

Hybrid

A hybrid between a contractually and a behaviourally predictable model can help compensate for the shortcomings of either of these models. The compensation sometimes can be viewed as a compromise in the never-ending growth versus revenue tug of war. Let us look at a scenario in which a startup has just launched a product for enterprises. The enterprises would use the software to enable consumers to perform transactions or distribute payments.

The business model for the startup could be simple licensing, transaction commissions or a licensing model with a commission on transactions. A licencing-only model is a contractually predictable model without tapping too much into the potential transactions that the enterprise could generate. A transaction commission model would scale without necessarily covering the risks of a low transaction scenario.

A combination of the two, in which a base licencing fee is charged and transactions beyond a threshold result in a commission, would ensure the startup can tap into the growth and cover the downsides. Several established corporates have started to explore hybrid models for similar reasons.

For instance, Nespresso by Nestle sold the coffee machines but also had a subscription for the coffee capsules. Despite the fact that they were priced targeting the luxury segment of the market, the coffee capsules offered them sustained revenues on top of the Nespresso coffee machines. HP's printer and printer ink is another such model that has demonstrated the merits of a hybrid business model.

Marketplace   The marketplace enables the supply and demand side to come together on a platform, helps them transparently see the requirements from the other side and then deliver them. In the process the platform typically takes a transaction commission. In the last decade we have seen an explosion of marketplaces.

Usual suspects such as Uber, Amazon, Airbnb have shown the world how to create value out of a growth-driven strategy. Amazon made its first quarterly profit in 2001, 7 years after it first incorporated. It was a survivor of the dot-com crash, and the rest is history. However, marketplaces are hard to execute. It is quite difficult to get the balance right between growing the supply side in line with the demand side.

The marketplace model really makes sense only after the 'network effect' has been achieved at scale. The network effect can be seen when a rise in the supply side is starting to bring growth to the demand side and vice versa. It becomes a self-reinforcing virtuous cycle of growth. It can be a capital-intensive game until and even after the network effect is achieved.

Marketplaces can be a really good example of a hybrid model that offers the upsides of stickiness and velocity while being able to grow insanely fast, too. I have also seen platforms take an SaaS approach to start with, and once the model has been established, pivot to a marketplace model successfully to tap into the growth. The reverse can also happen during crunch times to get stickier revenues.

In a marketplace, the startup makes money when there are transactions between the supply and demand sides. But, one or either of these sides can also be charged a monthly fee to stay listed on the platform. Amazon Prime is an excellent example of that. Amazon has also introduced financial products for the small businesses listed on their platform. I have known several small businesses that have managed to benefit from these products. Many of these businesses couldn't receive these financial services from high street banks or even fintechs.

Now, Amazon sells its own products, you have Fire and Kindle. But they sure as hell make a lot more money selling other people's stuff than they do their own. On the other hand, banks have deluded themselves into thinking that a platform means just adding more and more products into the product set. If all you're doing is adding your own products, you're not really a platform. It's like, we have our own checking account and our own mortgage, but we'll sell some mutual funds. That doesn't count.

By contrast, you look at what Starling Bank does. It's moving towards a model in which it is simply an aggregator. It's a distribution channel. You know, if you're not the one providing the core checking account, then you have to make your money somewhere else.

Richard Turrin
Author of Innovation Lab Excellence

There are several ways to make a marketplace a stickier platform from a consumer behaviour perspective. A hybrid business model can enable stickier revenues as Amazon Prime reminds us.

Mix, Match and Moonshot   Sorry, I couldn't write a book without using the word 'moonshot'. We have seen innovative business models being explored by startups across the world in a quest for world dominance. Some of them have been focussed more on sustainable revenues, and others have taken a Silicon Valley-style approach of 'winner take all' and 'grow at all cost'. That approach works well when capital is in abundance, and we have enough evidence of that.

Firms which do not have the luxury of capital, either due to the lack of an ecosystem like Silicon Valley or because of the industry they focus on, have had to get creative with business models. They have often mixed and matched these depending on their risk appetites and their cash flow needs. Some business models have also been found to be more effective based on their go-to-market strategies.

We have B2C products that have adopted either transactional or subscription models depending on the balance between growth and revenues they wanted to achieve. We have seen B2B products take enterprise software and SaaS approaches. Some of these products have also worked well with a hybrid approach that combines an SaaS and a transactional model.

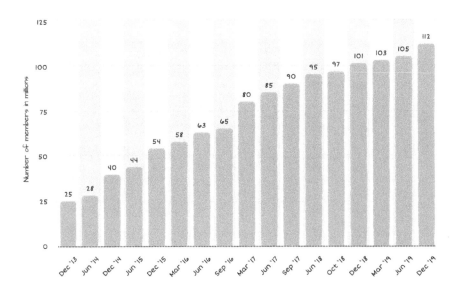

NUMBER OF AMAZON PRIME MEMBERS IN THE UNITED STATES AS OF DECEMBER 2019 (IN MILLIONS)

In recent times, we have seen D2C (direct to consumers) and B2C2B (business to the community to business) models emerge. The Graze and the Dollar Shave Club examples we discussed previously in this chapter can be grouped under a D2C model. The B2C2B model is interesting because it relies on first building a community of users before signing up enterprise clients through them.

The B2C2B model is typically used by product firms that see enterprises as their clients and the employees of these enterprises as a community of their users. Therefore they first build a community of these users, who also help them refine their product. As this community grows, typically through a free subscription, they expect premium features of the product. That need is the foot into the door for these firms into these big enterprises. But thanks to the community of users that they have built for their product, the penetration into these enterprises has already begun.

These firms usually give away their software free of cost to the community, but charge the enterprises when they need more from the software, such as a server component. However, in this model growth precedes revenue, so an enterprise software business can have a shorter sales cycle, longevity and sticky revenues due to the sheer nature of the business and the community model.

Therefore, it is important to mix and match the different business models based on their risk profiles, but also based on the go-to market of the firm. If you are one of the firms that is exploring business models that do not fall under these categories, you are in luck, and so is the innovation ecosystem. You are on a voyage to develop a new business model that can create value. These business models are called moonshots. Let us now look at Figure 7.1, the chapter summary in a sketch.

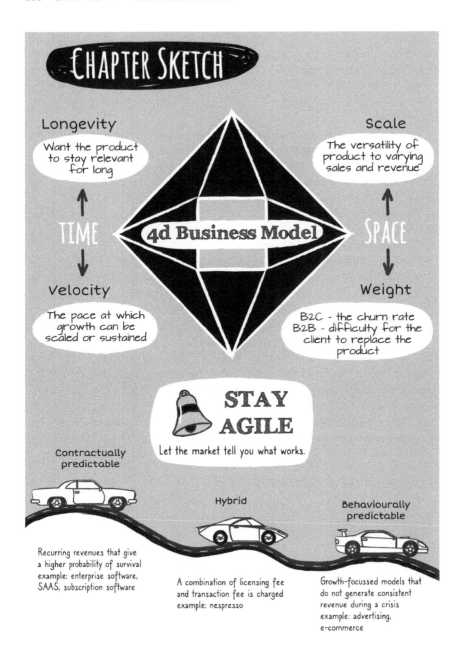

FIGURE 7.1 Chapter Seven Sketch

Conclusion

This concludes the second-order optimisation process. By now, you should be able to think through the three key pillars of the process: consumer behaviour, infrastructure and business models. In Chapters 5 and 6 we covered consumer behaviour and infrastructure. In this chapter we have examined business models at length.

The purpose of this chapter wasn't to describe every single business model out there. It was to help you understand the pros and cons of business models in the context of a crisis. Therefore, we first looked at a simple framework against which we could evaluate business models. That covered the time, scale, speed to scale (velocity) and stickiness aspects of business models.

We then looked at a number of business models categorised across three main buckets. The contractually predictable business models have sustainable revenues and are stickier for longer periods of time. As a result, the lifetime value of a customer tends to be high in this model, but the time taken to sign up a customer in these models is higher, too.

We looked at behaviourally predictable business models that perhaps might not have stickiness and longevity of customers. But they can be growth engines that can bring in billions of users, as we have seen with firms such as Amazon, Alibaba, Tencent, Google, Facebook, Uber and many more. These are considered the sexy Ferrari of the startup world by VC investors. Yet, during times of a crisis, if you are in preservation mode, find ways of being more capital efficient and cash flow conscious.

The last decade has created several innovative business models. Mixing and matching these categories of business models have helped optimise growth and revenues. Many businesses have attracted investors by carefully choosing the right business models in the context of the broader economic cycles they find themselves in.

However, if you are in the right industry, solve an important problem and have a differentiated solution and a stellar team to execute the business, a business model can often be the easiest variable that you can evolve through an exploratory journey. Let the market tell you what works, stay agile, stay on top of your customer and competition, and the rest will fall in place.

We have now completed second-order optimisation. In the next chapter, we will discuss third-order optimisation. We have so far addressed the bulge of the bell curve and ignored the tail. The bulge of the bell curve comprises businesses who have been adversely affected by a crisis and are finding their feet with cash flows and identifying ecosystem relevance and continuity. The third-order optimisation process is for businesses who have completely lost relevance due to a crisis and have to reinvent themselves.

CHAPTER 8

Hit Refresh

But doth suffer a sea-change,

Into something rich and strange.

William Shakespeare, The Tempest

Introduction

In summer 2005, three great minds came together to launch a podcasting platform. They had set up a product that would convert a phone call into .mp3 format and host it on the internet. The firm was called Odeo, and they even got funded for their product from VC investors. However, within a few weeks of launching the product, the mighty Apple announced iTunes would be rolled out with their iPods.

The founders of Odeo knew they had to act because their product wasn't seeing much traction. They had to reinvent themselves to stay relevant. The organisation of 14 employees came together to brainstorm ideas on how they could get out of jail. One of the top employees of the firm, Jack Dorsey, came up with the idea of creating an app in which people could share their status. It took until February 2006 for the idea to resonate with the rest of the management team.

The idea was named Twttr initially and then ended up becoming Twitter. Although the idea came from Jack Dorsey, the efforts to make it happen were led by Noah Glass in the initial days. Jack Dorsey and Evan Williams were still involved in moving the project forward. By March 2006, Twitter's prototype was ready. Twitter's own employees found the product increasingly addictive. In summer 2006, when an earthquake hit San Francisco, it became the first major product validation moment because several people used Twitter to spread the word of the earthquake.

Once Twitter had about 5000 users, Odeo's investors, who had chipped in with about $5 million, were notified about it by Evan Williams. He wrote to them saying that the podcast application wasn't taking off, and therefore he was happy to buy back the shares of Odeo and make it even with the investors. He had also mentioned about the Twitter project in the investor communication and highlighted that it was still early days for the project. Investors were happy to get their money back.

Twitter's founding team went through some reshuffling and rebranding after that transaction and rose to the tech giant we know today. In some ways, Twitter could be one of the most successful pivots in the history of technology startups. A pivot doesn't necessarily need to be as drastic as the Odeo–Twitter transition. It could be a more modest course correction.

Irrespective of the nature of the pivot, a decision to do so comes from a good understanding of the landscape the startup is operating in, consumer uptake and the potential upside post-pivot. Most of all it also requires a lot of self-awareness if not humility from the founders to look inward when things don't quite work to plan and chart out a course correction.

At the start of the first-order optimisation process, we discussed the startup bell curve. We looked at three categories of startup. One category comprised those that benefited from a crisis. The second category and the ones that formed the bulge of the bell curve were ones that still were relevant, but saw a dip in revenues and cash flows. The third category of startup was ones that were made irrelevant due to the crisis.

In the previous chapters, we largely focussed on the middle part of the startup bell curve, which is the group of startups that have challenges growing during a crisis. In this chapter, we will look at the tail of the bell curve: startups that are mostly irrelevant due to market shifts that are outside their control.

We will look at what options these startups have through the third-order optimisation process. This involves a detailed discussion on how to assess if they have to seriously consider a pivot. We also cover what would typically constitute a pivot. Beyond pivots, this chapter also touches on the key strategic and operational habits a startup could develop to be sustainable through economic dips. Let us look at some ways of confirming that you might need to look at pivoting.

Third-Order Optimisation

In Chapter 5, we looked at ways a startup can look to acquire customers. We have several distribution channels that startups can use to acquire and onboard customers. With a focussed approach, they should be able to identify their core distribution channel and support channels. However, during a crisis, markets might drift in different directions and that could affect the success rates of your acquisition and retention of customers.

We will need a scientific approach to assessing if a pivot is needed. Through this book, we have come up with several original, yet simple, frameworks and mental models. There is already a holistic framework that can help you spot the need for a pivot. The model that can help measure and monitor customer traction is called the AARRR model, also known as the pirate metrics. The model was first proposed by Dave McClure, the founder of 500 startups.

The Pirate Metrics

AARRR stands for *a*cquisition, *a*ctivation, *r*etention, *r*eferral and *reve*nues. Acquisition is the process of wooing customers to your product and taking them through the journey to sign up. Activation is about getting past the sign-up process and giving customers their first product experience, climaxing with the ah-ha moment. This is precisely when customers realise that the product is what they needed and perhaps didn't even know beforehand.

The acquisition doesn't necessarily mean that the customer is actively using your product; activation is what identifies and actuates customer use. Depending on the type of product, acquisition might be more important than activation. Activation is also correlated with the next step: retention. A customer who has signed up and used the product is less likely to churn; therefore, retention identifies the subset of your customer base that you have kept versus the ones you have lost.

The most important question is. Why should we pivot? That is the question you need to ask yourself before you pivot. 'Pivot' is being misused in this industry, sometimes as an excuse. If you are trying to do several things, just trying to make something work without a strategy and science behind it, it's not the right approach. You should be very honest with yourself that the pivot is an attempt to change the current status quo in a new direction.

In our (Swipii's) case, it was very clear the hardware model was not scalable. Ironically we did find product market fit for the hardware model. Customers were seeing value and big brands were starting to look at us. We had many big brands ready to roll with us. I think the big reason to pivot to a pure software-only model was the cost of scaling. It was making and delivering high-quality customer service difficult as well. So those were the two big problems. The decision to pivot Swipii's delivery model was right.

Chitresh Sharma
Former CEO at Swipii. Entrepreneur and Advisor

Retention is considered a very important metric for growth. If you are acquiring and activating at a fast pace, but have a high churn rate, then you are using a leaky bucket to fetch water. Acquiring customers can be compounded if you have a good referral rate. If you want to put your growth on steroids, come up with a very good referral plan and execute it.

If you are a B2C business, keep an eye on the 'viral coefficient', which is the number of new customers that an existing customer brings to you. If your viral coefficient is less than one, then the referrals are not going to bring virality. But if every customer brings in two customers, the compounding effect it has should put your growth on steroids. To create a sticky ecosystem to ensure retention, have a 'frequent flyer' programme to reward loyal customers, but most importantly, have a killer product suite that customers can't live without.

With growth and use in place, it is now time to focus on the viability and sustainability of the business and bringing in revenues. You need to find a way to monetise the growth that you have managed. Once you have identified monetisation, it is then about fine-tuning it. Here we start looking at lifetime value (LTV) and cost of acquisition of customers (CAC). The LTV-to-CAC ratio can help you optimise customer traction.

We cannot offer prescriptive measuring techniques that can scale industries and product lines. Depending on the type of business you run, you might have to use this framework to identify the right operational numbers that reflect the health of the pirate metrics. If you had this setup in place and have regular number crunching and reporting, that would help determine when your product is no longer relevant.

As a crisis sets in, the first metric that would typically dry up is revenue as customers become cost-sensitive. Consumers typically kill their subscriptions to products and services that they don't 'need' in times of crisis. I have done it in the past myself when a sudden financial crisis hit my life and I had to sustain.

A pivot scenario really comes in when use and retention falls. If you have a freemium model, customers can downgrade their membership and still use your product. Therefore, it might be useful to understand behavioural changes so that you can assess the degree of pivoting required. A crisis can sometimes kill all these metrics. Let us now look at the different types of pivot you could consider.

Shades of Grey

Pivoting doesn't necessarily mean you shut down everything you are doing and start from scratch again. The transition from Odeo to Twitter can arguably be viewed as starting a new company. But in my opinion, it was a proper pivot. Post the pivot came a rebranding and reshuffle at the top, depending on who really believed in the Twitter use case.

Therefore, pivots can come in different shades and shapes. Through the COVID-19 crisis one of my portfolio companies cut down their product suite to focus on just one product and another firm killed one business line altogether and focussed on another. Some ways that firms can pivot are as follows:

- Targeting a new market
- Targeting a new industry
- Changing the revenue model
- Focussing on a subset of your product suite
- Switching focus from one product line to another
- Expanding the breadth of product to make it more generic
- Using a new technology
- Using a new go-to market strategy

Let us quickly look at the second-order optimisation criteria to think through the considerations before you decide to pivot. As mentioned previously, you go through this process only when your AARRR (pirate metrics) have turned hopeless.

Consumer behaviour alignment needs to be tested through the pivoting process. Identify the metrics you want to capture to gain comfort that the pivot is gaining traction. My portfolio firm FrontM, which has a platform for remote communication and collaboration, was focussing on airlines and maritime before COVID-19 hit us. Their platform allowed for seamless development of AI and Edge-based applications for these industries.

Before COVID-19 they focussed on e-commerce and transactional applications. The assumption was that airline passengers would perform transactions in-flight. However, once COVID-19 hit, they quickly shifted focus to maritime with remote health applications to stay relevant. Within 8 weeks, they were able to test consumer uptake for the application and expand aggressively through partnerships from there.

Through the entire process of identifying traction with your customers, ensure you follow a framework such as the AARRR.

As the government declared a moratorium on lending, we had to find ways to survive. We realised pretty early that we could become a SaaS business. Apart from the strategic thinking about the decision, it is this survival instinct as an entrepreneur to just find revenue, right? So you're like, Where can I just find revenue?

I remember very early on, a senior person from a top-tier bank called me up and said, 'We're really struggling and we're completely locked down. We can't do any business right now. Is that anything you can do to help us do digital business?' And I was like, 'Oh my God. This is revenue'.

Lizzie Chapman
CEO at ZestMoney

Infrastructure support is required to perform pivots. Even though I have ordered consumer behaviour ahead of infrastructure, consumer behaviour metrics are often lagging indicators of traction. By contrast, infrastructure assessment has to lead the decision of pivoting. If you are planning to focus on another industry, check to see if you have the necessary infrastructure support. Infrastructure support might have to be reviewed across policy, technology, skills and investments.

If you are in a highly regulated market and planning a pivot, consult with your regulatory body to ensure there are no red flags. Just because your previous product was fine from a regulatory perspective does not mean your new one will be. The regulatory policy can also help accelerate product expansion. If you are pivoting, you should assess if the regulators have any rails that you can use to accelerate product traction.

Technology infrastructure will have to be identified before you decide your pivot. For instance, if your product relies on mobile internet and if your pivot involves focussing on Asia, Africa or Latin America, where internet penetration is low, you might have to go back to the drawing board. You will have to discover the parts of these regions where internet penetration is higher and slowly expand as mobile internet becomes the norm in other areas.

Many entrepreneurs and firms I know have described expanding or moving to a market with a different cultural and infrastructure setup as 'starting a new company'. Study the skills infrastructure when you are moving into a new industry or market. If your product needs specialist knowledge, such as a PhD in life sciences or quantum computing, you might have to identify ways of acquiring and integrating that talent into your organisation before deciding on the pivot.

Finally, you will need to understand the appetite and maturity of your investor ecosystem towards your new direction of travel. If you are in London, you wouldn't have to think twice about making a pivot into fintech. If you are in Switzerland, you are well supported by an amazing network of investors and policy ecosystem for a pivot into a Blockchain-based use case. If you are in the Bay Area, you will be just fine as long as you have a mask for the smoke and the virus.

A **business model** will also need to be checked to ensure the pivot is successfully complete. A good look at your competitors and understanding what has worked and not worked for them would help. If you already had a working business model before deciding to pivot, you might want to test that out first.

The pivot in our portfolio is going on with Sokowatch who are basically a last-mile distributor of fast-moving consumer goods to informal retailers in East Africa. They basically bring e-commerce to the small mom-and-pop shop in these small communities in Africa. Their business model was always targeted to the merchant. Through the COVID-19 crisis, they had to think about the viability of a merchant-based business model. Until that point there was no B2C in their business model at all.

They had to actually add a B2C line so they actually started doing digital food stamps. They started delivering emergency aid to people being laid off. That got them thinking about how they could make a B2C model work. And I think that's because fintech has shown good adaptability to COVID-19. But it was a big decision move from a B2B to a whole different engagement (B2C) model.

We were at a board discussion thinking about how much of a point in time versus a strategic pivot is this change. We have been through the process of analysing the pros and cons, what the viability of the new direction looks like and actually modelling an NPV and IRR analysis at the board.

Monica Brand Angel
Cofounder of Quona Capital

Remember, a pivot doesn't have to be about reinventing the wheel across the board. The more you can reuse what you already have, the better it is. However, please test every aspect of what you already have without assuming everything will work in the pivoted world because it worked before the pivot.

Preserve the Soul

One thing you want to preserve through the pivot is the culture of the firm and the values that it has been built on. The firm's values must remain in addition to its foundations. To a firm culture is like the steel rods that hold the structure of a building together. Pivoting your business can be compared to changing the layout of the rooms, getting new floors, remodelling your kitchen or adding a conservatory. You still need to have both the foundation and the structural strength intact.

Let us look at a technology startup building a product to serve farmers in emerging markets. You are most likely going to have a strong social impact angle to your business model, but, more important, it would be ingrained in the firm's culture. If you are pivoting and your new focus area is all about making money without a strong social impact dimension to the business, you would struggle to stay passionate about the new direction.

On a similar note, if you have been an organisation with a strong growth mindset in a B2C space and you have pivoted to become an SaaS organisation for large enterprise clients, you might struggle to cope with the change. Therefore, the cultural elements of the firm have to be tapped into through the pivot.

If you see there is a mismatch between the culture of the firm and the new direction, work with your management team to identify ways of tapping into the culture of the firm. If you don't see any ways of doing this in the new direction, identify ways of first pivoting the culture of the firm, or rethink the direction of the pivot.

Although you need to keep tabs on the cultural alignment, you also need to check if your core team is passionate about the new direction of travel. If you have ensured value alignment, that should largely take care of the passion dimension too. However, if you have specialists on your team who have come on board because of your previous proposition, and that has changed, it might be necessary to ensure that they are equally passionate about the new direction.

In summary, start with confirming that 'if' the current direction of the firm has become irrelevant to customer metrics. Once you have decided to pivot, understand the landscape of operation and ensure there is enough infrastructure support in the direction of travel. Review business model options and make sure they are in line with the values of the firm. Start testing consumer behaviour while making sure that the culture of the firm is aligned with the new direction of travel. Keep testing until you hit gold.

Continue Experimentation

A pivot is not a new solution; it is a new direction. The ruthlessness in coming up with hypotheses for traction of your products, and testing them continuously in a feedback loop, has to remain. There is no dodging that process. However, with the lean and mean base you created early in the crisis, it might buy you some time and allows you to get creative in the new direction. You will be less worried about the time pressures that fast-depleting cash flows will bring.

Therefore, set up a data-driven engine that will keep testing market traction as the firm navigates its way through the crisis. A continuous data collection process will ensure you will make the necessary adjustments and course corrections required to adapt to the market shifts that keep happening around you.

If you have a company that all of a sudden is irrelevant because of a crisis, or is incredibly under duress and distress because of the crisis, very aggressively deal with your situation. The first thing you want to do is extend your runway to as long as possible.

Airbnb is an example. I think they fired 1,000 people or so. They didn't necessarily need to do it because of the amount of cash they had. But because what the crisis dynamics were going to be was so unknowable, they very quickly decided that they were not going do a bunch of things. A few months later they may start expanding again because things have settled down. But if things don't settle down, they are as affected as they think they are.

I think the existence of a business, especially a startup, is trying to find what works in a series of experiments, many of which fail. So you just have to be comfortable as a leader embracing that fact. You want them to be short and rapid experiments rather than slow and long experiments. You want plenty of them to fail so that you free up time and can run new experiments. You just want to learn from each of those experiments. So when something suddenly is not working in your business, trying to get it to work through force of will is usually futile, not always, but usually. Not confronting the reality that it's not working is usually futile.

As a leader, it's not just you dictating the experiment. Use your team. Use the data from customers. The force multiplier of having a team in which people are running multiple experiments and trying different things and learning from not just their current reality but also from their collective experience is powerful. Having your customers and trying to get the system to tell you what's going on, or discovering what's going on through these experiments is better than you trying to come up with the answer.

Brad Feld

Managing director at Foundry Group and Founder at Techstars

As described in Chapter 5, you'll want to tap into market and consumer behaviour after you pivot. But you should also focus on how consumer values are evolving through the crisis. As we saw through the financial crisis of 2008 and the COVID-19 crisis, consumer behaviours are often driven by shifts in values. Values might be driven by a sense of security or the lack of it, a sense of fear or just the arrival of a digital generation wanting to transact over the internet.

As Brad Feld mentions, a CEO's role can also be defined as 'chief experimentation officer'. Create the culture of data-driven culture in the organisation to ensure you are on top of major trends and market movements.

Let us now look at what key elements can help you build an organisation that would have a high chance of survival during a crisis.

Build for a Crisis

Over the last four chapters, we have discussed how first-order optimisation can be done to create room for the survival of the firm. We then followed it up with second-order optimisation, in which we saw the three dimensions to look at: consumer behaviour, infrastructure and business models. In this chapter, we cover how pivots work and your considerations before and after the decision to pivot has been made.

The third-order optimisation is not just about identifying what you need to survive through the crisis, nor it is just about pivot. It is also about looking at ways that will make you more crisis ready. Remember, every crisis is different. You can be culturally and operationally prepared, but it is not possible to predict the market shifts that a crisis can create.

You need to make realignments as you go through a crisis depending on how the market shifts affect your firm. However, cultural and operational readiness should make that process easier. During our interviews with the VC community and startup founders, one comment we continuously heard was, 'Good startups are built for a crisis'. That explains why the survivors of a crisis often become great organisations.

Here are a few tips that will make an organisation more resilient. I call them tips deliberately because there is no such thing as a recession-proof strategy. You can only be more prepared, but be ready to be surprised when the crash comes. These are some of the best practices that you can put into business-as-usual mode at your firm to help you weather a crisis.

Tip 1
Discover your values
Tip 2
Assemble a kick-ass team
Tip 3
Empower your team with decentralised decision-making
Tip 4
Expect data-driven accountability
Tip 5
Gamify cost-consciousness
Tip 6
Grow responsibly
Tip 7
Lean into a support network
Tip 8
Mind the mind

Tip 1: Values Make or Break Firms

As a startup, you have to be clear about the value system your firm will be built on. Values are often not discussed when you are a small team working out of a coworking space or a garage. But as you start growing it must be clear where you will compromise and where you won't as the founding members of the organisation. As discussed previously in this chapter, a good understanding and articulation of your values will help you make better decisions during tough times.

I find many entrepreneurs very clear about their vision for their organisation. But when you ask them what values they want to stick to, they often don't have an answer. Therefore, when they explore business opportunities or business models that could potentially conflict with their values or vision, they struggle to stay on course. Therefore, it would help to define values that you can't compromise on so that it is clear to your investors, board and team.

As much as it sounds like b-school bull, values are what help you define the rest of this list. If your vision, strategy and execution are in stark contrast to what your values are, you will struggle to carry on when times get tough. A clear definition of the firm's culture can help ensure that the values are stuck to. To get the right organisational behaviour you need the right culture evangelised across the firm. As Ben Horowitz suggested, sometimes creating a 'shocking rule' can help with setting the right culture, such as these examples:

- Amazon – If the feature doesn't improve the metric (product KPI), the entire feature must be rolled back. This would give you a chill if you were a product manager at Amazon.
- Gmail – Every interaction should be faster than 100 milliseconds. Google apparently loses $4 million of revenues for every millisecond delay.[1]
- VMWare – Partnerships should always be 51:49, and the partners should always be better off.

Each of these rules reflects not just values and the culture within these firms but also how operationally and strategically aligned their organisations are to their values. But remember, if you are setting rules because your team is doing the exact opposite, assess if the goals you have set for your team are in stark contrast to your values.

A little personal story to help with this point, and it is not to talk about my benevolence. A few weeks back, I was driving my daughter to school. We were extremely delayed due to an accident on the road. The scheduled drop was at 8:35 am, and I was still a mile away at 9:00 am. I had informed the school that she would arrive late. Yet, when I saw an old couple trying to cross the road at a point where they shouldn't be trying to, I stopped for them.

---

[1]*Source:* https://akfpartners.com/growth-blog/what-is-latency#bs-example-navbar-collapse-1:˜:text=How%20fast%20is%20100ms%3F%20Paul%20Buchheit,the%20threshold%20%E2%80%9Cwhere%20interactions%20feel%20instantaneous.%E2%80%9D

There would have been a few parents in their cars fuming at me for doing so. Yet, I was happy to let the couple take their time. I was willing to compromise on the time of the school drop for my daughter, I was willing to let a few cars honk at me or stay furious but wanted to let the old couple cross the road. This applies in an organisation set-up, too. If your team knows what rules they or their organisation can break, what rules they can bend, what rules they can't even think of compromising, it will clearly tell them what the firm's values are.

Are you asking for high-quality code while setting extremely challenging timelines? What does your team perceive as the organisational values? Getting there on time, getting there with very few bugs or getting there with bugs that doesn't affect value delivered to customers? All these have different cultural approaches, operational processes and hence perceived values. You must set your rules in line with what you believe are the firm's values. It will also help your team decide what rules they can break and what they can't.

There are different ways of identifying values that really resonate with you. I have a process to do that with my clients. I have a list of about 30 words that I share with my clients. I just go through those words and just start to pick up the ones that are important to the client, the ones that resonate with them and keep doing that until they prioritise them

Natasha Chatur
Personal coach

Tip 2: It's the Team, Idiot

If there is only one thing that you want to do to keep you going in good and bad times, it is getting the right team in place. There is enough and more written about how you can hire a stellar team and keep doing it time and time again. There are a few things you will want to consider as you build your team. When you found a firm, you are most likely to lean on people you know quite well as the first few members. That is understandable because you want people you know will stick with you during thick and thin.

The weight on familiarity should start going down as you start expanding your team though. Weight on similarity must also go down as you grow your team. Avoid the temptation to hire people who are like you. Look at what you lack and hire people who bring that. If you are an aggressive go-getter, look for some thinkers for your team and vice versa. If the entire team leaps and then looks, it is not going to help during difficult times.

It's hard not to talk about diversity when I talk about the team. Diversity is not a vanity metric that you create for PR purposes. It is not something you should consider to be politically right either. Running a business involves making decisions across different levels in the organisation on a regular basis.

You need people with different exposures, backgrounds, mindsets and risk appetites to make optimal decisions.

Although diversity could be considered a vanity metric, inclusion is definitely not. You might have a well-diversified team from age, gender and race perspective. But if you do not create a platform that allows people to chip in with their ideas and make decisions that are driven from these ideas on pure merit, diversity is meaningless.

As discussed in Chapter 4, the COVID-19 crisis has shown that countries led by female politicians have managed better than those led by men. Research by Utah State University of Fortune 500 firms showed that women and men of colour are chosen to lead firms in trouble. That is partly because they had to take on riskier roles throughout their career to get the recognition they deserved. Therefore, they have a higher chance of turning things around for the firm. There is enough evidence to show that diversity can be a differentiating factor in a technology startup.[2]

Tip 3: Decentralising Decision-Making

During the COVID-19 crisis, many organisations had to quickly adjust to the remote working model. The ones that have really succeeded in staying operational while still keeping their culture intact are the ones that have managed to create leaders across different levels in the firm. If you have created an organisation that understands its core values and goals, it will be capable of making decisions without the founders necessarily being part of it.

Effective decentralisation of decision-making in the organisation can be the litmus test of how well it has kept its DNA intact. Founders and the management team should be able to see that decisions being made without them involved are similar to those that are made when they are involved.

This does not mean that the founding team is not involved in key decisions made by product managers. For instance, since the Blockchain age began, decentralisation has often been misunderstood as a precursor to anarchy. That is not what decentralisation decision-making is about. It is about knowing what the values of the firm are and being able to make quick decisions. But it is also knowing when to reach out to the management and create transparency at the right levels.

The Japanese technique of Nemawashi, in which there needs to be consensus across the board before moving forward with a decision, might be seen as the antithesis of what decentralised decision-making stands for. When the organisation can execute this principle successfully, it can stay nimble and move fast during a crisis.

---

[2]https://www.usu.edu/today/story/studies-show-women-amp-minority-leaders-have-shorter-tenures-tenuous-support

Tip 4: Data-Driven Accountability

The process of creating leaders across the firm can be quite empowering for the team. At the same time, it can sometimes start creating hierarchies within the organisation. To ensure that decisions are in line with the expectations of the management team and the direction of the firm, decision-makers in the organisation must feel accountable. Accountability can be created by evangelising a data-driven culture.

If a product team is rolling out new feature, decisions about the roll-out must be data-driven. If there has been a personnel decision on hiring a few team members or reshuffling a product team composition, then that must be clearly communicated and justified with data. Therefore, it goes without saying that any strategic decisions on the go-to-market, product pricing or pipeline management will need to be data-driven. That creates objectivity and makes decentralisation easier.

The challenge to this particular element is, what should you do if a decision must be made without enough data points? That is often the challenge in a fast-changing world, because some decisions might have to be made on a hunch. But two aspects to consider are when there are no data and you want to move forward so you are still in the process of experimentation. Then you might want to call it a hypothesis rather than a decision, create the right level of visibility in the organisation and move forward with that.

Remember, if you are at a crossroads and are asked to make a decision, and if you do not have data to justify a course of action, you just have to keep moving forward in one direction with your eyes wide open and ears to the ground. As long as the organisation is aware that you are in a mode of experimentation, it is fair enough.

Tip 5: Embracing Cost Consciousness

In Chapter 4 we discussed the process of cost-cutting and achieving cost efficiencies during a crisis. In order for decisions to be made quickly during crunch times, the organisation needs to have a cost-conscious culture. This must not be confused with cost efficiency. If you are an organisation that is experimenting with your customer base or going full-on with a growth strategy, you will likely have a high-cost base and that's okay.

Cost consciousness means that the organisation understands where the cash is being deployed aggressively and where optimisation is possible at any point in time. This must be the case at all levels of the organisation. Be it the management team looking to expand into a new market, a product manager looking to procure expensive infrastructure or an engineer looking for a subscription the company might not necessarily need – all stakeholders must understand the impact of these costs even though they might not necessarily refrain from spending the money.

As a cost-conscious organisation you will devise strategies to keep your fixed costs low and your contribution margins positive. This will help you stay efficient from a cost perspective. A consistent reporting mechanism on costs will also help understand the viability of product lines. If cost centres seem to be adding too much burden, consider turning them into profit centres as Amazon did with AWS for instance. In essence, staying cost conscious is not just for operational excellence; it provides strategic optionality, and in times of crisis, this optionality dictates survivability.

Tip 6: Growing Responsibly

This is my pet peeve with VC-backed firms across the world. Achieving growth on steroids and going for a winner-takes-all approach has definitely done wonders to the technology industry since the new millennium. However, it might not be the right thing for customers in some scenarios. For instance, if you are a technology-driven lending platform, following predatory lending practices to acquire customers might not be sustainable.

Growth that doesn't keep customers' welfare and values at heart won't last. It can be slapped with regulatory fines in some industries or take a huge reputational hit in others. The other aspect of growing responsibly is testing the viability of business models. As a startup in early, venture or growth stages, unless you are raising funds through crowdfunding, you are largely raising capital from qualified investors. Even with crowdfunding, there are certain regulatory hurdles that will ensure investors have an understanding of your business before they invest.

When you decide to go public through an IPO, you will be taking capital from retail investors who might not have the same level of understanding or expertise in assessing if you are running a viable business or not. Therefore, it might be in everyone's interest to ensure that the business model is scalable and viable before an IPO at least.

Ideally, you would want to check for business viability pretty early on in the firm's life cycle. But it must be the responsibility of the management team and the board to ensure that the business is profitable before it goes public. You would assume regulatory and reputational risks if you fail to demonstrate viability.

Proving business viability early on will help if growth stalls or falls during a crisis. You can go back to basics and still find your way through tough times.

Tip 7: Tapping into a Support Network

As discussed in Chapter 3, a support network can go a long way in helping you through a crisis. Remember that all of us need help to get there. Support networks can be a group of entrepreneurs you reach out to as a sounding board, a mentor network or just your own investors and board members. It is useful to also be close to your innovation ecosystem, which includes investment hubs, incubation and accelerator programmes, corporate innovation, and even government-supported innovation programmes.

All these can come in handy during a crisis if you have the right relationships. The relationship might be built through a rigid time timetable involves socialising through events and informal meetings. Alternatively, it could be accomplished by just building rapport with key stakeholders through social media channels. Consistent engagement with them through content creation can build familiarity and credibility in a relatively short period of time. A support network can help you with keeping your ears to the ground during a crisis to understand market shifts, investor appetite and the general direction of the industry you are operating in.

A support network must not be mistaken for an advisory pool or a bunch of people you lean on emotionally or to discuss ideas alone. It can also be viewed as the system that you plug yourself (and the firm) into so that it is in the best interest of this system to ensure you are successful. An admit into VC cohort or a cheque from Sequoia or A16Z or a huge corporate VC arm can fall into this category of plugging yourself into the right system. These organisations have the might to change the fate of their startups by virtue of their network.

Tip 8: Mind the Mind

I wanted to keep the best for last. Mental health is very critical for entrepreneurs. That has been the biggest takeaway for me through the process of writing this book, the research we have done and the interviews we conducted. You don't expect Usain Bolt to set a world record without a personal trainer. Entrepreneurs are like top sportspeople who have to be able to hit peak performance at crucial times. Their decision-making capabilities must be quick, unbiased, instinctive and as data-driven as possible. Their communication needs to be effective in the context of where it is delivered.

A healthy mind can make better decisions, be more empathetic and help connect with its team and stakeholders more effectively. Innovation communities across the world are still not matured enough that entrepreneurs can discuss and understand mental health issues openly. However, this must be something that you should sensitise your board and your investors to quite early in the firm's life cycle.

An empathetic culture within the firm amongst employees can help with mental health challenges. During my discussion with Onfido's CEO, Husayn Kassai, he mentioned that they had a mental health programme as part of their benefits package for their employees and it was the most used and popular benefit. We need more startups to be part of mental health discussions in a supportive environment.

Engaging in team activities to create an informal environment and build rapport can help ease those discussions, too. When team members find it difficult or delicate to discuss issues openly, create a private channel or a programme that they can be part of within or outside the organisation. On top of the support with mental health, as your startup becomes cash-rich, explore performance coaching sessions for at least the founding team members.

With that, we come to the end of the third-order optimisation process. Although the topic of pivoting is largely applicable to firms that have become irrelevant, strategies suggested for pivoting can be used on a regular basis. Adopting practices that give you the capabilities to be nimble during a market crash can be used by all firms.

Mental health is paramount. Running a startup is like running a series of marathons. You have to pace yourself. You have to ask yourself if you can last for IPOs. The average number of years to get to an IPO is 14 years, I think. Can you pace yourself for a 14-year marathon? It's not a sprint. Therefore, I think a performance coach is a way to do it. It is also important to create a culture where you can talk about it, acknowledge it and work on it and basically not ignore it.

We recognised mental health as a big factor very early on. Our most popular team perk is the Sanctus app, which is a mental health coach, which every team member has access to. They can book an appointment for an hour a week, as long as they want it.

Husayn Kassai
CEO at Onfido

Figure 8.1 shows a sketch note summarising this chapter.

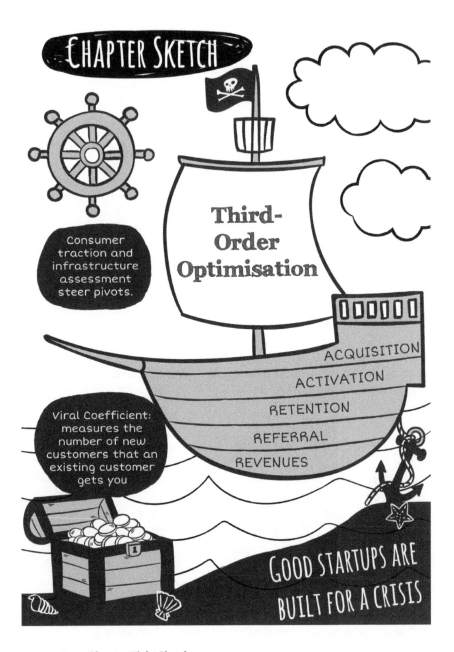

FIGURE 8.1 Chapter Eight Sketch

Conclusion

We have now reached the conclusion of the strategic pillar of this book. We went through the first- and second-order optimisation of your business in the previous four chapters. This chapter covered the third-order optimisation process. The first part of the third-order optimisation was about identifying if you needed a pivot.

Your customer traction can be measured using the pirate metrics or the AARRR framework. These metrics enable you to break down the process of acquiring, engaging and retaining customers. Referrals help with achieving growth and revenues are really the proof of the pudding, demonstrating that you have a viable business model that can scale.

When the pirate metrics start to look bad, and you haven't been able to turn them around after a couple of iterations, it's time to look to get your thinking hat on. Gather data to understand why the metrics have started to look bad. If it points to fundamental market shifts, changing customer behaviours and values, consider a pivot.

We then discussed what pivots could look like. Pivots do not necessarily mean reinventing the wheel or redoing everything from scratch. Pivots can be a change in strategy, revenue model, target consumer segment, target market or just the underlying technology.

We also looked at factors to protect through a pivot. If something has worked well for your firm before the pivot, try to keep that aspect intact. If you have been successful in building a sales culture, protect that through the crisis. You must also ensure that the pivot is in alignment with the values of the firm and passions of the core team members. A pivot might not work if the team is not passionate about the new direction of the business or product.

Beyond pivoting, we also looked at best practices that entrepreneurs should consider to prepare them for a crisis. Remember, it is not a major crisis if it doesn't have the surprise factor. As mentioned in previous chapters, the surprise often hurts you more than the market shifts themselves. However, looking after the firm's values and building a good team that understands the culture can help stabilise the firm faster during a crisis.

The operational aspects of the firm need consistent attention as well. A cost-conscious team will be able to get to a lean and mean base faster during a crisis. Business viability must be continuously tested to make sure customers and investors are protected. A viable business can keep its head above water for longer during difficult times.

Finally, we touched on the importance of the mind. A healthy mind makes better and quicker decisions during a crisis. Entrepreneurs must be at the top of their game in problem-solving mode, and mental health is critical to achieving that. Every startup should prioritise mental health as a key success criterion for its teams to look after. Investors and board members must be inculcated with a culture of embracing mental health issues.

We have now covered the three main pillars of the book: an understanding of the macro environment in Chapters 1 and 2, mental health in Chapter 3 and the three orders of strategy optimisation in Chapters 4 to 8. In the next chapter, we will bring it all together with mind maps and flowcharts summarising key concepts and takeaways from this book.

CHAPTER 9

Winner Winner Chicken Dinner

Introduction

The conundrum of crisis management for startups is an ocean. During the process of writing this book, we came across several experts challenging us on how we could create an exhaustive framework for startups wanting to deal with a crisis. We weren't trying to do that at all. Our objective was not to provide a framework that could be both broad and deep. Every business situation is different and often warrants creative solutions. Our objective was to help you think in most of these challenging situations.

If you are just starting up, we believe this book is a great way to look at different aspects of keeping your firm as recession resilient as possible. Nobody can predict market shifts that a crisis can create, but we can definitely prepare ourselves with a set of tools and techniques to deal with these tectonic movements in a nimble yet decisive manner.

We did not plan on covering the depths of identifying product market fit for every industry use case possible. We did not plan on covering all the mental health management modalities. Neither did we plan on covering every single business model out there or distribution channels that startups can tap into.

What we hopefully did in this book is to help you think through each aspects of building a startup during a crisis, especially in the context of a crisis. In this chapter, we bring together all the key points of consideration we have put forward throughout this book. It is beneficial for entrepreneurs to study these factors, internalise and customise them to their context of business. Ideally that could result in a set of values, strategies, metrics and operational processes that make their firm resilient and sustainable.

This book can be broadly summarised across three key pillars. One is the understanding of the macro environment that a startup operates in. Tech startups should not look at VC investors as their end game. There is more to capital markets and getting smart capital. An understanding of the motivations of capital market players can help you find your way through or in some cases, ride the highs and avoid the lows of this system.

The second aspect, and in my opinion the most significant aspect of this book, is mental health. Although we cover that topic only in one chapter, I cannot exaggerate the importance of viewing mental health as a core operational success criterion for your business. Once you integrate mental health into the culture of the firm, it helps several other aspects, such as consistent decision-making, humane communication, time management ... and the list goes on.

The third part of the book is strategy. We look at how to go lean and mean very fast and then consolidate from there. We touch on how you stay on top of consumer behaviour and value changes, infrastructure shifts and business model implications for your business. Of course, if everything is screwed up, think about pivoting.

We closed off the strategy part of the book with some tips on how to make your firm more sustainable and resilient to crisis. Let us now look at the key takeaways from the book across these three dimensions.

The Macro Environment

When a crisis hits while you are running a startup, the stress can be hard to manage. You are dealing with a lot of moving pieces and are responsible for a lot of people's livelihood, and that can be overwhelming. It might seem like the end of the world. But, just like everything else in life, this too shall pass. Instead of focussing on things that you do not have control over, you might as well focus your efforts in the moving parts that you can influence to potentially change the outcome for the better.

Even when the crisis passes, it doesn't mean your job in dealing with the crisis as a founder is complete. Some of the tactical decision debts need to be resolved before it snowballs. The more prepared you are before the crisis, the less bloodbath you have to go through during a market carnage. As we researched for this book, we saw companies react to problems differently. Companies that coped well had a few things in common. They were better prepared, acted decisively and moved swiftly.

In Chapter 1, we looked into how capital markets works and discussed the top-down flow of money through the five-tiered pyramid. At Tier 0, the central bankers regulate the cash flowing through the system. In times of calamity, more often than not, regulators are required to inject sufficient liquidity to help stabilise the economy.

Next level down, Tier 1, you have the blue chip firms and big banks distributing this cash, directly or through the markets, before it gets to the hands of the general public. Traditionally, blue chip firms employed a big slice of a country's population. Thus, the deployed capital gets to society through these blue chip firms. You then have the pension funds and endowments next in line in to tap into the capital flow from the top of the pyramid.

Although we hear more about money managers in healthy economic times, crisis times can be quite different. Funds that money managers run can work only with what they have, if, and only if, their limited partners can fund their crusade during these unholy times. Individual investors displaying high risk appetite in healthy economic times help high growth tech startups. Investors' desire to invest and spend is directly proportional to their asset size. This behaviour is known as the wealth effect. Conversely, during a crisis, liquidity can and will dry up in a blink of an eye. It's a socially contracted domino that we all signed up to.

If you are operating in the venture capital industry, you probably know that the power law dictates survival of a venture fund. In general, there is more capital than good ideas and even more capital than good teams that are able to execute these ideas. VC investors make money betting only on a grand slam rather than a home run. And, every year, there are only a handful of outsized winners. Thus, VC investors are always competing to get into the most competitive deals. The signal-to-noise ratio can be disproportionately in favour of negative externalities.

In good times investors have the noise to deal with. During downtimes, they have to ensure their limited partners have the risk appetite and there is liquidity in the system. Investors face the same dilemma that most startups face: should or should I not invest during times of crisis? What if this is going to be the next breakout firm? Should I just focus on preserving the current portfolio? It comes down to their risk appetite and often that is dictated by market conditions.

What History Tells Us

Eager to explore more about how successful technology firms survive and thrive in a market crisis, we turn the clock back four decades and revisit some of the modern-day market crises that have affected technology companies. We place most of the market crisis into two buckets: (1) structural crisis or (2) event-driven crisis.

A structural crisis is an internally induced market crisis, in which the culprit is typically found within the market. Portfolio managers' overconfidence in portfolio insurance and lack of oversight on trading algorithms were both commonly cited causes of the 1987 Black Monday. Both of these issues live within the financial markets. Similarly, the dot-com bubble in 2000 and the subprime mortgage crisis in 2008 were the product of internal inefficiencies. The irrational exuberance of technology execs caused the former whereas the bankers created the latter. Both the participants and the structural problem in the market were the leading causes of the crises.

Conversely, the COVID-19 crisis blindsided the world with a healthcare disaster. At the time of writing, there are a total of more than 40 million people infected, and more than 1.1 million people died from the pandemic worldwide. A large part of the world is still in lockdown, and most businesses are shut, with some countries showing early signs of easing the government-imposed mobility restriction. Most citizens of the world have been in lockdown for at least 6 months. The root cause of the crisis as such has nothing to do with the internal market factors, but it has everything to do with forces at play outside of the mechanics of a functioning financial market.

A few patterns emerged as a result of reliving all these market crises through research and conversations. Usually, the first sign of trouble is overvaluation. Despite it being pretty self-evident, it can be hard to separate the wheat from the chaff. Living and breathing in a market where Gordon Gecko's 'greed is good' flourishes can result in undetected mischiefs.

As soon as investors get wind of potentially seismic shifts of macroeconomic trends, they might reduce or hold off funding to the extent that they will pull out from previously committed rounds when the market corners them. Startups are forced to take a down round to raise the funding required in light of future economic uncertainties. When investors are unable to increase their commitment and improve their shots on goal, they naturally gravitate towards a few more significant sure-bet deals, investing per the power law. Lucky for a few, unlucky for most. This investing norm creates a funding gap, and it is especially prominent when looking at the number of deals made instead of value invested.

Ever heard the saying 'The more you sweat in peace time, the less you bleed in wartime'? We believe that there are a few internal and external sources that might come in handy when spotting potential market crises. In the tech industry, the word *ecosystem* has been thrown around a lot as a buzzword. Yet, the ecosystem pulse can be a vital seismograph for an earth-shattering crisis. Actors within your ecosystem can be the perfect radar to spot a potential catastrophe. Understanding the shift in the market positioning of competitors and funding landscape enable entrepreneurs to take an outside-in view and make an informed decision on their next step.

Internally, founders can rely on product feedback by splitting down features into three broad categories – market-driven, experimental and product debt – to gauge their adaptability in case of a market downturn. Understanding the ratio among these three buckets will help to uncover what proportion of developments are corresponding to revenue opportunities, product enhancement and unproven bets. This enables entrepreneurs to quickly have a snapshot of their product development and decide swiftly on the best space to invest their increasingly scarce resources as a result of a crisis.

As history suggests, many times during an emergency, management's knee-jerk response is to cut cost. It is no surprise that talent is the first line item to look at when, on average, the human cost amount for the majority of a startup's cost base. But, mindlessly cutting cost can prove to be even more costly down the line. Tangible barriers to entry have increasingly diminished, in some cases, even evaporated overnight. This is especially true during a crisis. An intangible asset such as talent is the only warrant to better outcomes. Hence, entrepreneurs have to identify and hold on to the talents that are core to the business at all costs, contrary to popular belief.

Here is a checklist that can help you with a regular data collection process, which can come in handy during a crisis.

Wear Your Mask First

When you board a plane, the emergency procedure announcement before every flight always repeats the same thing: 'In case of an emergency landing, always put on your oxygen mask first before you help others', even if it means there is a more vulnerable passenger sitting right next to you. This specific instruction is to ensure those who are 'able' will not get into trouble. Only then, the 'able' can help the 'unable'.

Similarly, when a crisis hits, the founding team needs to help themselves before they can help the company. As trite as it sounds, it is also true. One will often hear VC investors stressing how the founding team makes or breaks a company, but it often stops there. The individuals' mental well-being are not usually discussed. And, many times, it is willfully ignored, like a taboo.

That is also why we dedicated an entire chapter to mental fitness and self-introspection. We think it is one of the most underrated, under-spoken but vital building blocks when it comes to dealing with difficult situations, such as a market crisis.

When you are lucky enough to lead a team, everything that you as a leader say and do will have ripple effects across the organisation. Emotions drive decisions, which lead to actions. And, actions has consequences. Therefore, it is essential to engage the entire company consciously and mindfully. CEOs have to be self-aware of their thoughts and actions. Some subconscious subroutines might bring out the best or worst of people within an organisation.

In this chapter, we discussed the whole brain concept, essentially, putting both your left and right brain to work, addressing analytical needs with the left while the right picks up the empathetic and creative work. One has to make cold, hard decisions but execute them with warmth during a crisis.

In the middle of building a rocket ship, one can easily forget the initial mission. The punch line: a crisis is a great time to self-evaluate. This evaluation is when one needs to separate self-worth from work. We proposed a 360 evaluation model to tease out (1) passion, (2) skills and (3) demand through three questions.

- Are you still passionate about the business?
- Do you think you have the skills to drive the business forward?
- Are you still relevant in a crisis ridden world?

Asking yourself whether you are looking forward to what you are going to do every day is probably the best passion acid test. You don't have to like 100% of what you do, but there has to be a significant drive deep down to make it all worthwhile mentally.

The circle of competence concept best illustrate one's skills. If what it takes to drive the firm forward is within or not far away from the edges of one's circle of competence, chances are that person can prevail in the crisis. The remedy to lack of required skills can be to hire someone with that skill set to complement your strengths.

Last, gauge the demand for your leadership within the firm. Use external factors to help with self-evaluation. Gather feedback from your management team and board members and make sure they want you as a leader as much as you want to lead them.

If, by any chance, you decide that this is not what you want to do going forward, you can choose to step away. Do so with integrity and with pride. The trick here is to be honest. Only by recognising the problem can one solve the problem.

On the contrary, if you decide to fight the good fight, it is imperative for you, as an entrepreneur, to keep a healthy mind. Switching off when you are out of office and looking for a mentor and/or an executive coach are all valid measures one can take. Also, engage investors and operating team in a dialogue. It can be revealing and soothing. After all, people who go through shit together stick together.

Here is a framework to help you think through this topic.

Cold Decisions and Humane Execution

A crisis often blindsides us. When it arrives, it might not be immediately clear what one should do. Worst of all, financial indicators might belie the actual severity, leaving a big gap to fill when it's too late. Thus, it is imperative to at least know where your startup stands in the middle of it all.

An acid test of using the revenue growth rate and the business model relevance would help to distinguish where a startup stands in connection to the crisis. Statistically, most startups fall in the middle of a bell curve. Notwithstanding the slowdown in revenue growth, their business models are still relevant. Next, startups that are crashing have seen their revenue diminish; some evaporate overnight as a result of the crisis. To add salt to injury, their business models are no longer applicable due to the recent market shift. As Journey, the American rock band, had it in their song 'Don't Stop Believin,' 'Some will win, and some will lose,' There will be a group of businesses that become super relevant as a result of the crisis and consequently accelerate their revenue, growth or both.

A clear demarcation of where the business stands helps founders to concentrate their energy in devising a proper plan of attack. Based on our experience and research, we have condensed multiple factors into a three-pronged approach. First-, second- and third-order optimisation to survive, normalise and thrive, respectively. Some startups will only go through part of the process, whereas some might need to go through multiple cycles of it to stay relevant.

To put it simply, the first-order optimisation – survive – is to protect core assets, such as business and talent, while lowering cash burn. To a startup, cash flow is akin to what oxygen is to a human being: indispensable. Getting your financial affairs in order helps to paint a clear picture of how much cash one startup has after taking into account all relevant payables and receivables, cash conversion cycle and so on.

Subsequently, with enough supply of oxygen, an entrepreneur needs to look into the heart of the business to determine what are the core and non-core business functions. Before proceeding to scenario planning, amassing information such as product value, optimal cost structure and market knowledge will help with accurately reflecting the lay of the land. As a general rule of thumb, one should always plan for the worst.

When you are in a crisis, time is not on your side; everything needs to be done swiftly. Maintaining a healthy cash position more often than not requires cooperation from every level of the organisation. Albeit being a rather cold and objective decision, cost optimisation has to be humanely executed. Thus, communication becomes a critical lever to effectuate cost-cutting measures smoothly.

Humans value bonafides. Communicate to your team with authenticity and investors with transparency. They must know what you are up to and why. Concurrently, infuse confidence in external stakeholders, such as clients, suppliers and social following. It helps corroborate the fact that you are sticking around despite the hard times.

To improve cash position, you can expand product offering, renegotiate for quicker payments or work out favourable pricing models with clients. Additionally, one can also decrease outgoing from office space to operations and tech. One thing to bear in mind is to cut costs mindfully and not make haphazard decisions that might sacrifice your long-term goals for short-term gains. As the saying goes, take care of your people, and they will take care of your business. It is especially true in times of crisis. Treat your team with empathy, and they shall reciprocate. In essence, financial capital will sustain you, and human capital will unchain you.

Here is a framework to help you think through this topic.

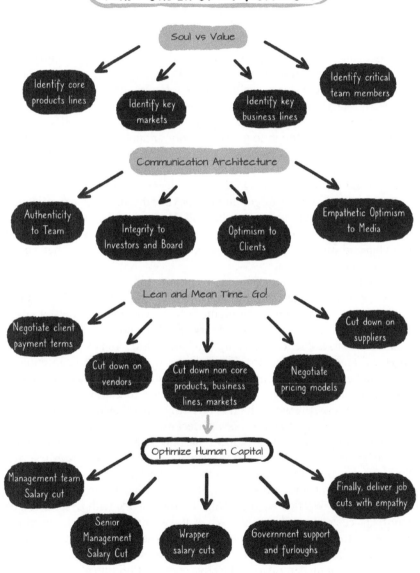

FIRST ORDER OPTIMISATION

Soul vs Value

- Identify core products lines
- Identify key markets
- Identify key business lines
- Identify critical team members

Communication Architecture

- Authenticity to Team
- Integrity to Investors and Board
- Optimism to Clients
- Empathetic Optimism to Media

Lean and Mean Time... Go!

- Negotiate client payment terms
- Cut down on vendors
- Cut down non core products, business lines, markets
- Negotiate pricing models
- Cut down on suppliers

Optimize Human Capital

- Management team Salary cut
- Senior Management Salary Cut
- Wrapper salary cuts
- Government support and furloughs
- Finally, deliver job cuts with empathy

Customer Is King

In Chapter 5, we begin the process of second-order optimization. When you are trying to get from the point of origin to your destination, there are three steps that you need to take.

First, you check the map to gauge the distance and route required. The map contains information about the services en route. From a startup point of view, a map will help you to evaluate if the infrastructures your business rely on are still intact. These foundations can either be technology- or policy-led.

Then, you check your car, making sure that the vehicle is well-serviced or at least functioning enough to get you to your endpoint. In this instance, the automobile is similar to a business model. It is how your organisation creates and captures value. Further probing will help to uncover the feasibility of your business (car) when seeing it in the context of a crisis (driving).

Last, unless you have forgotten most of your driving courses, you tend to check the mirrors right before you take off. During a drive, the mirror serves as a tool to realise your surrounding and your positioning. It is analogous to observing and studying the market and consumer consumption when you are going through the motion.

As our first pillar of second-order optimisation, we propose a four-step framework to figure out consumer appetite. Starting with the 'Who?', unveil your ideal customers. Then figure out the 'Why?' - what problems customers are trying to solve with your product and services. Next consider the 'How much?' a quantitative assessment of the 'Why?' and the 'Who?'. And finally, think about the 'How?', an operating methodology to figure out customer consumption.

We talked about building an avatar to flesh out all the aspirations and frustrations of your customers. It serves as a way to detect changes in customer motivations, the why, which in turn drives purchasing decisions. Given the context, we thought Zoom was a perfect example. When the government implemented the pandemic lockdown, users were hit with physical communication barriers. Zoom happened to alleviate users from these hurdles, virtually. Their user base grew by 20 times in a few weeks.

Next, we spent some time talking about the why, the drive behind every decision to buy. We floated the MEDDIC framework with a specific goal, identifying customer pain points. When there's no fire, there is no money. The idea is to identify the pain flame that burns the strongest. Through a need matrix by scoring customer segment needs against product capabilities, the illustration can turn a subjective conversation into a relatively accurate snapshot.

To be truly objective, we need to quantify the impact it has on the business, which then brings us to the next step of the four-step framework: the how much. Instead of relying on one source of data, we recommend overlaying external market data with internal usage data and illustrating the results on a value-need graph. For low-value and low-need features, kill them. Conversely, if products have high value and a high need, go for it.

It gets complicated when you have a part that has low value but high need. We have seen companies prioritise features as such only if there are significant ancillary revenues make up for it. When met with high-value and low-need products, companies tend to double down a lot on sales and marketing channels to educate users. In the context of a crisis, this strategy might not be the best use of the resources.

Finally, the how. Most problems that a startup product faces could have been easily mitigated if only companies speak to their customers. If a picture is worth a thousand words, then primary research is worth a thousand secondary studies. Empathetically listening to your customer is the best way forward. Some clues are obvious, and some are subtle. Listen attentively and record furiously throughout the research.

Although customers are willing to try on new things in general, the inertia for a behavioural change can be a hurdle in times of crisis. It is vital to understand customer behaviours on top of the value-need frameworks. Given that inertia could overpower their need to try new things, it is also sensible to relook at your current customer base and leverage your existing knowledge to expand adjacent offerings.

Here is a framework to help you think through this topic.

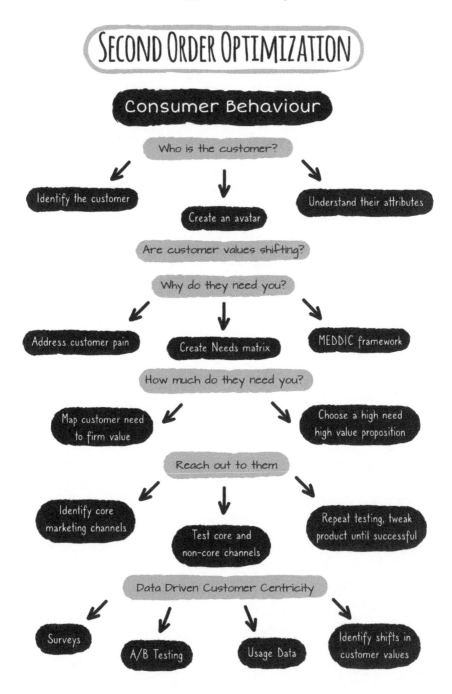

Infrastructure Catalysts

If you are like most of us, before you start driving, you will spend some time looking at Google Maps or SatNav to help determine what's ahead. You will probably drag the screen along the whole route; some of us might even zoom in on specific services along the route. Similarly, in this chapter, we are zooming in on 3 distinct infrastructure layers on your startup journey: policy, technology, and ecosystem. They can either be a bolster or a booster for your startup when employed correctly.

First, as of 2020, the world has 195 countries, all with their own set of policies. As you can imagine, running a business in the US is very different from running it in Japan. The consequences of not complying with local regulations can be severe and devastating to a company and its employees. As such, it is essential to keep an eye out for potential rules because you never know what might make or break your business model.

While discussing policy infrastructure, we looked into how the European Banking Authority (EBA) used policies such as the Payment Services Directive (PSD II) to promote competition in the financial market. As a result, a phenomenon known as open banking fueled the ascent of fintech companies around the continent. Conversely, global regulators found themselves on the other side of the fence when dealing with the cryptocurrency market crash. Investors, retail and institutional, lost thousands if not millions on pump-and-dump schemes.

Worldwide regulators have been criticised for policy frameworks not marching at the same speed as innovation. The lag creates the perfect breeding ground for mischief and deceit. On the other side of the globe, however, you have the Indian government mandating the use of a national digital identification service, Aadhar. Together with the unified payment initiative (UPI), these initiatives provided the necessary propellant for e-commerce and payment adoption in India.

Next, since the vacuum tubes made way for transistors in the 1950s, the introduction of microprocessors in the 1970s and the proliferation of graphics processing unit (GPU) technology has become more powerful and more affordable. Consumer electronics and the internet have become part of society's everyday life. With half the world's population connected via the internet, it is undisputedly one of the most important infrastructures of modern civilisation.

The technical innovation founded by the Defense Advanced Research Project Agency (DARPA) in the 1960s disrupted the traditional way of life and altered industries. Fifty years later, it continues to change how businesses create and capture value. The maturation of the internet gave birth to household names that we love and adore today, such as Amazon, Google, Facebook and

Twitter. Had they not had the foundation of the internet, these companies might not have formed, and the world would look quite different from what we have now.

Similarly, the social media era created a tonne of data, structured or unstructured, which, in turn, helped reinvigorate machine learning and artificial intelligence discipline. More recently, the relentless innovation for cheaper and faster internet speed has enabled seamless video streaming across the globe. Although technical infrastructure is an important enabler of an entrepreneur's startup journey, the lack of it should not deter one's will to solve a burning problem. Google, for example, created Chromecast with the goal of bringing TV experience with YouTube even when smart TVs weren't around. The constraints from infrastructure can breed creativity and lead to further innovation.

Last, ecosystem infrastructure has the power to supercharge a rocket ship, namely through talent and funding. A multigenerational entrepreneurial ecosystem passes business wisdom from one generation to another. This approach not only lowers the probability of a newborn entrepreneur repeating similar mistakes as their predecessors but also propagates experienced operators into working in newly founded startups within the community. They will bring their experience and knowledge to further enrich all the nodes within the network and further improving the odds of success.

Within the startup ecosystem, VC investors are commonly known as the main funders. However, if one is willing to look further than traditional funding sources, there are also angel investors, debt providers, grants from a government body and so on. Knowing and executing on the right funding source is fundamental to the long-term success of a startup. To successfully raise a fund, entrepreneurs also have to work on the quality of their pitch, research investors upfront and find common ground with the investors. These will all improve the chances of the fundraiser.

Here is a framework to help you think through this topic.

INFRASTRUCTURE

Policy Infrastructure

Policy Restrictions

Are you restricted by regulations?

Can you innovate to overcome the restrictions?

Is it too expensive to overcome restrictions?

Can you collaborate with regulators to derisk?

Policy Opportunities

What policy gaps can you exploit?

Can you collaborate with regulators to accelerate?

What policy support exists?

Technology Infrastructure

What infrastructure do you need?

Do you have a maturity map of infrastructure dependences?

Are you limited by a low maturity technology infrastructure?

Can you overcome the limitation?

Do you need to innovate to overcome the limitation?

How much will it cost?

What are the alternatives?

Can you scale with the limitation?

Ecosystem Infrastructure

Talent

Do you have the right talent nearby?

Do you need to rely on global workforce?

Can you keep culture intact with a distributed workforce?

What are the best ways to inspire talent?

Investments

How strong is your investment proposal?

Do you have a supportive investment ecosystems?

Do the key investors know you?

If not, what can you do to get on their radar?

Have you shortlisted investors with similar backgrounds?

Innovation Support

What incubators and accelerators exist?

Are they good enough to help your growth?

Are there corporate innovation hubs that you can tap into?

Have you got operational support? Legal and financial modelling

Business Model Evaluation

Following the analogy for driving, a business model is similar to a car. Depending on the context, each car will have features that favour one terrain over another. The same is true for business models. We define it as how a firm creates value for its customers and captures value in return.

Then, we introduced a four-dimensional lens to investigate business models in detail. Reduced to its core, a successful business model has to withstand the harshness of time and space. The longevity of a business model creates a sustainable income stream for a relatively long period. From a time perspective, one would also want to get to a steady state in the shortest amount of time, so evince the importance of velocity when thinking about a business model. Additionally, a business model also has to have scale, the versatility to apply across a broad spectrum of customers, and weight, the ability to attract and retain customers with its value exchange mechanics, commonly known as stickiness.

To keep things simple and representative, we condensed business models into three categories based on the predictability of contracts, behaviours or both. The world of businesses is governed by tangible forces, contract, and intangible force, trust. A contractually predictable business warrants smoother revenues as outlined in the contracts themselves, although in practice, contracts can and will be breached as a result of unforeseen circumstances or ill intentions. That is, however, the exception rather than the norm.

With a concrete judiciary system, a signed and enforced contract is the closest representation of revenue that a firm has. Business models as such are rife in the B2B space, such as enterprise software and SaaS. In recent years, the subscription model has slowly emanated in the B2C landscape to better align the value exchange between a provider and a consumer, generating fixed sources of income for startups and reducing variable costs for consumers.

Alternatively, you have growth-focussed business models that rely on consumer trust rather than contracts. Unlike contractually predictable business models, behaviourally predictable models typically don't have a recurring stream of income. Instead, they rely on use, interaction and prediction to gauge user interest and generate a variable income for the startups. Advertising, for example, is a business model that utilises behavioural predictability to drive revenue. Platform such as Facebook, Google and Twitter, provide their core services to end users for free, in turn, the brands and enterprises pay for the service to reach end users.

The mechanics of value exchange are less linear, and it often involves more than just two parties. At the precipice of disruptive innovation, we also find a combination of contractually and behaviourally predictable business models. These models often derives from parts of both contractually and behaviourally predictable business models. For example, Slack employed a B2C2B approach where it built a community for its messaging product. Then, they started selling to enterprises from the bottom-up, using key behavioural data from their product to inform their enterprise go-to-market strategy. As crises disrupt traditional industries, entrepreneurs continue to employ myriad business models to create value for and capture value from end users.

Here is a framework to help you think through this topic.

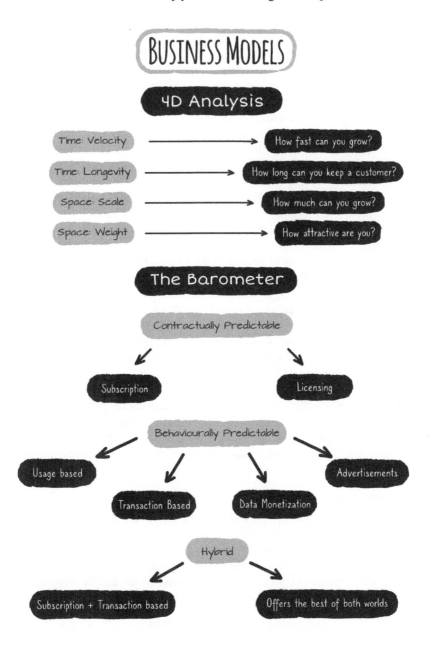

All Change

Finally, in Chapter 8, we explored the third and final order of optimisation: the pivot, an instant turnaround point to prevent a business from slipping into helplessness and cataclysm. Instead of coming up with novel and less dandy frameworks, we think that the pirate metrics works well in evaluating the need to pivot, because it is commonly known as the AARRR framework. It captures the customer funnel in one snapshot. Please note that this is not the only framework to measure and manage customer traction. The decline in every stage of the funnel indicates the need to reevaluate current approaches and, if need be, course correct.

A pivot need not be a full 180 degrees; it could be a couple of degrees of course corrections, which will sufficiently yield an enormous outcome. Imagine taking a flight from London, travelling to Tokyo at a certain angle. When the pilot calibrates it by a few degrees off, one might end up in North Korea instead. When pivoting a startup, entrepreneurs have numerous options, starting with a new market, altering revenue model, killing off less cardinal business lines and more.

Founders can align their pivot with an imperative such as consumer behaviours, availability of infrastructures and a sustainable business model to increase their chances of success. Or, at least, reduce the probability of a catastrophe happening during a pivot. If you want to go fast, go alone. If you want to go far, go together. It is important to keep the team at the centre of it all. Their motivation induces execution and sets the direction. When it comes to team welfare, ignorance is not bliss; it is an abyss.

Over the course of writing the book, we managed to interview some of the keen minds and entrepreneurial practitioners around the world. Their insights made this book. One of the key discernments we commonly got from almost all our interviews is that a good startup is built for a crisis. And, if I were to sum up one key takeaway: chance favours the prepared mind. Whilst one is unlikely to predict a market crisis, one can prepare for it operationally and culturally. The map is not the territory, but with a map, you can create some building blocks to understand the lay of the land. Here are some of the bricks that might help you construct your palace:

- Values make or break a firm.
  - When your startup is a five-man band, the culture of the firm is the makeup of five personalities. As your company scales, the influx of personalities will enrich or dilute the way things are done within the company, setting organisational behaviour in motion. Values are set to guide everyone in the company to execute in symphony. To realise the one advantage that startups have over big corporate, speed,

everyone on the ship needs to row in the same direction. Values are like the beat of the marching drums, guiding and leading actions of everyone onboard.

- It's the team, idiot.
  - To sail through the crisis, we need all hands on deck. Those hands need to be willing and motivated to get the deed done. Rome wasn't built in a day, and it certainly won't be built with just a pair of hands. It takes the whole civilisation to lay the foundation and another civilisation optimises it. Without the divergent experiences and ideas, we risk slipping into an echo chamber and dive straight into a precipitous cliff. Having a great team does not warrant a safe exit, but it sure does lighten the load and pressure. As Sam Altman at YCombinator alluded to in his tweets: 'The strongest teams have a lot of diversity of thought but do not have much diversity of values or goals'.

- Decentralise decision-making.
  - In times of emergency, such as a crisis, time is of the essence. The ability to decide is often better with the people on the front line, in this case, the employees who are responsible for the day-to-day operations of your startup. By empowering employees to make decisions on behalf of the firm, a company can respond faster to complications. Additionally, it is a great litmus test for culture dissipation within the firm. Ideally, the decision-making process will not differ when the founder is or isn't in the room.

- Use data-driven accountability.
  - Motivation and momentum can sustain the team only for so long. Without an accountability system, it is easy to blind ourselves from the real progress, especially when things go south. We've all heard the phrase 'data is the new oil'. As annoying as it might be, by embracing data, companies can turn a subjective matter into an objective discussion. Pair emotions and feelings with facts and figures to get to the desired outcomes.

- Embrace cost consciousness.
  - Euripides, an Athenian playwright, wrote, 'Chances fight ever on the side of the prudent'. Being cost-efficient during sunny days is as important as being cost-effective in rainy days. By keeping overhead low, extra cash enables startups to experiment in volume and double down on those with value. A startup dies when it runs out of cash or when the founders give up. Keeping an eye on the costs increases the number of experiments permitted, even under resource constraints, or reduce pressure for the founders under duress.

- Grow responsibly.
  - o A venture scale business is often identified as businesses with hypergrowth. Whilst it has done wonders with a winner-takes-all approach, there are very few businesses in the world that truly need hyper-scale. The dark side of a startup looking for hypergrowth is one without a tangible plan to sustain its growth and business. Without a tenable way to create value for customers and durable modus operandi to capture value from customers, growth could dwindle twice as fast as it burgeons.
- Support your network.
  - o Your network is your net worth. I doubt this phrase needs an introduction. Over the years, there have been dozens if not hundreds of books written about network and networking. But, in practice, a support network has the ability to lift you up during your lowest point. A network has the ability to provide time, money, expertise and connection when a startup needs it most. It acts as a sounding board, eyes and ears and oftentimes the yellow pages for a founder. Nurture it, contribute to it; it will reciprocate when you least expect it.
- Mind the mind.
  - o To solve a problem, we first have to acknowledge the problem. For too long, mental health has been a taboo within the technology industry. If people in the company are the only asset that matters, it pays to focus on their well-being. Their mental well-being affects the company's well-being. Mental health should be at the centre of a company's agenda. It is both a personal and business need. Engage, listen and learn for one another.

Here is a framework to help you think through this topic.

Conclusion

Figure 9.1 shows a sketch note that encapsulates the main messages of this chapter, and perhaps this book, too.

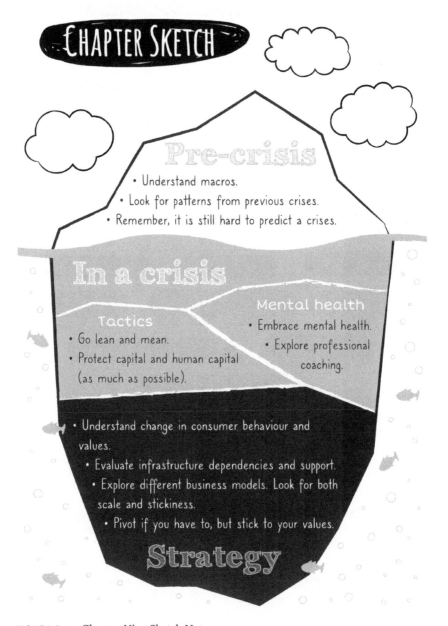

FIGURE 9.1 Chapter Nine Sketch Note

Entrepreneurs are creators, communicators, listeners and visionaries - but most of all leaders. They might be the most learned and mature practitioners in their technologies and sectors. They might be university grads trying to solve a problem they are passionate about, yet they have the child-like naivety to believe in their vision and the conviction to pursue it against all odds. In all my interactions with entrepreneurs, it is that mix of naivety and conviction that instills me with hope for a better future.

When we started writing this book, we knew it was about strategy, but we also felt it was about technology, the macro economy, mental health and business models. Now, as we close off this book, we realise that it is mostly about people and hope. When you have the right people with a lot of hope coming together, even a crisis can feel like a walk in the park. You might fondly look back at the time as a difficult period when you worked hard, learned a lot, had a lot of fun and emerged as winners.

We hope that we have contributed to this ocean of hope that keeps us going in uncertain and unreal times through this book. I thought finishing writing the final chapter of the book would feel like a nice closure to a great journey. It feels like we should close it off with 'All's well that ends well', but I must confess that it feels like the beginning of an exciting and a rewarding journey of hope.

True hope is swift and flies with swallow's wings,
Kings it makes gods, and meaner creatures kings.
William Shakespeare, *Richard III*

Glossary

Chapter 1

Macroeconomics The study of large economic systems, such as those of whole countries or areas of the world

Dry powder Refer to cash reserves kept on hand by a company, venture capital firm or individual to cover future obligations, purchase assets or make acquisitions

Burn Rate Describe the rate at which a new company is spending its venture capital to finance overhead before generating positive cash flow from operations.

Central banks financial institution given privileged control over the production and distribution of money and credit for a nation or a group of nations.

Wealth Effect Behavioral economic theory suggesting that people spend more as the value of their assets rise. The idea is that consumers feel more financially secure and confident about their wealth when their homes or investment portfolios increase in value.

Virtuous/Vicious Cycle a virtuous/vicious cycle is used to describe a chain of positive/negative events that reinforces itself.

Pension Funds Pooled monetary contributions from pension plans set up by employers, unions, or other organizations to provide for their employees' or members' retirement benefits.

Corporate Venture Capital is the investment of corporate funds directly in external startup companies.

Private Equity & Venture Capital Private equity is capital invested in a company or other entity that is not publicly listed or traded. Venture capital is funding given to startups or other young businesses that show potential for long-term growth.

Fear of Missing Out (FOMO) is a social anxiety stemming from the belief that others might be having fun while the person experiencing the anxiety is not present. It is characterized by a desire to stay continually connected with what others are doing.

Recession is a business cycle contraction when there is a general decline in economic activity.

Interest Rate is a percentage charged on the total amount you borrow or save. ... If you're a borrower, the interest rate is the amount you are charged for borrowing money – a percentage of the total amount of the loan. You can borrow money to buy something today and pay for it later.

Monetary policies are actions that a country's central bank or government can take to influence how much money is in the economy and how much it costs to borrow.

Fiscal policies refers to the use of government spending and tax policies to influence economic conditions, especially macroeconomic conditions, including aggregate demand for goods and services, employment, inflation, and economic growth.

Innovation Policies is the interface between research and technological development policy and industrial policy and aims to create a conducive framework for bringing ideas to market.

Runway It refers to how long your company can survive in the market if the income and expenses remain constant.

Chapter 2

Irrational exuberance unfounded market optimism that lacks a real foundation of fundamental valuation, but instead rests on psychological factors.

Quantitative easing a form of unconventional monetary policy in which a central bank purchases longer-term securities from the open market in order to increase the money supply and encourage lending and investment.

Valuation quantitative process of determining the fair value of an asset or a firm

Down rounds refers to a private company offering additional shares for sale at a lower price than had been sold for in the previous financing round.

Funding Gaps is the amount of money needed to fund the ongoing operations or future development of a business or project that is not currently funded with cash, equity, or debt.

Product Management is an organisational function within a company dealing with new product development, business justification, planning, verification, forecasting, pricing, product launch, and marketing of a product or products at all stages of the product lifecycle.

Debt financing occurs when a firm raises money for working capital or capital expenditures by selling debt instruments to individuals and/or institutional investors.

Grants is a quantity of money, i.e., financial assistance, given by a government, organization, or person for a specific purpose. Unlike a loan, you do not have to pay back the money.

Equity financing is the process of raising capital through the sale of shares.

Bull market a market in which share prices are rising, encouraging buying.

Bear Market a market experiences prolonged price declines.

Chapter 3

Mental Health a person's condition with regard to their psychological and emotional well-being

Self-care the practice of taking an active role in protecting one's own well-being and happiness, in particular during periods of stress.

Entrepreneurship a person who sets up a business or businesses, taking on financial risks in the hope of profit.

Self-awareness conscious knowledge of one's own character and feelings.

Self-inquiry is the constant attention to the inner awareness

Emotional fitness as the state wherein the mind is capable of staying away from negative thoughts and can focus on creative and constructive tasks.

Coaching Coaching is a form of development in which an experienced person, called a coach, supports a learner or client in achieving a specific personal or professional goal by providing training and guidance.

Chapter 4

Bell curve a graph of a normal (Gaussian) distribution, with a large rounded peak tapering away at each end.

Business model a plan for the successful operation of a business, identifying sources of revenue, the intended customer base, products, and details of financing.

Scenario Planning is a structured way for organisations to think about the future. A group of executives sets out to develop a small number of scenarios—stories about how the future might unfold and how this might affect an issue that confronts them.

Communication Architecture defines the frequency and fidelity of information flow between individuals in your organization.

Stakeholder management and communication is the process by which you organise, monitor and improve your relationships with your stakeholders. It involves systematically identifying stakeholder; analysing their needs and expectations; and planning and implementing various tasks to engage with them.

Pricing Model is a structure and method for determining prices.

Chapter 5

Regulatory Framework Regulatory Framework means any laws, regulations, decrees and policies officially developed and approved by the government, for the purposes of regulating a sector, a function, or more.

Disaster Recovery is an area of security planning that aims to protect an organization from the effects of significant negative events.

Customer Segment is a way to split customers into groups based on certain characteristics that those customers share

Micro Data points are unit-level data obtained from sample surveys, censuses, and administrative systems.

Ancillary Revenue is revenue that is derived from goods or services other than a company's primary product offering.

Sentiment Analysis the process of computationally identifying and categorizing opinions expressed in a piece of text, especially in order to determine whether the writer's attitude towards a particular topic, product, etc. is positive, negative, or neutral.

Touchpoints a point of contact or interaction, especially between a business and its customers or consumers.

Chapter 6

Policy Infrastructure Infrastructure are the basic systems that undergird the structure of the economy.

Clinical Trials are a type of research that studies new tests and treatments and evaluates their effects on human health outcomes.

Open Banking is a banking practice that provides third-party financial service providers open access to consumer banking, transaction, and other financial data from banks and non-bank financial institutions through the use of application programming interfaces (APIs).

Ethereum is a decentralized, open-source blockchain featuring smart contract functionality.

Quantum technologies Application of new physics dealing with the tiny energy levels of atoms and sub-atomic particles.

Machine learning is an application of artificial intelligence (AI) that provides systems the ability to automatically learn and improve from experience without being explicitly programmed.

Graphics processing units a specialized processor originally designed to accelerate graphics rendering

Drug Discovery In the fields of medicine, biotechnology and pharmacology, drug discovery is the process by which new candidate medications are discovered.

Chapter 7

Triage decide the order of treatment of (patients or casualties).

Key Performance Indicator (KPI) a quantifiable measure used to evaluate the success of an organization, employee, etc. in meeting objectives for performance.

Customer Relationship Management is the process of managing interactions with existing as well as past and potential customers.

Barometer an instrument measuring atmospheric pressure, used especially in forecasting the weather and determining altitude.

Recurring revenue is the portion of a company's revenue that is expected to continue in the future.

Sales Cycle is the process that companies undergo when selling a product to a customer.

Procurement the action of obtaining or procuring something.

Growth Metrics Growth metrics are used to examine a company's historical growth (and hopefully provide clues for the future)

Moonshot an extremely ambitious project or mission undertaken to achieve a monumental goal

Chapter 8

Pivot occurs when a company shifts its business strategy to accommodate changes in its industry, customer preferences, or any other factor that impacts its bottom line.

Freemium a business model, especially on the internet, whereby basic services are provided free of charge while more advanced features must be paid for.

Edge based applications Edge computing is computing that's done at or near the source of the data, instead of relying on the cloud at one of a dozen data centers to do all the work.

Moratorium a temporary prohibition of an activity.

Decentralisation Decentralization or decentralisation is the process by which the activities of an organization, particularly those regarding planning and decision making, are distributed or delegated away from a central, authoritative location or group.

Reputational risks is a threat or danger to the good name or standing of a business or entity.

Index

NB *Italic type* denotes illustrations